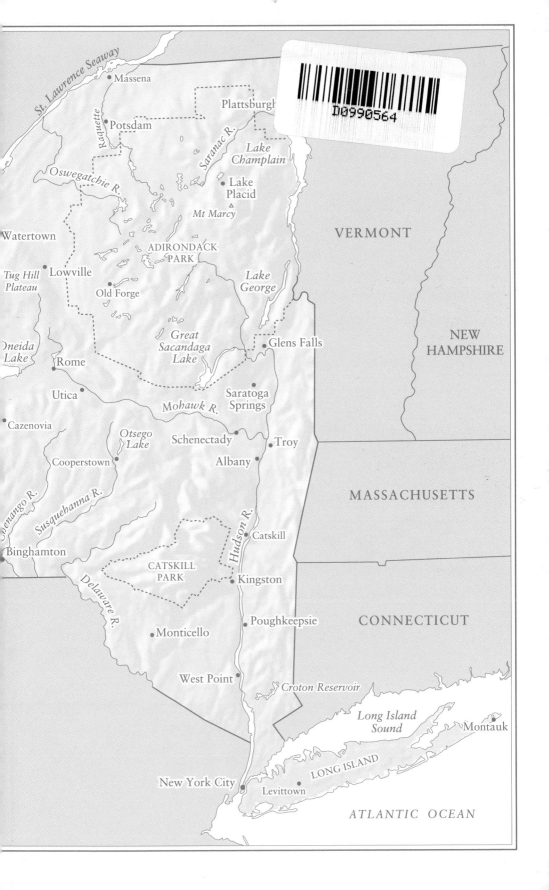

St. Lawrence Seaway

Massena

Plattsburgh

Potsdam

Raquette

Saranac R.

Lake
Champlain

Oswegatchie R.

Lake
Placid

Mt Marcy

VERMONT

Watertown

ADIRONDACK
PARK

Tug Hill
Plateau

Lowville

Lake
George

NEW
HAMPSHIRE

Old Forge

Oneida
Lake

Rome

Great
Sacandaga
Lake

Glens Falls

Utica

Mohawk R.

Saratoga
Springs

Cazenovia

Otsego
Lake

Schenectady

Troy

Chenango R.

Susquehanna R.

Cooperstown

Albany

MASSACHUSETTS

Hudson R.

Binghamton

Catskill

CATSKILL
PARK

Delaware R.

Kingston

Monticello

Poughkeepsie

CONNECTICUT

West Point

Croton Reservoir

Long Island
Sound

Montauk

New York City

Levittown

LONG ISLAND

ATLANTIC OCEAN

D0990564

—

The Nature of New York

The Nature
of New York

*An Environmental
History of the
Empire State*

DAVID STRADLING

Cornell University Press

ITHACA AND LONDON

Publication of this book was made possible, in part, by a generous grant from Furthermore, a program of the J. M. Kaplan Fund.

First published 2010 by Cornell University Press

Printed in the United States of America

Library of Congress Cataloging-in-Publication Data

Stradling, David.
   The nature of New York : an environmental history of the Empire State / David Stradling.
      p. cm.
   Includes bibliographical references and index.
   ISBN 978-0-8014-4510-1 (cloth : alk. paper)
   1. Human ecology—New York (State)—History.
   2. New York (State)—Environmental conditions.
   3. Environmentalism—New York (State)—History.   I. Title.
   GF504.N7S77   2010
   304.2'809747—dc22   2010006559

Cloth printing   10 9 8 7 6 5 4 3 2 1

For my parents,
Richard and Gail Stradling

Contents

4.
Tainted and Unwholesome Atmospheres:
Urban Environments, Government, and Reform
106

5.
A Sound Conservation Program: Theodore Roosevelt,
Franklin Roosevelt, and the Power of Individuals
138

6.
Tracing Man's Progress in Making
the Planet Uninhabitable: Environmental
Interest Groups and Postwar Threats
173

7.
We Live in This Filth: The Urban Crisis,
Environmental Justice, and Threats from Beyond
205

Epilogue:
Finding Places in History
235

Notes
243

Bibliographical Essay
251

Index
271

Acknowledgments

This book began with Alison Kalett at Cornell University Press, who approached me with the idea of writing an accessible, comprehensive environmental history of New York State. I was excited by that prospect from the very beginning, and I was grateful for the invitation and Alison's enthusiasm and support. I hope that what follows meets her expectations for what this book might be. Michael McGandy took on the project with the same level of enthusiasm, and as this book took shape he offered wonderful advice and guidance. Also at Cornell, I have benefited from the patience and good advice of Emily Zoss. Ange Romeo-Hall and Amanda Heller have guided the book through its final stages.

Most of my intellectual debts are expressed in the bibliographical essay, but several scholars have been especially important in shaping this book. Phil Terrie, with whom I've had many e-mail conversations but whom I have never met, has been an important supporter of this work. He read and commented on my original proposal, commented on chapter 3 in draft form, and, perhaps most important, he read the entire manuscript and offered dozens of wonderful suggestions for improvement. In other words, I am deeply indebted to Phil. I am also indebted to Neil Maher, who read and commented on the book proposal and read and helped me improve chapter 5. Neil was also generous with his own collection of materials and writings related to the CCC and the history of the Hudson River Valley. I have benefited from the aid and support of my colleague

Roger Daniels, who is at work on a biography of Franklin Roosevelt, and who read and commented on chapter 5. I have also benefited from the counsel and support of Joel Tarr on this and other projects. Joel is a remarkably generous scholar; he read and commented on an early draft of chapter 4. Sara Gronim read chapter 1 for me and offered both support and valuable suggestions for improvements. I am also thankful to a second, anonymous reader who read my manuscript for Cornell University Press and made valuable suggestions for improvements.

Many other historians played significant roles in shaping this work, albeit less directly. Bill Cronon has been my most important mentor over the last fifteen years; he continues to influence my thinking on environmental history and our craft generally. Zane Miller has also been my teacher and colleague for nearly twenty years, and I still learn from our regular correspondence. Among my friends and supportive colleagues I am fortunate to list Marty Melosi, Peggy Shaffer, and Andrew Hurley. Here at the University of Cincinnati I have benefited from the innovative work of the environmental historian Rob Gioielli, who is now at Towson. I have also had the support and good cheer of many colleagues, including Wendy Kline, Willard Sunderland, Maura O'Connor, Chris Phillips, and Man Bun Kwan.

I received important financial support from the Taft Memorial Fund, which allowed me to travel through parts of New York I had not visited before. Taft also partially funded a sabbatical, during which I drafted much of the book. I am also grateful to the Rockefeller Archives, which supported this work with a research grant, and the J. M. Kaplan fund, which generously supported the production of this book through its Furthermore program.

I also received considerable aid in finding and acquiring images. Special thanks to Suzanne Maggard, of the University of Cincinnati Archives, Peggy Hatfield and Dan DiLandro, both of the Buffalo State College Archives, Kasi McMurray of the UCLA Department of Geography, and John Hart, of the New York State Historical Association. I would also like to thank the very efficient staffs at the Museum of the City of New York, including Melanie Bower, and the New York State Archives, which provides wonderful services to the residents of New York—and anyone else who comes through their doors or visits their Web sites. Davin Hall created the fine map of Adirondack wilderness, and Bill Nelson created the map inside the cover. I am also grateful for the assistance and generosity of Michal Heron, who shared photos of her Catskills farm and took a wonderful photograph for inclusion in the book.

Finally, I thank my family. My daughters, Sarah and Nina, are always generous with their observations about my work. My wife, Jodie, has been as supportive as ever, reading my work, accepting my travels, and forgiving my absentmindedness. My brother Richard has patiently awaited the completion of this project, so that the two of us might tackle another together: a study of the Cuyahoga River and industrial Cleveland. This book is dedicated to my parents, Richard and Gail Stradling, upstate New Yorkers, who showed me the state during the many vacations that collectively constitute my fondest childhood memories.

The Nature of New York

Introduction

Nature Is on the Side of New York

New York State abounds in places of national, even international, significance. From New York City's Central Park to the expansive Adirondack Park, from Niagara Falls to the suburban community of Levittown, the state contains myriad places where critical environmental history has occurred. On its completion in 1864, Central Park became the national model for the nineteenth-century urban landscaped park. The creation of the Adirondack and Catskill forest preserves in 1885 represented the first significant forest preservation in the nation's history. Some sixty years later, Long Island's Levittown would become the quintessential postwar suburb, as it sprang up seemingly overnight, famously replacing thousands of acres of potato fields. In the early 1970s, Love Canal turned the city of Niagara Falls into the poster child of the anti-toxics movement in a story that revealed the human cost of industrial growth.

New York's history abounds in important personalities, too. In 1823 James Fenimore Cooper penned one of the nation's earliest laments on the frontier's passing, set in a fictional version of the town his father founded—Cooperstown—and featuring one of the great characters of American literature: Leatherstocking, the archetypal woodsman who longs for the liberty afforded by living in a wild land. Over the following decades, Thomas Cole and dozens of other Hudson River School artists created the imagery of American romanticism, and in the process their many canvases cast the New York landscape as the American wilderness ideal. John Burroughs, one of the nation's most famed nature writers, featured the Catskills and his Hudson River home, Riverby, in a body of work that spanned fifty years. Theodore Roosevelt, the consummate New Yorker, both lover of the city and devotee of the wild, did so much as president to set aside the nation's remaining natural resources that his administration has become synonymous with conservation. While wearing a number of different hats, Robert Moses remade the city of New York and nearby Long Island, pushing highways through neighborhoods and parkways into distant counties. Late in the twentieth century, Lois Gibbs turned her concern for her children's health into a lifetime of environmental activism, working tirelessly to uncover the connection between disease and toxic chemicals in her neighborhood around Love Canal and then beyond.

The stories of these places and people—combined with many others—touch upon all the significant themes in American environmental history: the changes to the land wrought by European settlement, the growth of commerce and an urban network, the power of romantic notions of nature, and the development of industry with all its benefits and detriments. New York has been a leader in natural resource conservation, urban and regional planning, and zoning. The long-cultivated fruits of environmental activism lie plainly upon the landscape. The state's landscape also readily reveals the ecological costs of industrial development and the flaws of an automobile-centered suburban culture. In the nineteenth century, New Yorkers helped set cultural trends in American romanticism and tourism, which together redefined nature and wilderness. For what they did in their state and beyond it, New Yorkers became leaders in environmental thought and activism, spreading the romantic appreciation of nature, encouraging conservation, and developing modern environmentalism. For two hundred years New York State has been an incubator of environmental philosophy and a training ground for environmental activism. Since so much of the state's history has had national significance, a study of New York can serve as a primer of the nation's environmental history.

WHAT IS ENVIRONMENTAL HISTORY?

In the summer of 1842, Dr. B. W. McCready investigated an outbreak of typhus among a group of African Americans who were living in a "double frame house." The home was set in the middle of a yard, and a number of pigsties and stables surrounded it on three sides. McCready made special mention of "the quantity of filth, liquid and otherwise," that had filled the yard, and a "thick greenish fluid" he observed as he inspected the premises. In response to the outbreak of fever, "the inhabitants took the alarm, and the house for a time was deserted." McCready called the authorities, who removed several pigs, spread lime about the yard, and whitewashed the house. Most likely because of the evacuation, the outbreak subsided, but only after nine people had become ill and two had died.

In McCready's quick telling of this story we find important lessons in environmental history. An outbreak of typhus, caused by an as yet unknown bacterium, spread by a not yet understood vector (lice), led the physician to implicate the environment directly. The recommended remedy: the cleansing of the yard and the building's walls, and the removal of animals. In and around this home, humans interacted with a wide variety of nonhuman life—bacteria, domesticated animals, lice, and, no doubt, a variety of other vermin—and these interactions had multiple implications for their lives. Environmental history attempts to explain the consequences of these interactions, not just with nonhuman organisms but with all aspects of the environment—including the soil, the weather, and, in this story, the filth in the yard and that "greenish fluid."

As the prominent historian William Cronon describes, "Environmental history tries to reconstruct the endless layers of change that we and the earth have traced upon each other." I have interpreted this definition broadly. This book concerns the full diversity of environments in New York—wild, rural, suburban, and urban—as it must, since environmental history happens in all types of places. For instance, even though the yard in McCready's typhus story "had been completely boarded over, so that the earth could nowhere be seen," this is still an environmental story. And even though another building, inhabited by several Irish families and a liquor store, occupied the front of the lot where the outbreak occurred, and even though this lot was at 49 Elizabeth Street on Manhattan's Lower East Side, just four blocks from the already infamous Five Points immigrant slum, this is still an environmental story. To the minds of many people—both then and now—nature had long since fled the dense working-class neighborhoods of mid-nineteenth-century Manhattan, but in truth it had not, as the description of 49 Elizabeth Street should make clear. In the history of New York's environment that follows, every place is worthy of study, from the deep woods of the Adirondacks to the gloomy tenements of the Lower East Side.

Not surprisingly, defining environmental history as the study of human interaction with place, the physical and biological world, necessitates a very broad scope for this book. Many scholars have resisted the evolution of environmental history into the study of all types of environments, fearing that by moving away from a more traditional focus on wild nature, especially in the great expanses of the American West, environmental history would simply become the history of everything, since the interaction with place is so fundamental to human existence. Most environmental histories describe the interaction of culture with something called nature—the nonhuman world. But this approach requires ignoring two fundamental lessons of environmental history itself. The first is a lesson that echoes a central tenet of ecology: everything is connected. All places are connected, too. I learned this indelible lesson while on a field trip in Cronon's environmental history seminar many years ago. Driving west out of Madison, where the city's farthest reaches blended into the agricultural landscape of central Wisconsin, Cronon pulled the van to a stop. He asked us to locate the place where the city ended and the country began—a task destined for failure. In the same way that no discernible boundary separates city and country, no boundary can keep environmental history beyond the city's limits.

Fittingly, this lesson overlaps with the second one: the boundaries between nature and culture are porous. In many ways, history is the story of how nonhuman nature and culture blend over time. Indeed there is a fundamental problem in thinking of nature as a unity, a single entity, sometimes even described as having goals and intentions. This is especially problematic when humans are kept outside this unity. This way of thinking perpetuates the description of human actions as almost necessarily diminishing nature's integrity or, in an oft-used phrase, disrupting the delicate balance of nature. This philosophy has helped create powerful narratives in which European Americans found untouched nature—wilderness—and dismantled it over time. Narratives of environmental degradation can be morally and political instructive, but they can also be simplistic and inaccurate, especially if they claim that the arrival of humans or the development of human economies meant the gradual disappearance of nature. Deforestation, extirpations, the draining of swamps, the introduction of nonnative species: these and other human activities clearly altered New York's environment, but never did nature, as a unity, retreat. It changed.

Nature persists everywhere and at all times in New York's history, and so in describing the state's landscape I avoid the typical bifurcated categorization: natural versus built environments. In doing so, I hope to erase the artificial boundary that historical narratives have traditionally placed on the landscape. Although the Lower East Side's tenements may seem completely unnatural, they are in fact no more removed from nature than Central Park, less than four miles away, or even Lake George, just under two hundred miles to the north. The rain that falls on Five Points obeys the laws of gravity, carrying with it the dust and trash that it lifts as it runs off. It dissolves water-soluble chemicals, just as it does in Lake George. Water that falls in Five Points makes its way to the ocean, just as the water from Lake George does. The smoke that rises from the chimneys of urban furnaces behaves much the same as the smoke from campfires along Lake George, since the carbon cycle is as alive in Manhattan as it is in the Adirondacks. Many of us may prefer the calls of loons on an Adirondack lake to the cooing of pigeons roosting under the Brooklyn Bridge, but that should not prevent us from recognizing both as part of nature. Both are also legacies of culture: the pigeon imported from Europe and the loon preserved as part of the Adirondack Park. Environmental history must remove the boundaries that have so often placed nature and culture in distinct realms in order to see how thoroughly humans shape all types of environments and how much nature—the physical and biological world—influences even the most constructed of places. The rules of ecology operate on the streets of midtown Manhattan as surely as on the slopes of Mount Marcy. So too do the forces of culture and economy.

This book covers a great diversity of topics. The narrative covers trends in culture, since environmental history must address changing ideas of nature, especially those created by the romantic movement. Landscape paintings gain special attention here, since Hudson River School art did so much to establish the ideal American landscape. Economic history is equally important in what follows. Clearly environmental history must take into account the development of private property, the profit motive, capitalist markets, and industrialization, all of which have been prime forces in shaping New York's landscape. Since New York's places have been transformed by the development of and investment in new transportation, energy, and pollution control systems, this book also includes some consideration of the history of technology. Several of the chapters consider politics at length, since environmental history must include an understanding of public policy and political activism. The histories of science and medicine, too, play a role, given the importance of disease, human health, agricultural science, and the evolving and increasingly influential science of ecology. All of these disparate topics and methodologies come together in this volume because each tells us something about human interaction with place.

What follows is not a comprehensive history of New York, but the degree to which it approaches comprehensiveness is a testament to the centrality of the environment to New Yorkers' lives and the state's culture and economy. *The Nature of New York* does not support a single thesis, but it does support two broad themes. First, environmental history has implications for understanding all aspects of the past—not only how humans have interacted with nature, but also how all humans have occupied and changed the places where they live. From geology to climate, ecology has always exerted influence over culture; place has been much more than a setting for the events of the past. Over time, places intertwine with events and ideas, and so all histories that make claims to comprehensiveness must pay significant attention to place. Second, since New York's history contains all the significant themes in environmental history, what follows reveals the utility of a state as a unit of study.

THE STATE AS A UNIT OF STUDY

A glance at the map reveals the degree to which the state has been defined by natural features, which constitute many of its boundaries. New York's borders contain only a few straight lines drawn by politicians. In the northeast, Lake Champlain separates New York from Vermont. In the south, the Hudson River, Long Island Sound, the Atlantic, and the complex New York Harbor separate New York from Connecticut and New Jersey. The Delaware River forms part of the border with Pennsylvania. Lake Erie, the Niagara River, Lake Ontario, and the St. Lawrence River form much of the western and northern border of the state. In an ecological sense, these are not boundaries that separate these places at all but ecosystems that join them. Lake Erie connects New York to Pennsylvania, Ohio, and Ontario. The Delaware River rises in the foothills of the Catskills and runs south, out of the state and between Pennsylvania and New Jersey. New York shares Long Island Sound with Connecticut, and so both states have immediate concerns there. New York's boundaries also include a small portion of the Atlantic Ocean, the ecological health of which is of great interest to the state.

Just as ecosystems cross state boundaries, New York's interests also extend well beyond state lines. New York's cultural and economic links to oysters, lobsters, and whales, for example, reveal just how connected the state is to ecosystems that it does not wholly contain. Indeed, countless species move across state boundaries, including waterfowl, songbirds, and other migratory animals. Sometimes species move more freely than we'd like, including zebra mussels and Eurasian milfoil, both of which have altered New York ecosystems since their arrival from Asia. Microbes also move across state lines, of course, including the *Rickettsia* bacteria that cause epidemic typhus. These are just the most obvious ways that ecosystems and individual species cross political borders, and they suggest serious limits to a state-bound environmental history. What follows, therefore, cannot fully contain the stories that run through the state's past. The porousness of human boundaries is, after all, a central theme of this work.

More than just nature fails to abide by state boundaries; people, too, move back and forth. Many New Yorkers have had an influence well beyond the Empire State. John Burroughs, Theodore Roosevelt, and Laurance Rockefeller were all New Yorkers, but they had even greater influence on the nation's environmental history than on that of their home state. Bob Marshall was born in New York City, fell in love with wilderness in the Adirondacks, and then lived mostly outside the Empire State, becoming the nation's most important wilderness advocate while living in the American West and Washington, D.C. Similarly, other important actors in the history of New York were not native New Yorkers, including the English-born Thomas Cole, who arrived in New York City at the age of twenty-four, and Connecticut native Frederick Law Olmsted, who moved to Staten Island to be a gentleman farmer at about the same age. Olmsted eventually set up his landscape architecture business outside Boston. Unfortunately, given the scope of this book, it cannot fully account for human movements across New York's state lines, even when central characters continue their careers beyond the Empire State.

State boundaries are porous in other ways, too. The products of culture and economy move easily across them. The cultural trends I examine are national in scope, including romanticism and tourism. Hudson River art depicted more than just New York scenes, and its influence was international. Travelers from around the nation took the waters at Saratoga Springs, and they took home with them ideas about tourism and health. Chemicals, flatware, clothing, and hundreds of other products of New York's industrial economy found markets outside the state, as did wheat, cheese, apples, and dozens of other agricultural products. By-products also move across boundaries. Over the last half-century New York has inherited sulfur and nitrogen emissions from the Midwest, inheriting along with them the problem of acid rain. And there are many other examples, including threats to the ozone layer in the 1970s and the ongoing dangers of global warming. Clearly pollution does not abide by state boundaries.

All of this is a reminder that a state, even one as large and populous as New York, cannot fully contain its own environmental history narratives. Perhaps this is why no important environmental histories use state boundaries to set their geographical limits. Many studies focus on smaller places like Concord, Massachusetts, or Georgia's coastal plain. Some important books have followed ecologically defined boundaries, such as the Columbia River Basin or the short grass prairie. Both of these approaches make good sense, of course, and they allow authors to tell important stories with tight arguments and broad implications. Other historians have taken on larger geographies, often telling regional or national stories, including those of the developing "Great West" and national parks and federal policies.

National boundaries matter. Indeed, national policies have greatly influenced New York State's history, including the passage of the Clean Air Act in 1970 and, a few years later, the creation of Superfund. The federal government has also negotiated international treaties that have significant bearing on New York, including agreements signed by the United States and Canada concerning water quality in the Great Lakes. International events, such as the spread of epidemic disease, the arrival of plants and animals from around the world, and global warming, all reinforce the idea that any boundary placed on an environmental history must exclude some aspects of the story.

Even with all this said, the state is a useful unit of study. State policies have mattered in environmental history, and in New York especially so. The state built the Erie Canal and other canals that followed, opening up the central and western parts of New York and binding the Empire State together. More than one hundred years later the state built the New York State Thruway, and again initiated dramatic changes in land use and development. New York established the nation's first state forests, even writing preservation into its constitution in 1894. Since then, ongoing acquisition of state land has made the Forest Preserve a tremendously valuable resource and a point of pride for New York residents. Since purchasing land around Niagara Falls in 1885, New York State has created an expansive public recreation system, with nearly 170 separate parks. In 1901 the state also passed one of the nation's earliest comprehensive tenement laws in an attempt to improve the living conditions of the state's working poor. And as the following chapters relate, dozens of other state actions, from pollution control to reforestation, have directly affected the environment. Over time, state agencies have become important actors, especially the Department of Environmental Conservation.

Just as important, the state's boundaries have created a cultural bond, a New York identity. Despite long-standing rivalries, especially between New York City and the rest of the state, residents generally do identify themselves at some level as New Yorkers. Residency in the Empire State matters. Some symbols of New York's identity reflect the state's cultural success; the Statue of Liberty, the Empire State Building, and, more recently, the World Trade Center, are important examples. But perhaps more important are the state's natural landscapes, such as Niagara Falls, the Adirondack High Peaks, the Hudson Highlands, and Long Island's many beaches. From Manhattan Island to Grand Island, from Chautauqua Lake to Lake Champlain, an attachment to place has long constituted a large part of what it means to be a New Yorker. New York's environment has played a fundamental role in shaping the state's culture and economy, and as the double meaning in this book's title suggests, nature has been instrumental in creating New York's identity.

GEOGRAPHY

Clearly the state of New York is not a meaningful ecological unit, but it is home to a remarkable variety of ecosystems. New York contains two significant mountain ranges, the Adirondacks in the north and the Catskills, west of the Hudson River. The Adirondack High Peaks reach above the timberline, where an alpine zone shaped by low temperatures and high winds features bare rock, lichen, mosses, and heaths; dwarf willows and birches find rootholds in crevices. The state contains fewer than one hundred acres of this type of ecosystem, much of it atop Mount Marcy and nearby Algonquin Peak, both now contained in the High Peaks Wilderness.

The Adirondacks may be better known for aquatic ecosystems, the vast numbers of lakes and streams that lace the North Woods. The Raquette River meanders north, carrying the dark, acidic waters of beautiful Raquette Lake through the aptly named Long Lake, then through Tupper Lake and on up to the St. Lawrence River. Every part of New York is well watered, and in addition to rivers, lakes, streams, and springs, the state is dotted with bogs, swamps, and marshes, including Nine Mile Swamp along the headwaters of the Chenango River, north of Hubbardsville, and the larger Montezuma Swamp at the northern tip of Cayuga Lake, an important stopover for migrating waterfowl, many of which feed on the crop waste left in the cornfields that surround the swamp. There are numerous bay ecosystems as well, for example, Sodus and Black

River bays on Lake Ontario, and Long Island's Shinnecock Bay and Jamaica Bay, where a large estuary and salt marsh harbor 330 bird species, most of them migratory. The bay also shelters healthy populations of horseshoe crabs and diamondback terrapins.

Farther out on Long Island, the sandy soils of the Pine Barrens are home to dwarf pitch pines and scrub oak; this is an ecosystem that needs to burn now and then to maintain forest health. Back north, the Tug Hill Plateau rises due east of Lake Ontario. This heavily wooded area receives a huge amount of lake-effect snow—more snow on average than any other place east of the Rocky Mountains. Heavy snowfall there, and throughout much of the state, helps create damp springs and moist summers, and a deep-green landscape with lush vegetation. The Tug Hill Plateau's maple, beech, and birch forest is nearly all second growth, some of which is so young as to give the area the appearance of still being farm fields that are slowly returning to woods. Like much of New York, the Tug Hill region is punctuated by lands reforested by the state, as is evident in the thick stands of evergreens, including white pine, red pine, Norway spruce, and white spruce, all of which might seem out of place if planted patches of evergreens weren't so common around the state.

Even this extremely cursory description of the state's geography gives a sense of the great diversity of ecosystems in New York. It also affords a glimpse into the stories that follow. All of these places have a human and a natural history. Even above five thousand feet, at Marcy's peak, the footsteps of humans—literally the footsteps—have helped shaped the landscape by trampling some of the fragile plants. At the Montezuma National Wildlife Refuge, the federal government controls water levels in the swamp, and New York's Department of Environmental Conservation issues the permits sold to hunters hoping to bag the waterfowl. On Long Island, humans have extinguished the periodic fires that the Pine Barrens require, setting off unanticipated ecological changes. Human actions aren't the only causes of environmental change, of course. Oak, maple, chestnut, and elm hardwood forests once occupied much of the state until diseases decimated the chestnuts and the elms, dramatically shifting forest composition. Other tree species have declined for different reasons. White pine and hemlock are still plentiful in the state, but they were even more abundant before the logging and tanning industries targeted these species. The declining fortunes of chestnut, elm, white pine, and hemlock are all reminders that none of the state's many ecosystems is timeless. Climate, soil, and drainage all contribute to the creation of plant communities, but humans have altered them all, adding nutrients to thin soils, draining swamps, and, sadly, even altering the climate. We can easily recognize the persistence of nature in New York, a theme that runs through this book, but no place in the state is static; no place is without a history.

In much of what follows I describe how human action has shaped the environment, but nature's role in shaping New York cannot be forgotten. Twenty thousand years ago the Wisconsin Ice Sheet spread over much of what would become New York, and in its presence and its retreat the ice shaped the landscape. Retreating glaciers created the Great Lakes and the Finger Lakes—and hundreds of other lakes, large and small. Glaciers smoothed the Adirondack and Catskill peaks, and as the ice retreated, it dropped the erratic boulders that dot New York's landscape. Larger collections of debris, known as moraines, also shaped the landscape, most obviously through the creation of Long Island. It took ten thousand years for the ice to withdraw fully from New York State, and as it did, new watercourses drained the landscape, new soil developed from glacial till and bedrock, and ecosystems began to take shape. Geology, topography, and climate largely determined the natural changes that continued even as human beings arrived, perhaps twelve thousand years ago. Natural forces continued to shape the landscape as the Owasco Indians began to practice agriculture in central New York about a thousand years ago.

And of course those natural forces have never stopped shaping the landscape and the events that have taken place upon it. In reporting for the New York State Natural History Survey in 1846, Ebenezer Emmons waxed rhapsodic about the state's geographical diversity, thanking Providence, rather than nature, for the state's good fortune: "If variety of surface and climate favor's multiplicity of productions then may the state of New-York be said to be fitted by Providence for that end." The state reaches from sea level to altitudes of over five thousand feet, and as Emmons wrote, "she extends her arms through a large portion of the temperate zone," a climate well suited to agriculture. From Emmons's perspective, this climatological and geographical diversity ensured that New York's agriculture would also remain diverse and productive, as it has.

We often overlook the fundamental way in which culture is shaped by the natural world; many of New York's regions are defined primarily by geography. The distinctiveness of the North Country comes from its harsh winter climate and its distance from downstate populations, a distance reinforced by the intervening Adirondacks. Long Island's comes from its isolation by water, as does Manhattan's. But the most important regional distinction in the state is wholly cultural: the differentiation of New York City from a place called *upstate*. Some New Yorkers use that term to describe everything north of the city—Westchester and Rockland counties included, and sometimes even the Bronx. I use *upstate*, however, to mean places north of metropolitan New York, and so north of the suburbanized counties. This means, of course, that *upstate* is a somewhat vague and mutable term, since the suburbs have moved farther and farther north over time.

PLAN FOR THE BOOK

What follows is a modified chronological telling of the state's environmental history. Each chapter carries the narrative forward, while also introducing an important theme. Chapter 1 concerns Native American cultures and the arrival of Europeans. While not ignoring other changes wrought by European settlement, this chapter stresses the importance of the market and the development of the profit motive in shaping New York's landscape after 1609. The shift in economic thinking toward "improvement" and the accumulation of wealth was fundamental to the many environmental changes that came thereafter. The second chapter focuses on the Erie Canal and the spread of agricultural and urban development in upstate New York. It continues the theme of economics and the market revolution, but it introduces an additional theme concerning the role of engineers, technology, and scientific advancement in environmental change. Chapter 3, which concerns the romantic movement and nineteenth-century tourism, presses the theme of cultural influence, especially the ways in which ideas of nature affect human interaction with particular places.

The fourth chapter addresses the topic of turn-of-the-century industrial cities. It introduces the theme of government regulation, especially through the dramatic expansion of governmental authority in the Progressive Era. Chapter 5 concerns the conservation movement from the late 1800s into the 1930s, but focusing particularly on Theodore and Franklin Roosevelt and the ability of individuals to shape environmental history through political skill and perseverance. The last two chapters address the post–World War II economic boom, suburban sprawl, and environmental activism. The sixth chapter discusses the mass environmental movement and the role of democracy in providing a check on big business after World War II. Chapter 7 focuses on the contributions of women and minorities to the environmental movement since the 1960s.

A final theme runs throughout the book, one well articulated by Basil Hall, who in 1829 explained why New York's Erie Canal would best other states' canal systems. Hall assessed the places where competing canals would be built, none of which was nearly as favorable as the route taken by the Erie, which passed from east to west with only a modest rise in elevation. "Nature is on the side of New York," Hall concluded succinctly. Building the Erie Canal along the Mohawk River, through the only substantial break in the Appalachian Mountains from Maine to Georgia, is just one of many instances of New Yorkers' putting nature's gifts to good use. Rich soils allowed agriculture to flourish in some regions; thin but well-watered soils allowed for logging in many others. All around New York, people turned falling water into mill sites to process grain and lumber. On Long Island, residents engaged in whaling, and in many places fishing and hunting augmented local diets and contributed to economic success. The beauty of the state's landscape—beaches, mountains, lakes, and falls—encouraged the development of tourism, long important to the state's economy. Over time, New York Bay became one of the great ports in the world. And from the earth New Yorkers mined iron in the southern Hudson Valley and the Adirondacks, quarried bluestone in the Catskills region, and mined talc in the North Country. Gravel, limestone, and sand are all abundant in New York, and together they constitute the concrete from which New Yorkers have built so much. A diversity of natural resources has allowed New Yorkers to create a diversified—and substantial—economy. Over the course of history, it does seem that nature has been on the side of New York, imparting wealth, pleasure, and meaning to the lives of millions.

1

This Comes of
Settling a Country

*European Colonization and
the Market's Arrival*

I
n September 1609 Henry Hudson and his crew sailed the *Half Moon* past
a sandy spit of land, through a narrow opening, and into a spacious harbor with large islands, expansive salt marshes, and several tributary rivers.
Searching for a passage that would lead them into the North Pacific, the sailors found instead a wide and beautiful tidal river that flowed into the harbor
from the north. They also found native peoples who almost daily approached
the ship in canoes during the weeks it moved upstream. At times the sailors
took these actions as aggression, and they kept the natives at bay, sometimes
even firing muskets and small cannon. At other times, however, the *Half Moon*
welcomed approaching natives, those who appeared interested in trading. The
natives brought with them pelts and a variety of goods that reflected the bounty
of the lands along the river. There were oysters from the harbor's many estuar-
ies, and from nearby farmland came tobacco, corn, and beans. From the forests
all around came venison, grapes, and currants. Some days the *Half Moon* sent
forth its own men in smaller boats to fish, gather chestnuts, and walk the woods,
which were altogether impressive to the Europeans, who took special note of
the massive hardwoods. As the journey's terse record keeper, Robert Juet, reported, "This country is full of great and tall oaks."

Hudson and his men may have been disappointed by their failure to find a
passage to Asia, but the Dutch, under whose flag Hudson had sailed, had gained
a valuable claim to "New Netherland" and one of North America's finest ports.
To help secure their claims to the harbor and the north river, which took the

name of its European explorer, in 1614 the Dutch built Fort Nassau near the future site of Albany. There they created a lively fur market, where the Iroquois presented pelts, mostly beaver, and received various European goods, including rum, knives, metal pots, and woolen cloth. The trade was fraught with hazards for both the Dutch and the native peoples, but it was most hazardous for the many furbearing species in the region. Combined with the French fur trade to the north, the Albany market was so successful at moving pelts that by the end of the century, Native American hunters had exterminated beaver from nearly all of Iroquoia, the extensive region controlled by a confederation of five tribes, a region that included most of what would become New York State. Sometimes using snares, at other times guns, native hunters, later joined by European trappers, removed beaver from the region's watery landscape. Sometimes hunters destroyed the beavers' dams, draining the water to make hunting easier; at other times the beavers' destruction ensured the eventual failure of the dam, since no animals remained to make repairs. Thus the removal of beaver from New York resulted in a noticeable remaking of the landscape, as the draining of beaver ponds and lakes created new streamside meadows with rich soil.

The long-term environmental consequences associated with the fur trade represent a small part of the great transition under way. New European arrivals put both indigenous peoples and indigenous animal and plant species under pressure. Over the next two hundred years, the Iroquois and other Native Americans would be defeated, forced westward, and confined. Forests would be pushed back from rivers and up hillsides, and in their stead Europeans would create landscapes of fields and fences. They would remove or threaten many native species, such as beaver, wolves, and panthers, and they would introduce species, including horses, cattle, and pigs, that would become abundant. This was a long transition, to be sure, one filled with significant setbacks for the European arrivals, but it could hardly escape notice, for it constituted the heart of nation building. This new landscape supported a new culture, steeped in religious belief and driven by the profit motive. In some ways the landscape would be made poorer by the changes, but the settlers would make themselves richer. And that was the purpose of all their hard work.

NATIVE AMERICANS AND THE ENVIRONMENT

As Native Americans garnered knives and guns through trade with Europeans, they became more effective hunters and warriors. In this way the fur trade increased the level of violence in the region, as conflict among various tribes grew, and more and more animals died. Indeed, trapping quickly diminished the populations of all furbearing animals. Beavers, martens, otters, and minks nearly disappeared from the region. Less marketable animals, such as muskrats and raccoons, also suffered because they wandered into the snares—and eventually the metal traps—that littered the landscape. The Iroquois so thoroughly removed furbearers from their own territory that they became middlemen mostly, moving furs caught well to the west and north to the Albany market. Eventually the Iroquois participated in the systematic removal of furbearing animals across the Great Lakes region. Their widening participation in the fur trade put them in competition—and therefore into adversarial relationships—with other indigenous groups, especially those who traded their furs to the French in Canada.

The fur trade gave Native Americans their first exposure to the profit motive and thus initiated a changing relationship with nature. Never before had native peoples hunted so completely for trade. Of course, hunters had long taken beaver—the Iroquois prized its meat and used its pelts—but they had always done so carefully, offering ceremonies of thanks for those they had taken and leaving most of the animals undisturbed. Like other native cultures, the Iroquois believed that spirits animated all of nature, and they explained events by attributing pleasure or displeasure to these spirits. One must live carefully in a world of spirits. Rituals helped villages give thanks and apologies to the animals that supplied them with meat and clothing and to the spirits that controlled the weather and made crops possible.

Enthusiastic Native American participation in the fur trade is difficult to explain. Since it required hunters to take so many more animals than they needed for themselves, participation in the trade ran contrary to native beliefs, given how completely Native Americans connected their material and spiritual worlds. A partial explanation may come from pressures exerted by European disruptions. The dramatic increases in hunting and trapping may reveal a spiritual crisis, in which Native Americans expressed anger at the spirits for the rising numbers of deaths they were experiencing from disease. Or perhaps they simply found the market too alluring, the guns and gunpowder too useful to pass up. For most tribes the fur trade constituted their first prolonged interactions with Europeans, and through increasingly regularized trading, natives purchased a variety of goods, including cloth, tools, and metal pots, all of which they quickly wove into the fabric of their culture.

Perhaps most important, through the contact required by trade, Native Americans acquired a number of European diseases previously unknown to them. Smallpox, measles, and influenza were among the most deadly. Since they had had no previous exposure to these diseases, and therefore had developed no immunity, the native peoples succumbed in much greater numbers than did the European carriers. In 1633 the worst epidemic in the Hudson Valley struck the Mohawks, the easternmost of the Iroquois tribes. The disease swept through their four settlements, home to as many as 8,100 people altogether. By the time the epidemic subsided, perhaps as few as 2,000 were left alive. The Mahicans, an Algonquian tribe that lived to the east of the Mohawks, saw up to 90 percent of their number die during the same epidemic.

Waves of epidemic disease over the long transition greatly reduced the military power of all indigenous tribes, leaving them susceptible to European conquests farther inland. By 1677 there were perhaps only three hundred Mohawk men left. Although historians have been more interested in describing the colonial era's many Indian wars, most Native American deaths came unaccompanied by war whoops; they occurred neither on warpaths nor in massacres. Rather, death tended to come quietly, at the hands of dreadful diseases, in dark longhouses and wigwams, with only loved ones nearby. Europeans were most likely to comment on the results of these epidemics as absences. As early as the 1660s, Europeans described finding nearly deserted villages and poorly maintained fields. With mounting political and cultural stress caused by the deaths, indigenous groups adjusted as they could, often by making new alliances, welcoming orphaned individuals into their own groups, or by becoming aggressive, attacking, kidnapping, and plundering to ensure survival. The acquisition of pelts for trade should be seen as another survival tactic employed by deeply disrupted cultures.

Despite the myth of the ecological Indian, which imagines Native Americans as living in balance with nature in cultures that had essentially no impact on North America's ecosystems, participation in the fur trade did not initiate the Eastern Woodland tribes' influence on their environment. They used a detailed knowledge of the world around them to exploit nature's bounty in each season. They could identify useful plants and animals, and they knew where and when these might be found. Even without European guns and knives, Native American men were effective hunters. Using snares and arrows, they took and made use of a wide variety of animals. Hunting was particularly important in winter, when animals were easier to track in the snow, and when other food resources dwindled. Deer meat provided critical protein, and deerskins provided clothing. Native Americans also prized bear and beaver meat. Migrating birds afforded seasonal meat; passenger pigeons, geese, and ducks all supplemented native diets. Natives also hunted turkeys, rabbits, and other small animals. New York's many lakes and rivers abounded in fish, taken with spears, nets, weirs, and hook and line. Especially in the spring, natives caught great quantities of salmon, striped bass, and other migrating fish. On Long Island, Algonquian tribes ate shellfish—most famously at clambakes—and hunted migrating whales. Along with hunting, gathering diversified diets, adding a variety of berries and nuts, and certain plants served as medicines, dyes, and poisons. Natives also cut sugar maples in the spring and collected sap, which they apparently drank without boiling it into syrup, a practice that became common among European settlers. Native use of Jerusalem artichokes and groundnuts undoubtedly encouraged the spread of these species, since digging for the nutritious tubers would have sparked further growth. In fact, natives probably protected and encouraged the growth of many useful species, even before they cultivated their own crops.

Hunting and gathering were critical to all Eastern Woodland tribes, but by the year 1300 they were also practicing a complex and very productive horticulture. The Iroquois used a form of slash-and-burn horticulture, which involved setting fires to clear the forest and then planting mixed fields of corn, beans, and squash. Ash from the fires provided some natural fertilizer. Beans added nitrogen to the soil as the corn removed it, also increasing the productivity and longevity of the fields. Native Americans had no plows but instead used sticks to make the holes into which they dropped seeds. This practice kept soil disruption—and thus erosion—to a minimum. It also helped fields retain productivity. Since dry corn and beans can be stored for months, these crops were especially important during the long winter season, when other resources dwindled.

This horticulture, practiced by women, produced the majority of the calories sustaining Iroquois communities and provided considerable stability, allowing villages to support up to two thousand people. By the time of European contact, the Mohawk had become well established along the river that bears their name. To the west, along the plains south of Oneida Lake, the Oneida and the Onondaga had established their communities, and along the lake that bears *their* name, the Cayuga planted their fields. Seneca fields and villages were found farther west, in the plain along the Genesee River. In the early 1600s the Iroquois Confederacy, or Haudenosaunee, consisted of perhaps fifty thousand people spread across the vast region that is now upstate New York. Other indigenous groups included the Lenape along the southern Hudson River and west to the Delaware River, and a number of Algonquian tribes, including the Mahicans, east of the Hudson, and the Montauketts and Shinnecock on Long Island.

Although Iroquoian hunting parties traveled great distances in the winter, they returned to wooden longhouses, sometimes surrounded by broad meadows, made and maintained by the community over many years. Still, Native American communities tended to move periodically. Iroquois villages apparently moved every ten to twenty years, though they did not go far. Historians have long assumed that communities moved primarily because fields began to lose productivity, but perhaps other resources diminished sooner, such as firewood or game. The rotting of village palisades, the logs planted side by side for protection, also may have encouraged periodic movement. Or perhaps growing concern about the accumulation of waste material signaled that it was time to find fresh ground. In other words, periodic movement could solve several problems, including those related to sanitation and the diminishing productivity of the surrounding lands.

Even beyond their hunting and horticulture, Native Americans significantly shaped their surroundings, especially through their many uses of fire. In addition to clearing fields, fire removed brush in forests to facilitate hunting. Fire was even employed in hunting, to frighten deer into an ambush. European travelers regularly commented on the quality of the woods created and maintained by these fires, how stately oaks and maples, unharmed by the flames, shaded open forest floors. Fire may also have encouraged the spread of nut trees, such as hickory and walnut, which are both fire resistant and produced important sources of protein.

Clearly Native Americans altered North American landscapes, but compared to the changes to the land that would come with European settlement, native influence over the landscape might be overlooked, and for good reason. Since native belief systems required a deep respect for other living things, ecologically destructive behavior was limited. Just as important, since native cultures did not place special value on the accumulation of wealth, in the form of either land or material objects, prior to European contact indigenous peoples had no cultural incentive to exploit natural resources beyond ensuring their own survival.

Other factors also limited natives' environmental impact, such as low population densities and scattered settlement patterns. Although what would become New York could be a bountiful land, late springs, early frosts, and droughts could lead to crop failures and food shortages. Deep winter snows could cause deer kills that kept numbers low for years. Periods of low caloric intake for Native Americans encouraged low birthrates, part of the reason why indigenous population densities remained low by European standards. Tribes were well separated by wild forests, not just because they provided resources but also because they served as safety zones, diminishing contact and thus conflict among different groups.

For all these reasons, as European settlers moved into former Native American lands, they found mostly forests. In the early 1800s, for example, as surveyors measured the former Seneca territory in western New York, they found few areas that were obviously Native American clearings—totaling less than 1 percent of the region. Although some effects of indigenous occupation had undoubtedly disappeared beneath new growth in the nearly twenty-year interval between military conquest and European occupation, observers determined that altogether the Iroquois had lived in a world dominated by forests.

In part because European settlers thought of indigenous people as part of nature, they undoubtedly underestimated the degree to which Native Americans shaped their environments. Similarly, colonists regularly described Native Americans as primitive. Europeans thought poorly of Native American men because they did not work in the fields as European men did. To Europeans, hunting was mostly sport; real work was done in agriculture and husbandry. Since women performed this work in native cultures, Europeans thought Native American men were lazy. Europeans also found Native American fields unkempt because they contained stumps and had no straight lines like those produced by settlers' plows or farmers' fences. Thinking of Native Americans as primitive and part of nature undoubtedly eased the minds of Europeans as they moved into native lands. To their understanding, Native Americans only partially and poorly utilized the gifts God and nature bestowed upon them. The colonists understood their mission to exploit these gifts more fully as the will of God.

Despite their denigration of indigenous peoples, European colonists borrowed extensively from Native American technology and horticulture. Iroquois horticulture was remarkably productive, and significantly, Europeans quickly learned the value of natives' crops. Corn, beans, and squash all became staples of settlers' farms. Early settlers widely adopted corn for the ease with which it might be planted without plowing; it was ideal for fresh fields that retained tree stumps. Europeans borrowed from indigenous cultures in other ways as well. On Otsego Lake, settlers learned how to build weirs made of woven branches to capture the fish that migrated by the thousands up the Susquehanna River. On Long Island, seventeenth-century European whalers required the labor and skills of Montaukett men to harpoon migrating whales and drag them onshore. On the beach, Montaukett crews processed the animals, turning the blubber into whale oil, the commodity Europeans desired. Settlers also commonly traded European goods for Native American food, relying on the productivity of indigenous people to get them through lean years.

Significant differences separated the kinds of agriculture practiced by the two groups, however. New York's soil and climate were suitable for European crops, including wheat and rye, which colonists much preferred to corn. Indeed, that European crops flourished in New York played a role in the marketing of the colony, the effort to attract immigrants who might make the enterprise profitable. As Daniel Denton wrote in his popular *Brief Description of New York*, published in 1670, Long Island was "very natural for all sorts of English Grain." Even when European farmers grew native crops, they generally did so using different techniques. Europeans used plows to till fields, which also meant that they needed work animals, usually oxen or horses.

The presence of animals constituted the greatest difference in the styles of agriculture. Native Americans kept no domesticated animals except dogs. Europeans brought with them hogs, which were remarkably resourceful and could forage in forests, where mast from oaks and other trees sustained them for much of the year. Pigs could also fend for themselves, especially after settlers removed the larger predators from the region. Farmers gathered hogs in the fall and fattened them on corn before slaughter. Pork was a versatile meat, too; it could be eaten fresh or cured by smoke or salt, providing protein through long winters. Cattle, too, were imported from Europe to provide meat, milk, butter, and cream. Since they also provided labor, pulling plows and wagons, they were essential to a successful New York farm. As early as 1632, the great Dutch landholder Kiliaen van Rensselaer wrote, "Our principal profit will come from cattle, for which there is plenty of fine pasture and hay for nothing" in the area around Rensselaerswyck, surrounding Albany. Cattle herds also flourished on the Hempstead Plains of Long Island, where native grasses nourished horses, too, and other imported animals. Cattle were especially valuable as the surplus product of a farm, since after being fattened on grass and grain, they could be walked to market more economically than other agricultural products. Though less common on early farms, sheep also became important members of the farmyard, providing wool to farm families and surpluses that might be sold or

traded. Domesticated animals thus allowed European farmers to create products designed to enter the market. These animals, at least those not turned out
into the forests, also produced manure, which farmers spread on fields to improve fertility.

To keep animals in yards—or, more commonly early on, to keep them out
of fields—farmers built (and constantly repaired) fences. Altogether, Dutch
and English farms looked very different from Native American fields, more ordered, segregated, and filled with straight lines. Some of these lines separated
properties, others marked off fields from forests, and still others distinguished
one crop row from another. These farms represented a literally reordered landscape, replete with new animals, new crops, and new wealth. Those property
lines revealed that settlers brought with them more than just new crops and
animals. Europeans had a different understanding of their relationship to the
land. Native Americans had a usufruct conception of landownership, meaning
that people had temporary and incomplete rights to land as they made use of it.
Europeans believed that individuals could gain outright ownership of land and
control its use in perpetuity. To Europeans, land was *real* property, to be bought
and sold like any other commodity. The control of real estate—the land—was
central to European settlers' beliefs about self-improvement through hard work
and the accumulation of wealth.

Surveyors, who measured and marked out properties, were critical to the
new Europeanized landscape. Only after surveyors had identified property lines
would most settlers make investments, mostly in labor, on their land. Dutch and
English settlers made these investments because they assumed that they would
recoup the profits from their improvements. Although some settlers moved repeatedly, when they left, they sold their land, improvements and all, and prof-
ited thereby—or at least so they hoped. Dutch settlers drained wetlands, for
example, using ditches and dikes to create productive fields in rich soil along
the Esopus Creek, the Mohawk River, and their tributaries. Every acre cleared
of forest represented an improvement that had value; every yard enclosed by
fencing, every barn and solid home represented stored labor and retained value.
Expectations of accumulating wealth kept settlers at work on their land, continually altering it, making it more productive, more valuable.

Not all people could profit from their own labor. African American slaves
toiled in many parts of the colonial economy, in both the city and the country.
Although New York had no large plantations worked by slaves, for two centuries the colony's agriculture relied at least in part on slave labor, especially at

harvest time, when reaping wheat required many hands. After 1711 a New York City slave market sold humans imported from Africa and the Caribbean, and through much of the eighteenth century, slaves constituted more than 10 percent of the colony's population. In addition to black slaves, some white New Yorkers also could not reap the profits from their work, or at least not all the profits. The Dutch granted large tracts of land to patroons, individuals who controlled much of the land up the Hudson Valley. Most famously, the Van Rensselaer family controlled Rensselaerswyck—roughly Albany and Rensselaer counties—for more than two centuries, during which they extracted rents from the thousands of settlers who did the hard work of clearing and farming the land. Farmers generally paid rent in the form of wheat and other agricultural products. Although the settlers who occupied the best lands could easily afford the rent, for others it posed a considerable hardship, especially in lean years. What was worse, since the land was not the farmers' to sell, they could not recoup the cost of their hard work if they moved. This arrangement lasted into the 1840s, when the Anti-Rent Rebellion finally forced a democratic solution, granting renters the lands on which they had toiled. Interestingly, when farmers protested their rents and resisted authorities, they often dressed as Native Americans, hiding their identities and, ironically, asserting their historical claim to the land.

IMPERIAL AND REVOLUTIONARY CHANGES

Dutch patroons and merchants made their profits, but they accumulated only gradually. New Netherland grew very slowly, with few Europeans making the long, difficult trip across the Atlantic. By 1630 no more than three hundred settlers lived in the entire colony, and periodic wars with the Esopus Indians along the Hudson retarded growth through the 1660s. In the intensifying conflict between the Esopus and the Dutch, both groups burned farm fields and surplus crops as a way of forcing their enemies to flee. Although both Native Americans and Dutch settlers lost their lives in the First and Second Esopus Wars in 1659 and 1663, the Esopus were much more likely to kill European animals, including cattle, horses, and hogs, all of which were essential to Dutch survival in New Netherland. By attacking livestock, the Esopus hoped to jeopardize the settlers' entire enterprise.

The failure of New Netherland to thrive did not make it less attractive to the British, however, who hoped to consolidate their colonial holdings in North

America. In 1664 they took New Netherland from the Dutch without a battle, and renamed it New York. Although the British colony grew faster than its Dutch predecessor, war and the threat of war continued to retard growth, especially in the north, where the fur trade kept colonial powers in conflict. In 1690 the French and their native allies raided New York from Canada and attacked Schenectady, killing sixty and capturing twenty-seven. The raiders burned the small village to the ground. These and other conflicts rightfully gained the attention of prospective settlers, who appreciated the danger of living on the seventeenth-century frontier. And so, until the 1780s, Euro-American settlement remained confined, clustered on Long Island, around New York Harbor, up the Hudson, and along the lower Mohawk near Schenectady. Settlers farmed the fertile flatlands along these rivers, taking advantage of periodic floods that eased the clearing of the land and kept the soil rich. By the mid-1600s the Esopus Valley had become one of North America's first great wheat granaries. The farming community centered on the small stockaded village of Kingston and the Hudson River docks at the mouth of Rondout Creek. As the stockades around Kingston suggest, the modest European expansion into the colony's uplands did not reflect Europeans' lack of desire to farm farther inland. Rather, the slow population growth in New York and the Iroquois Confederacy's continuing strength kept European settlements hard by the region's largest navigable rivers.

Despite the modest size of New York's population, especially north of Kingston, Europe's great colonial powers—France and England—understood the strategic importance of the region James Fenimore Cooper called "the bloody arena," where two valleys, one pointing north to the St. Lawrence River, the other south to New York Harbor, nearly meet in the eastern foothills of the Adirondacks. Travelers from French Canada could canoe up the Richelieu River from the St. Lawrence into Lake Champlain and thence into Lake George, from which a relatively short carry brought them to the Hudson. For more than a century this was the most important north-south route in the interior of eastern North America. Combined with the imperial desire to acquire the rich natural resources of the American interior, this geography ensured that colonial conflict would recur here. The British built two significant forts: Fort Edward along the Hudson and Fort William Henry at the tip of Lake George. After the French built Fort Carillon on Lake Champlain in 1755, the region's "forests were alive with men," as Cooper recounted in *The Last of the Mohicans*, his fictional account of the Seven Years' War. During the war, the

British took Fort Carillon, which they renamed Ticonderoga, and eventually they took all of Canada, too.

By the time American colonists began demanding their independence from the Crown in the 1770s, the British had long understood the strategic value of Lake Champlain and the Hudson in the defense of North America. Since the British controlled the Atlantic Ocean and Canada, if they could gain control of the Hudson and Lake Champlain, they could effectively cut the growing rebellion in two, preventing the movement of information, supplies, and personnel from New England to the rest of the colonies. When the American Revolution began, military action focused first on Boston and then on New York City, but control of the long valley separating New England from the rest of the colonies remained critical. As General Philip Schuyler noted to John Hancock in 1775, "To me, Sir, Every Object, as to Importance, sinks almost to Nothing, when put in Competition with the securing of Hudson's River." With the Hudson River at the center of George Washington's strategy to defeat the British, the Hudson Highlands took on special strategic importance. Running from Hook Mountain, just twenty-five miles above the tip of Manhattan, north to Storm King, another twenty-five miles upstream, this series of mountains afforded commanding views of the Hudson, which at points became narrow and winding as it passed through.

Protecting the Highlands from the British required the success of the large Northern Continental Army, which took Fort Ticonderoga early in the war. In 1777, as a British army traveled south from Canada, the Americans occupied Bemis Heights, on the modest Neilson farm, taking positions that reveal the importance of geography to military tactics as well as strategy. With clearings and sightlines in three directions to the upper Hudson River, Patriot artillery perched on a bluff, overlooking the Albany Road and blocking the British advance. Fittingly, the decisive battle at Saratoga took place in a wheat field, one of the few large clearings in the area.

As the British defeat at Saratoga secured the Hudson from the north, Washington set his southern defenses in the Highlands, where he built Fort Montgomery and Fort Clinton, among other batteries with cannon trained on the Hudson. In 1778 the Patriots strung a great iron chain—forged at Sterling Iron Works in Orange County—across the Hudson at West Point, where the river turned sharply to the west. Along with improved fortifications at West Point, the chain helped secure the waterway and allowed Washington to keep his headquarters in Newburgh for much of 1782 and 1783. After the war West

Point remained important to the young nation, even briefly housing the entire standing American army. In 1802 Congress established the nation's military academy at West Point, forever reminding Americans of the military significance of the Highlands and the Hudson in the Revolution. To the north, the Saratoga battlefield and Fort Ticonderoga became tourist destinations, even in the years immediately following the war. Indeed battlefields and fortifications across the state became a prominent part of the tourist landscape over the next century, auguring the intensifying demand for the preservation of meaningful natural and cultural sites.

SETTLEMENT

The American Revolution brought a wave of change in New York. In 1779 the Americans raided Iroquois territory, and four years later, with the defeat of their British allies, the Iroquois were forced into a series of treaties that systematically removed Native Americans from most of upstate New York. Confined to shrinking reservations, some groups eventually headed west or into Canada. Still, the transition from a landscape controlled by Native American cultures to one possessed by Euro-Americans was a long one. Some individuals held on and adapted to new circumstances. Many Montauketts, for example, participated in the Euro-American economy, hiring themselves out to the growing English community on Long Island. By the early 1790s, however, indigenous people constituted a small fraction of the state's population. Altogether the Iroquois tribes had declined to just 3,500 people in 1794. Native American influence over the landscape diminished significantly, as the Euro-American economy and culture supplanted indigenous ways of living. In one respect, however, Native American influence has persisted: on the map. Native American place-names appear from Montauk, borrowed from the Algonquian word meaning "place of observation or a fortified place," to the Adirondacks, generally believed to have been named by the Mohawks who derogatorily described the people to the north as "tree eaters." Literally hundreds of New York places, from Esopus to Chautauqua and from Setauket to Saranac Lake, remind us that this was a well-occupied land long before the Dutch arrived, a land with a deep human history that involved the purposeful shaping of the natural landscape.

The defeat of the Iroquois meant that upstate New York was suddenly available for settlement. At the same time, the young nation began an era of rapid population growth, and the newly opened lands of New York became attractive to Yankees leaving the long-settled farmlands of New England. Many of them sought to start their own farms on fresh lands, hoping to profit from increasing European demand for wheat. Indeed a strong wheat market in the 1780s and 1790s encouraged the rapid conversion of upstate from forests to fields. From 1790 to 1820 New York gained over a million residents, many of whom arrived from the crowded farmlands of New England. Much of New York's growth occurred in the northern and western reaches of the state.

Though relieved of the fear of native attack, the first wave of settlers after the Revolution experienced great hardship. Most arrived with little money and few tools. Since nearly all of New York was covered in forest, settlers arrived on their land, or the land they hoped to purchase, and found mostly trees, the clearing of which would be their first great task. Unfortunately it wasn't a particularly profitable task, and so the first months spent clearing the forest were only lightly rewarded. Since early crops generally couldn't sustain families, to stave off hunger settlers took to the woods, hunting for meat and gathering a wide variety of foods, including wild leeks, the smell of which became an emblem of poverty. After touring New York frontier farms in 1803, downstate resident James Kent gave up any romantic thoughts he might have had about "living in a new Country." Indeed, "There are very few Comforts in poor log Houses in the wilderness at a great distance from Markett & the Conveniences of Life," he wrote. "They are totally detached from all Elegance & Luxury & surrounded by [a] harsh & rugged natural Landscape, by rude woods & dreary naked Trees & Stumps, by a poor & rude race of the first Settlers, by muddy & impassable roads—In short by Poverty and hard labor." As Kent made clear, early settlers started poor and advanced only slowly, held back by the difficulty of their work and the relative isolation most of them experienced. For many seasons, settlers occupied a cultural middle ground that blended the wild with the domesticated and that mixed Native American knowledge and technology with European preferences. Native and European crops grew side by side in the fields; venison and beef mixed in stewpots. Settlers wore buckskin and woven wool, ate wild turkey and domesticated chickens. Some stored treasured pieces of fine English china in homes made of rough-hewn logs. Everything about their lives spoke to the great transition under way.

Although life on the agricultural frontier could be remarkably isolating, frontier families had to cooperate with one another. William Cooper, a speculator who had purchased lands around Lake Otsego, described his own efforts, noting that "the first difficulties are the greatest, and it is only by combination and cooperation that they can be surmounted. The more the settlers are in number, the more hands can be brought to effect those works which cannot be executed by a few." As Cooper well understood, success for one required the success of others. Farmers shared equipment, such as plows and even the teams of oxen that pulled them. They gathered together for barn raisings, road building, and other cooperative work. Even after the "first difficulties," after fields entered production and barns stored surpluses, only growing communities would build the edifices that proclaimed success: schools, meetinghouses, and churches. To settlers, forests represented work yet to be done, work that would mean success not just for individuals and families but for entire communities and even the nation as a whole. On the frontier, growth was the common goal, and individual success served the interests of the commonweal.

Since settlers thought of themselves as bringing civilization to the wilderness, much of their work involved subduing nature, taming the wild. In this task they brought their guns to bear, using them to clear out dangerous or troublesome animals, such as large predators. Wolves and panthers threatened livestock, especially sheep, which had no means of self-defense. Bears were troublesome in a number of ways. In 1786 one Otsego County settler thought bears had eaten so many of his apples that he blamed them for depriving him "of a hope of making one Barrel [of] Cider." Not surprisingly, panthers, bears, wolves, and foxes became special targets; rare was the armed settler who wouldn't shoot one on sight, since their removal was an important step in making the landscape safe for occupation. Clearing the landscape of dangerous animals became government policy as early as 1651, when the Dutch put a bounty on wolves, offering payments to hunters who could prove they had killed a wolf by offering evidence "in the shape of a head or a leg, or an ear." Bounties became common. In 1799 the town of Hamilton, in Madison County, voted to pay a bounty of ten dollars for a full-grown wolf, five for a whelp, and one dollar for killing a full-grown bear. The town raised the bounty on wolves significantly in 1801 and then repealed it two years later, an indication that local wolves had been cleared and town leaders feared having to pay for imported carcasses. Settlers hardly needed bounties to provide extra incentive to hunt predators, however. Some men even participated in hunting parties, in which they cooperated in daylong hunts designed to clear animals from nearby woods.

Undoubtedly the removal of predators led to increases in certain species, including deer and smaller animals such as squirrels and chipmunks. Ironically, without natural predators, rodents themselves became a threat to crops, so much so that by 1800 Otsego County farmers dedicated their hunting parties to clearing the woods of squirrels. In one 1807 competition, two hunting parties killed a combined 2,368 squirrels. They also killed one bear and a porcupine that happened to be in the wrong place at the wrong time. Perhaps the death of the porcupine—which posed no threat to the settlers or to their crops, nor was it prized for its meat or skin—tells us the most about hunting in the settler era. Literally any animal was fair game.

Some settlers hunted mainly to protect their farms or to augment their produce, but a few men dedicated themselves to hunting and trapping, living off the meat of wild animals and the proceeds from pelts and skins. One such man, Thomas Meacham of Hopkinton in St. Lawrence County, kept a tally of the animals he had extinguished throughout his life. At his death in 1850, he claimed to have killed 214 wolves, 77 panthers, 219 bear, and 2,550 deer. Not surprisingly, over time, hunting pressure affected nearly all wild animals, especially those that were edible. Game was an important supplemental source of meat for early farmers; venison, turkey, goose, and duck all diversified frontier diets. Very quickly, then, hunting severely depleted wild fauna. But as we have seen, settlers brought a host of other animals with them, the taste of which they generally preferred to that of wild game. Through much of the state, forests and their wild creatures gradually gave way to fields stocked with domesticated animals.

Since an average farm family might clear five to ten acres of forest per year, depending on how many hands could be put to work, even rapidly settling areas remained largely wooded for a decade or more. In western New York's Holland Purchase, west of the Genesee River, by 1815 few farms had more than twenty-five acres of cleared land, meaning most of the landscape remained forested. As late as 1825, none of New York's seven western counties, including Genesee, Niagara, and Erie, had more than 25 percent of its acreage "improved." In central New York, too, clearing forests was a long, arduous process. Traveling out of Albany and up the Mohawk Valley in 1831, Alexis de Tocqueville jotted in his pocket notebook: "Man still making clearly ineffective efforts to master the forest. Tilled fields covered with the shoots of trees; trunks in the middle of corn. Nature vigorous and savage." To European eyes, American landscapes were especially wild—"savage," in Tocqueville's terminology. Like other travelers, then, Tocqueville may have been disposed to see frightful disorder in the landscape. Still, he was surely right about vigorous nature; the settlers' struggle should not be underestimated.

But over time the settlers gained the upper hand. In 1849 Orsamus Turner captured the heroic national narrative of the frontier struggle in a four-panel illustration of settlement in *A Pioneer History of the Holland Purchase of Western New York*. In the first panel, labeled "The first six months," a log cabin, smoke issuing from a small chimney, sits in a tiny clearing littered with stumps. In the second panel, representing the second year, the woods have been pushed back and a worm fence has appeared. Ten years later, in the third panel, the house, with clapboard addition, is now surrounded by an orchard, a barn, and post-and-rail fences. A large wagon overloaded with hay travels down the new road in the foreground. By the fourth panel, "The work of a lifetime," a fine Federal-style home sits on a completely reordered landscape, with straight lines demarcating fields, and most trees relegated to orchards and woodlots. A steam locomotive pulls a train across a long horizontal line in the mid-ground.

Although these were idealized portraits of progress, Turner's images would have looked familiar to many frontier families. Certainly William Rumsey and

Figure 1. "The first six months." Orsamus Turner, *A Pioneer History of the Holland Purchase of Western New York* (1849).

Figure 2. "Ten years later." Orsamus Turner, *Pioneer History of the Holland Purchase* (1849).

Figure 3. "The work of a lifetime." Orsamus Turner, *Pioneer History of the Holland Purchase* (1849).

his family, who arrived in Genesee Country from Vermont in 1802, would have seen a familiar struggle for success in these panels. Having heard of the region's excellent land, Rumsey purchased 150 acres near Batavia, home of the Holland Land Company's land office. He built a small house on the Genesee Road and went to work on his farm, which by the time of his death eighteen years later included fourteen head of cattle, more than a dozen pigs, a small flock of sheep, and an ox to work the fields, of which forty acres were under plow. Although he grew for the market, his farm retained the diversity necessary to early agriculture. He raised wheat, corn, rye, and oats, but also peas and beans in smaller quantities for his family. This was "the work of a lifetime." It was also a world remade.

POTASH, FIREWOOD, LUMBER, AND LEATHER

Not surprisingly, early farms were great consumers of wood. In most cases farmers likely consumed most of the wood on their properties simply by burning it. In an environment of ample land but scarce labor, settlers used fire to remove unwanted trees. Live trees burn poorly, of course, so often settlers girdled them, taking the bark off all the way around the trunk. The dead trees stood and dried, and they could be felled later, piled up, and burned. Ash from these fires served as an important though fleeting fertilizer for recently cleared fields. Ash could also be used to produce lye and potash, which themselves were important export products from new farms, and for many settlers their only cash crop for the first season or two. As the name suggests, potash required the boiling of ashes, usually in a large iron pot which itself was so expensive that most settlers did not own one. Instead they transported their ashes to "asheries," small establishments where heated water leached out the desired chemicals, which were then prepared for market. Potash, used in the manufacture of everything from soap to glass to gunpowder, became one of North America's leading exports to Britain, and by the 1770s, New York City had become the second-largest handler of potash, behind Boston.

Hardwoods, especially oak and maple, yielded the highest quantities of potash when burned, but its production was largely a by-product of the fires. The primary product of the fires was usually a farm field. Indeed one might track the movement of the farming frontier by counting the number of asheries. In the first half of the 1820s Beekmantown, on Lake Champlain, had just over twenty asheries, indicating both the great number of trees being burned along the lake and the access settlers had to markets via water route. In 1845 Madison County, in the middle of the state, contained twenty-one asheries, but ten years later it had just two, an indication that the removal of forests had slowed. Over the same period the county's sawmills increased, however, to seventy-five, suggesting that the consumption of wood for other purposes had surely not declined.

Some of the first settlers planned only to take the trees. These "woodchoppers," as Holland Land Company officers derisively called them, removed hardwoods and burned them, often leaving the property even less valuable for their efforts. Abandoned lands quickly filled with brush and small trees, which were difficult to clear and provided no reward for the work. Other early settlers removed trees and relied on their livestock to keep new growth from overtaking the clearing. Generally cattle and pigs had free run of the landscape; fencing was used to keep animals out of planted fields rather than in pastures and yards. Livestock ate grasses, wild leeks, selected saplings, and other tasty vegetation, but they left behind other plants, such as thorny shrubs and Canadian thistle, which was actually a European native, one of many nonnative "weeds" that thrived in the disturbed soils of the frontier. These nuisance plants became so numerous that local governments went so far as to pass legislation requiring property owners to cut them before they went to seed.

Settlers may have turned most wood to ashes, but they consumed wood in a number of other ways as well. Everyone burned wood for cooking and for heating small but drafty homes. Cutting cordwood could consume as much as a month of labor, as farmers replenished woodpiles in early spring so it could season over the summer. If time and market conditions permitted, farmers sent some wood to nearby villages and cities. Farmers also used wood for buildings and fences. Indeed one popular fencing style, the worm fence, became emblematic of settlers' wastefulness with wood, for it involved laying rails on top of one another in a zigzag pattern, a process that made digging postholes unnecessary. This type of fence used much more wood than a post-and-rail fence, both initially and over time, because the bottom rails, laid directly on the ground, tended to rot more quickly. Settlers sent some wood to sawmills for the production of lumber, though most of this wood would not have traveled far in the colonial era. In swampy areas, settlers used wood to make corduroy roads, with the logs laid side by side, creating a bumpy but generally less soggy roadway.

Late in life William Reed published an account of his North Country childhood, offering a detailed description of frontier life. In the early 1820s Reed's family moved from New Hampshire to Bombay, near the Canadian border, where they occupied a cabin set in the middle of a dense forest. The farm—though still mostly woods—was seventy-two acres, and they could see no neighbors through the trees. The family undertook the arduous work of turning forest into productive farm, a process that also required that they and their neighbors build a road to connect them to the outside world. After several years of intermittent work, they opened a one-mile road cleared of trees and stumps. The predominant task of the family, however, was "to fight the forest with the axe," as Reed put it. Fields for plowing needed to be stumped, but corn might be planted "right among the logs" left rotting on the ground. The axe was the "indispensable tool," and "year by year the forest fell in all directions." Soon neighboring farms came into view.

Farmers burned so much wood when clearing farms largely because they had no incentive to mill logs for market—at least not a market beyond the local one. In some areas, however, lumber did find more distant markets, especially where rivers could be used to float out logs. Early lumbering involved selective cutting, since some species were quite valuable, others worthless. The easily milled softwoods, such as white pine, were especially valuable, not least because they floated. Pine forests along larger rivers were logged most extensively.

As early as the 1750s Albany had become an important lumber market, as settlers along the northern Hudson and many of its tributaries milled their wood and placed it on rafts for transport. In the high waters of springtime the rafts arrived by the dozens in Albany, where workers loaded the lumber onto schooners for the trip down to New York City. When settlers moved into Delaware County in the 1790s, both branches of the Delaware River carried out lumber on spring freshets. By the 1830s, as the timber industry peaked in the Delaware watershed, more than two thousand rafts ran down the Delaware every year, headed for Philadelphia. Some of these rafts were tied together at Deposit, so named because it was a good place to leave logs awaiting their trip down to market. After 1800, settlers rafted timber down the Susquehanna and its tributaries, hoping to sell it all the way down in Baltimore. Some lumber headed north on Lake Champlain and out the Richelieu River to Canadian markets. Later, New York lumber traveled down the Allegheny to Pittsburgh, or even farther down the Ohio River. Lumber floated down the Genesee River to Rochester, where it was milled and, after 1825, sent to market on the Erie Canal. In sum, New York lumber headed out of the state in all directions, though almost always by water, the only means of transportation that made shipping wood profitable, at least until the construction of railroads.

White pine was the most valuable of lumber species, but it wasn't the only tree selectively cut from forests. Throughout the state men sought hemlock because the bark possessed an essential ingredient, tannin, used in making leather. Bark peelers felled the hemlock in the spring, removed its bark, and stacked it. The bark could then be taken out of the forests when convenient, often after snowfall allowed sledding. Bark was too expensive to transport far, so tanneries clustered near hemlock forests. Hides could travel considerable distances, mostly by water. Not surprisingly, tanneries consumed hemlocks along the Hudson River first, since that river facilitated the transport of hides, often in both directions, up to the tanneries and then back to the city. Tanning was by its nature a fleeting industry, however, since operations gave up as soon as the nearby hemlock stands gave out. In this way the industry cleared upstate New York of much of its hemlock, acre by acre, leaving only the least accessible stands. By the 1830s, tanning had moved into the Catskills, and would eventually move north and west. Hemlocks fell at greater and greater distances from New York City, the business center of the leather industry, which clustered in the Swamp, an area of Manhattan that had formerly housed tanneries.

MARKET CONNECTIONS

The New York frontier did not move precisely from east to west, because topography and climate directly influenced settlement patterns. Settlers skipped over rough terrain, preferring flatter lands with richer soils, even if they were farther from the well-populated areas. Settlers also preferred lands along waterways, even those not large enough to provide transportation, and they avoided the highest lands nearly altogether; the Adirondacks and the Catskills gained comparatively few residents in the early 1800s. In 1819 Henry Dwight was surprised to find a thriving little community in Hunter as he toured the Catskills. Farms lined the upper Schoharie Creek, while the mountainous acres nearby had few takers. Poor farming situations did provide opportunities for the poorest settlers, who could acquire these lands on favorable terms or, as was common in remote areas, simply occupy them as squatters, eking out a living on someone else's land.

Most migrants, however, preferred to move farther west in the early 1800s, to the fertile soil of the Great Lakes Plain. The difficulty of transportation left the pioneers largely supplying their own needs in the first years, principally through crops of Indian corn that sustained them and their animals. In 1810 Nathanial

Rochester joined the westward migration, arriving in the Genesee Valley via the Susquehanna River. He and his family operated a large farm and purchased land around the falls of the Genesee as an investment. Although it was several miles from the shores of Lake Ontario, this was an ideal spot for mills. When peace between Britain and the United States arrived in 1815, Lake Ontario offered easy access to markets via the St. Lawrence River, and the city at the falls, platted in 1812, began to grow. Rochester's development could be sustained only through market connections, as was the case everywhere in the state. Settlers struggled to establish and maintain these connections. Some opened stores and built warehouses; waterfront communities built docks and wharfs. Just as important, settlers combined their labor to build roads, the fundamental means of reaching markets for most upstate farmers.

Although property owners and towns built most local roads, private companies built many longer routes. These private turnpikes charged travelers at a series of tollgates as a means of recouping the great cost of building the roads. The Susquehanna Turnpike, for instance, had nearly twenty tollgates along its route from Catskill to Unadilla, a major road completed in 1806. In that same year construction began on the Skaneateles Turnpike, which soon linked Otsego and Madison counties to the settlement for which the road was named. And work was already under way on the Cherry Valley Turnpike to the north, which provided an important segment of the road that eventually linked Albany and Batavia by way of Cazenovia and Manlius.

While turnpike companies hoped to prosper by charging travelers, the Holland Land Company built roads in an attempt to profit from its expansive holdings in western New York—more than 3.2 million acres. It contracted for the construction of key roadways, knowing that they would increase the value of nearby land. By 1802 the company had built 170 miles of roads running out of Batavia. The most important of these, the Buffalo Road, connected Batavia with what would become a major port on Lake Erie. Altogether, by 1822 New York State had four thousand miles of road—both publicly and privately owned. Many of these roads were critical for farmers hoping to reach markets. Still, road builders had to be careful not to overextend their labors. An untraveled road could quickly fall into disrepair, as stumps resprouted and new plants grew densely in the sun-splashed openings created by the initial cut. The turnpike between Bath and Angelica, for example, fell into disrepair after the War of 1812. Only state intervention could keep it open.

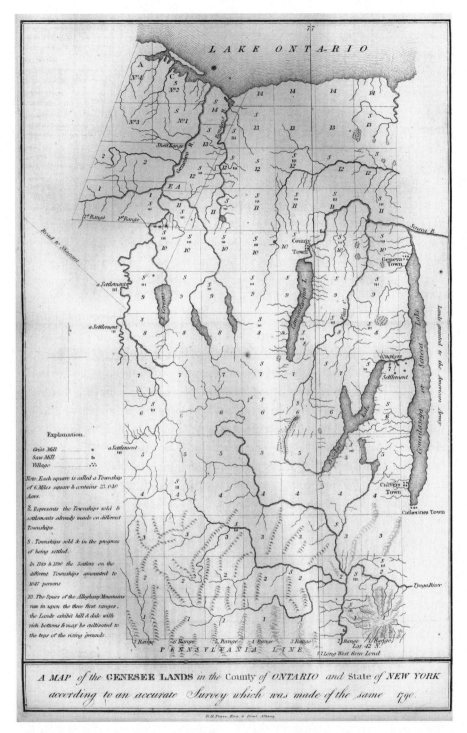

Figure 4. Gristmills and sawmills were critical to early settlers, as is made clear by this early map of the Genesee Valley and the western Finger Lakes. Map of the Genesee Lands (1790). From "Description of the Country Between Albany & Niagara in 1792," in *The Documentary History of the State of New York*, ed. E. B. O'Callaghan, vol. 2 (Albany, 1850).

If roads connected farmers to markets, usually waterways connected markets to one another. Water transportation was much more efficient, especially for moving bulky goods. Grain could travel only short distances by road; greater distances required water. This was also the case with wood. On some waterways, lumbermen began to send their logs to market without first milling them. Log drives down mountain streams were especially common in the Adirondacks, the western Catskills, and Allegany County.

In 1806 the state declared the Salmon River, which runs into Lake Ontario, a public highway so that logs could be floated on floodwaters down to Pulaski unimpeded. The next year the state granted the same designation to the Allegheny River so that settlers might float their rafted logs without obstruction. By midcentury most rivers that flowed out of mountain forests were designated public highways, including the Raquette, Oswegatchie, and Black rivers in the north. Although inaccessibility slowed logging through much of the Adirondacks, by the early 1800s Glens Falls had already become an important mill town, and the Hudson River had become the state's leading lumber thoroughfare.

Market connections also influenced the creation of early industry, including tanneries. Although they popped up around the state, exact locations were determined by specific variables. William Edwards, who founded a Catskills tannery in 1818, explained his reasoning: "I explored the Schoharie Kill from where Prattsville is now to the height of land in Hunter, wishing to find a good mill seat and plenty of hemlock bark; and as near the Hudson River as I could find these advantages." Edwards's needs mixed natural resources (falling water and hemlock stands) with market requirements, namely, access to New York City via the Hudson River. His establishment of a large, successful tannery, and the subsequent removal of thousands of hemlocks nearby, illustrates how thoroughly the market—and market connections—influenced when and how New Yorkers would exploit the state's natural resources.

MILLS

The Edwards example also reveals how both navigable water routes and obstructions on waterways shaped settlement patterns. If frontier life centered on the farm, its economy literally turned at the mill. Early settlements clustered around falling water, even on minor streams, where small dams could hold back enough water to turn a variety of wheels that themselves turned a variety of equipment. Farmers looked for rich, flat lands, but they judged distances to good mill seats, too. Joseph Ellicott well understood the need for mills in a successful farming community. Under his direction the Holland Land Company built three mills, two of them in Batavia, where a sawmill opened in 1802 and a gristmill two years later. Gristmills were nearly essential, allowing farmers to prepare surplus grains for market. New York was home to over 2,250 gristmills in 1825, the peak year for the number of establishments grinding grain. Over the next several decades, as transportation improved, milling would begin to concentrate at larger mills in larger cities. Sawmills, too, provided necessary services, allowing communities to replace log homes with houses built of prepared lumber. The 1825 New York census found nearly 5,200 sawmills, a number that would continue to grow for another twenty years. Other mills prepared wool for market, prepared bark for use in tanneries, and worked trip-hammers and bellows at small forges.

Ample precipitation falls throughout New York, and a great number of streams provided power to fledgling communities around the state. The best mill seats often became sites of successful cities, including Rochester, Ithaca, Troy, and Glens Falls. But much more than we recognize, manufacturing spread throughout the countryside along with agriculture, as small businesses produced for local markets or transformed local products, including wool. For example, the hamlet of Poolville grew up around a wool-carding business after 1825, and later gained a shoe manufactory. Like many small towns, Poolville also gained a tannery, although the tannery and the other two concerns all failed in the depression of the mid-1830s. Indeed many of these early manufacturing establishments failed quickly, and in some places even good water power could not ensure long-term growth. This was the case at Trenton Falls, where mills captured the power of falling water, but the unsuitability of the surrounding land for farming and the distance from major trade routes limited growth. Some of these old mill sites eventually became sites for electric power generation, such as at Trenton Falls and Heuvelton.

EARLY CITIES

Cities were critical to the colonial and early national economy, but New Yorkers had built no great metropolis before 1820. Many prominent New Yorkers made a great deal of wealth in commerce and manufacturing, but land was so inexpensive that cities grew only slowly, since most early immigrants were intent on acquiring the economic self-sufficiency that comes from farming. After

120 years of growth, New York City was still just a large village. "I found it extremely pleasant to walk the town," wrote visitor Peter Kalm in 1748, "for it seemed like a garden." New Yorkers could be proud of Broadway's beauty and of Trinity Church, one of the finest edifices in the New World. Still, New York had just 10,000 residents in 1740; London, by contrast, was eighty-four times larger. Eighty years later New York had grown into the country's largest city—with a population of 124,000—but it was only then poised for its mete-oric growth over the next century. Albany, the second-largest city in the state, ranked eleventh in the nation, with not quite 13,000 residents in 1820. Situated in between the state's two largest cities, Kingston, which dated to 1658, had grown to just over 1,000 residents by 1820, many of them still living essentially rural lives on large properties in and outside town. Others supplied services to the farmers nearby. There were blacksmiths and saddlers and a wagon maker, and a cider mill produced for the local market.

The urban environment posed few special challenges at this size. New York City residents could easily walk out of town, up Manhattan Island, and into the countryside. Few complained of the stench and din that plagued larger cities, though these complaints would eventually come to New York. Still, even small colonial cities faced two significant threats: fire and disease. Fire may have been the greatest danger. Most buildings were made of wood, and firefighting was limited by water pressure and the professionalism (or lack thereof) of firefight-ers. In 1731 New York City even passed a law requiring homeowners to hang a bucket by the front door, allowing them to join in a bucket brigade quickly when the inevitable fire broke out. Eighteenth-century New Yorkers were particularly aware of the potential for arson at the hands of slaves, who had previously used fire as a means of rebellion.

Contagious diseases also posed a grave threat in the colonial and early national periods, since smallpox and yellow fever epidemics could carry away so many souls so quickly. New York suffered through a series of yellow fever epidemics in the 1700s and early 1800s. During the last major yellow fever outbreak in 1822, residents burned coal, creating a dense smoke they hoped would purify the air. By the end of the summer nearly everyone had fled the city, with businessmen reestablishing a commercial district in Greenwich Village, then well outside the densest part of the city. A visiting Glasgow businessman described the disorder he found, with "nearly the whole of the business-part of the city being removed out to the fields which skirt the suburbs." No one knew of the mosquito's role in spreading the disease, but observers did remark on the connection between deaths from the fever and low, swampy ground, a connection that helped confirm the notion that wetlands were especially unhealthful.

Unnatural wet areas in cities also gained the attention of public health advocates. Colonial New York City had no sewers, and water collected in city streets, regularly augmented by human wastes dumped by residents uninterested in making the walk with their buckets to one of the rivers, where city ordinance required waste disposal. Even as sewerage improved, the lack of sanitation ensured recurring epidemics of yet another deadly disease, cholera, beginning in 1832. Limited understanding of how diseases spread led to the development of the miasma theory, which connected standing water and vapors to epidemics. Some New Yorkers blamed the moral failings of disease victims, who were likely to live in low-lying, poorly drained areas. This theory of disease neatly linked ideas of poverty, filth, and morality. Interestingly, the theory suggested that drying swampy lands and improving drainage would remove the threat of disease, and no doubt these steps did help by eliminating mosquito breeding grounds and reducing contact with human waste. Swamps and marshes were drained in the name of public health throughout the 1800s; not coincidentally, yellow fever became rare in the North. The primary public health lesson of the early 1800s was that urban environments contributed significantly to the spread of disease and poor human health generally.

Throughout the 1700s another typical urban problem developed in New York City: supplying ample fresh water. Since Manhattan was surrounded by salt water, its supply of fresh water was limited to cisterns, wells, and a seventy-acre pond called the Collect, located just north of where City Hall now stands. By the mid-1700s public wells had become infamous for their poor quality, having been spoiled by wastes discharged into city streets and privy vaults. Most colonists, even those who lived in the country, drank little water straight, preferring to boil what water they had to prepare tea. Colonial stomachs also tolerated beer and cider better than water, although rum was perhaps the most popular drink, much to the chagrin of moralists. In Manhattan the wealthy could send their slaves to more distant wells to fetch water in kegs, thereby reducing their own risk of dysentery or other ailments.

The Collect remained the city's most reliable water source into the late 1700s, but in the 1780s it had also become home to a growing number of industries, from tanneries to breweries. In 1785 the *New York Journal* declared the Collect "a very sink and common sewer," where both whites and blacks washed their "cloths blankets and things too nauseous to mention." The *Journal* also feared

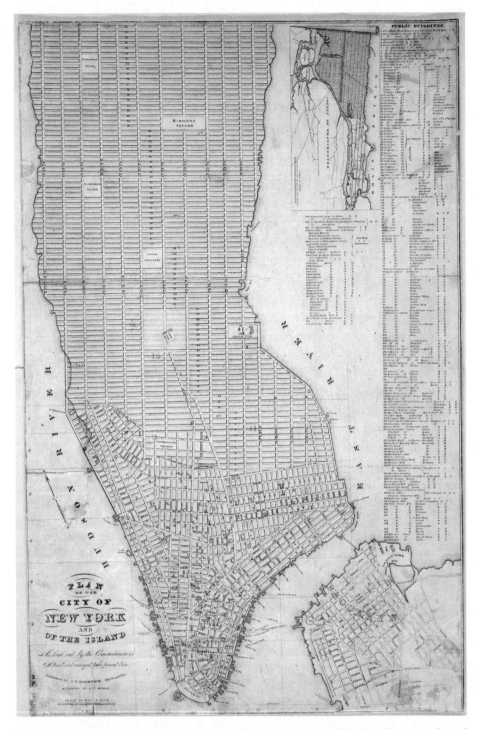

Figure 5. The commissioners' 1811 plan ignored all natural variations in Manhattan's topography and instead cast a grid over the entire island, perfectly symbolizing the dramatic reorganization of the state's landscape in the nineteenth century. John F. Morin, "Plan of the city of New York and of the island: as laid out by the commissioners, altered and arranged to the present time" (1828). Engraving. Lionel Pincus and Princess Firyal Map Division, New York Public Library, Astor, Lenox and Tilden Foundations.

that the Collect's neighbors were throwing "many buckets"—of human waste—into the pond. Between 1802 and 1813 New Yorkers systematically filled in the Collect, long since considered a nuisance. Cartmen brought refuse, soil, and rock, and the city paid them by the load. Poorly filled, low, and unstable, this new land was centrally located, just north of City Hall, but it remained an undesirable neighborhood. Buildings constructed on the settling fill listed, basements stayed wet, and foul smells filled the air. The neighborhood, eventually called Five Points, became home to immigrants and African Americans, who paid too much for small apartments in ill-kept buildings. It also became one of the nation's first slums, plagued by crime and prostitution. Five Points was an object lesson in the connection between low urban lands and undesirable neighborhoods, and at least for nineteenth-century New Yorkers, it provided ample evidence of how degraded environments encouraged immoral behavior.

By 1820 the small cities of New York State only hinted at the great changes that would take place in urban environments over the next century. Relatively weak urban governments had little power over urban spaces, but they had begun the process of reshaping the landscape, filling in low spots to prevent the collection of foul waters and filling in nearby wetlands to prevent the creation of unhealthful fogs. In New York City, for instance, the Common Council buried a ditch under Canal Street in the hopes of draining troublesome waters from the Five Points slum. More significant, a few years earlier, in 1811, a state-appointed Streets Commission began the process of planning a more orderly expansion up Manhattan Island, in the hopes of promoting "the health of the city" and allowing for the "free and abundant circulation of air." The Commissioners' Plan was nothing short of a grand vision of the city Gotham would become. It famously proposed a rigid street grid, with twelve major avenues racing up the island, laced by more than a hundred regularly placed cross-streets, all the way up to a proposed 155th Street. The plan completely ignored the topographical realities of the island and took no account of natural watercourses. According to the plan, everything would be reordered, with natural features suppressed by the city builders. The plan was as clear an announcement of Americans' intention to subdue nature as any the young nation made. As of 1820, of course, it remained lines on a page; the lines on the landscape would come over time.

"SETTLING A COUNTRY"

In 1823 Otsego County's most famous son, James Fenimore Cooper, wrote his first Leatherstocking novel, *The Pioneers*, in which he offers a fictionalized version of the settlement of his hometown, Cooperstown, in the 1790s. Cooper's rich description of frontier life makes clear its struggles and opportunities, and, most important, reveals how profound a transition the frontier represented, a transition that brought loss as well as gain. A lone Native American character represents an era already past—the lost world of Iroquoia. Another character, the old hunter Natty Bumppo, also known as Leatherstocking, represents the loss then under way. Natty looks upon the settlers with great suspicion. They are wasteful of wood and wildlife. Their growing numbers mean the end of Leatherstocking's frontier freedom, at least around Lake Otsego. Bumppo complains that game is becoming hard to find because of "clearings and betterments," but he knows that more than just the lack of game will force an end to his ways.

The most compelling and perhaps now most famous passage in *The Pioneers* describes the town's reaction to the approach of a seemingly endless flock of passenger pigeons, which traveled in huge numbers, perhaps as many as a billion birds. With the heavens "alive with pigeons," the whole town appears armed on the streets—guns, arrows, even crossbows at the ready. The crowd fires repeatedly into the flock. No one "pretended to collect the game, which lay scattered over the fields in such profusion as to cover the very ground with fluttering victims." Leatherstocking watches the proceedings with silent disgust, until someone introduces a small cannon to fire into the flock. "This comes of settling a country," Leatherstocking shouts, as he launches into a complaint against the settlers' "wasty ways." In this scene, and in another where the settlers haul in so many bass from the lake that many are simply left to rot on the shore, readers are reminded of both the bounty that nature once provided in New York and the profligate manner in which the early settlers consumed it.

Modern readers certainly find Leatherstocking's laments compelling, knowing as we do that the passenger pigeon has long been extinct and that Lake Otsego will never again yield seines brimming with bass. But early-nineteenth-century readers may have been more struck by other passages in *The Pioneers*, such as the opening scene in which Cooper paints a loving portrait of Otsego County, with its "romantic and picturesque character," "the limpid lakes and thousand springs," and the "neat and comfortable farms." At the time of Cooper's writing, Otsego County's valleys were rich and cultivated, its villages beautiful and thriving. This too came "of settling a country." Although the novel tells a less than heroic tale of the frontier, in the opening pages Cooper seems mostly proud of what has been accomplished around Cooperstown, which after all had been founded by his father. "In short," Cooper writes, "the whole district is hourly exhibiting how much can be done, in even a rugged country, and with a severe climate, under the dominion of mild laws, and where every man feels a direct interest in the prosperity of a commonwealth of which he knows himself to form a part." Hard work had wrought prosperous and attractive communities. And perhaps most astonishingly, Cooper concludes, "Only forty years have passed since this territory was a wilderness." Here he sounds much like his father, who also reflected on what had happened in the valley since his arrival. "I am now descending into the vale of life," William Cooper wrote in 1807, "and I must acknowledge that I look back with self complacency upon what I have done, and am proud of having been an instrument in reclaiming such large and fruitful tracts from the waste of creation."

We are left, then, with two very different views of this great transformation, one that emphasizes loss, the other gain. Not surprisingly, most Americans have chosen the latter perspective in telling their nation's story. Overlooking a much-altered environment, Americans, in Otsego County and a dozen other places in the state, would see native landscapes transformed and increasingly forgotten. Settlers brought with them entirely new ways of thinking about the places they occupied and new ways of acting to alter those places to suit their desires. They struggled to remove the forests, cutting and burning acres at a time. By 1825 New Yorkers had cleared more than 7 million acres of forest. They had also selected certain species for more measured removal—such as white pine, hemlock, and oak, each useful in its own way. Settlers had selectively removed wild fauna as well, greatly diminishing the population of all furbearers, panthers, wolves, and bears. But they brought their own animals: horses, cattle, pigs, sheep, as well as rats. Fields filled with species from Eurasia: English grasses, wheat, and rye, but also dandelions and ragweed. The cutting plows and heavy hooves of European-style agriculture turned the soil, drying it out and subjecting it to erosion. Those fields were productive of their desired crops and of a new culture on the American frontier. From the perspective of the 1820s, few Americans would doubt that this was anything but progress.

2

This Wilderness Becomes a Fertile Plain

Engineering the Empire State

With great expectations a young Nathaniel Hawthorne climbed aboard a boat on the Erie Canal, the "watery highway" Governor DeWitt Clinton and thousands of workers had strung between Albany and Buffalo. Like many Americans, Hawthorne traveled in order to experience the "Grand Canal" as a tourist. He hoped the remade New York landscape would inspire him to write poetically about this magical stream. "Surely, the water of this canal must be the most fertilizing of all fluids," Hawthorne wrote in his 1835 essay "The Canal Boat," published five years after his trip, which itself had taken place five years after the canal's completion in 1825. As he headed west toward Utica, though, Hawthorne was underwhelmed. The boat moved at a leisurely pace, about five miles per hour, through "dismal swamps and unimpressive scenery." Still, there was variety in this landscape, even if it passed too slowly. In Utica the boat moved "amid piles of brick, crowded docks and quays, rich warehouses and a busy population." Then, moments later, it was "threading an avenue of the ancient woods again." He had entered the "long level," where workers had begun digging the ditch on July 4, 1817. For nearly seventy miles the canal had "not rise or fall enough to require a lock."

As Hawthorne recounted, the effects of the canal's construction were still evident even as he passed in the dark. The damp forest of cedar and ash had dried out, the swamps having been partly drained by the canal, and the trees now stood "decayed and death-struck"; the "tall stems and intermingled branches were naked, and brought into strong relief, amid the surrounding gloom, by the whiteness of their decay." In some spots, Hawthorne wrote, "where destruction had been riotous, the lanterns showed perhaps a hundred trunks, erect, half overthrown, extended along the ground, resting on their shattered limbs, or tossing them desperately into the darkness, but all of one ashy-white, all naked together, in desolate confusion."

Here in Hawthorne's chaotic and dying forest was evidence of the disorder wrought by rapid change. In the mid-nineteenth century, this disorder could be found through much of upstate New York. Many travelers on the canal would remark on the receding forests and on the draining of swamps, but most offered nothing but praise. After all, the purpose of the canal was economic growth, which surely followed. The canal transformed upstate New York, connecting millions of acres to distant markets, encouraging settlement and export, the growth of villages and cities, of agriculture and manufacturing. At either end of the canal, Albany and Buffalo became sizable cities, and down the Hudson River, the Erie turned New York City into the "granary of the world," just as DeWitt Clinton had promised in 1824. Despite Hawthorne's judgment, by 1830 the canal was already an obvious triumph. The Erie's success sparked a canal building boom in New York and other states, helping to draw the nation together in the market revolution. Although the Erie would have implications well beyond the state's boundaries, encouraging settlement in Ohio and the growth of dozens of Great Lakes cities, changes were felt first and most deeply in New York, which by the time of Hawthorne's writing had become the Empire State, the largest in the union in population, in agricultural production, and in manufacturing. But as Hawthorne reminds us, this growth had its costs, as the remade economy required a remade landscape, one with fewer forests and swamps, and more farm fields and cities.

The story of the canal also reminds us how thoroughly nineteenth-century New Yorkers engineered their environment, applying scientific knowledge to the pursuit of wealth and opportunity. Even beyond transportation, the application of science helped transform New York. Experimentation and innovation increased agricultural production, as New Yorkers participated in what became known as scientific farming. Burgeoning cities required governmental and technological innovations to provide basic services, especially in the construction of new systems to supply potable water and carry away human waste. Engineers applied their talents to these tasks. Altogether, through the mid-1800s, New Yorkers engineered a new environment. The disorder Hawthorne witnessed in

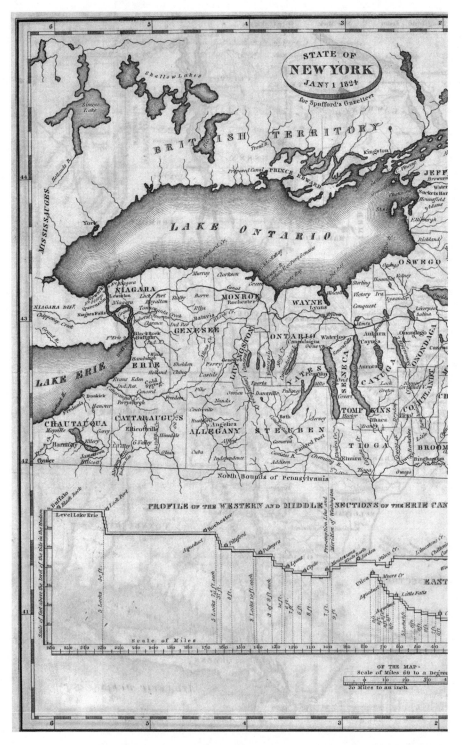

Figure 6. Early-nineteenth-century maps featured watercourses, including the artificial river, the Erie Canal. "State of New York, Jany. 1, 1824," *Spafford's Gazetteer* (1824). Lionel Pincus and Princess Firyal Map Division, New York Public Library, Astor, Lenox and Tilden Foundations.

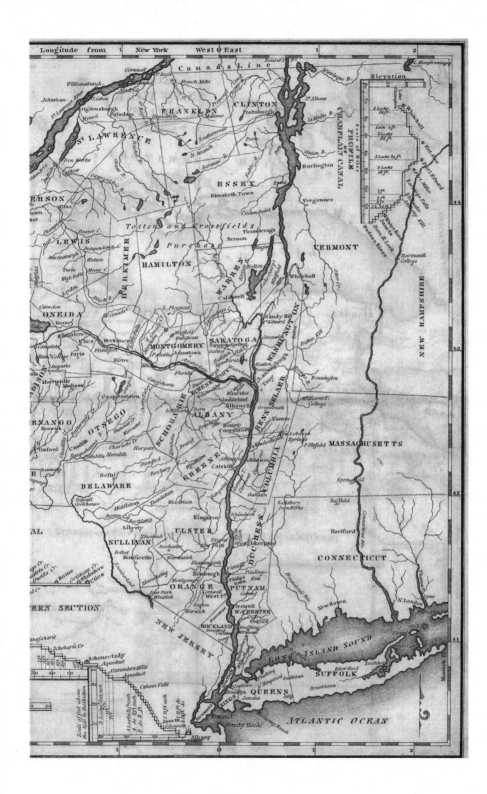

1830 was but a stage. The desired result was a new order—an increasingly integrated and networked civilization—built to replace a receding wilderness.

BUILDING THE CANAL

The Erie Canal was a technological wonder, but observers also thought of it as an extension of nature, and not just because it relied on water, gravity, and workhorses to operate. The canal was an "artificial river," placed by engineers at a break in the Appalachian mountain chain. The term neatly reflected the blending of nature and art in the canal, the way the structure revealed the ability of engineers to improve the landscape, to make gravity work, to find the level spots in an uneven landscape. Although it required eighty-three locks to overcome elevation, the canal traveled through a relatively flat region, along the easiest overland route from the Atlantic coast to the Great Lakes. Other states tried to replicate the Erie's success, but none could come close. Most famously, Pennsylvanians filled their mountainous state with canals, some of which proved very successful; but none could compete with the more efficient Erie in transporting goods east and west. Farther south, not even federal aid could turn the Chesapeake and Ohio Canal into a rival to the Erie. After twenty-two years of halting construction along the Potomac River, that canal had only reached Columbia, Maryland, and it never connected to its namesake, Ohio. The southern Appalachians were simply insurmountable by canal. As Basil Hall wrote in 1829: "The various attempts now making to outdo the Erie Canal must inevitably fail. Nature is on the side of New York."

Despite the advantages afforded by nature, the Erie Canal was much more than a 363-mile, forty-foot-wide ditch across the state. The New York landscape posed challenges to engineers and workers alike. The canal required reliable water sources to feed water continuously at highpoints, so engineers diverted streams for that use, making it possible for Lake Erie waters to keep boats afloat through much of the canal's western section. Since the canal didn't require the waters of most of the streams it traversed, eighteen aqueducts were built to carry boats over waterways, including the stunning aqueduct that carried the Erie across the Genesee River in Rochester. In addition, as Hawthorne reported, the canal's construction required the draining of swamps and the building of embankments. For two summers, workers stood in the waters of the Cayuga marshes, facing illness and exhaustion, but digging the ditch all the same. To the east, the Irondequoit Valley posed an even greater challenge, solved by the construction of a great embankment that raised the canal bed more than two hundred feet above Irondequoit Creek, which passed through a culvert below. Perhaps the biggest challenge, however, involved the breaching of the ridge that separated the Genesee plain from the Niagara Frontier. Here workers blasted away a deep cut, seven miles long, culminating in a flight of five locks that surmounted the sixty-foot rise.

During the summer of 1821 perhaps nine thousand men labored on the canal, joined by hundreds of work animals. Fortunately for engineers and workers, continuous technological innovation eased construction. As workers prepared the long level west of Rome, they developed new technology for clearing trees, using an endless screw, cables, and a crank. With this device, men could pull down the largest of trees so that they might be dragged away by teams of oxen or horses. Another contraption, involving chains attached to large wheels, served as a stump puller. At points workers used spades and wheelbarrows to move the earth, but in another innovation, animals pulled large plows back and forth along the canal line, peeling back the earth to make the four-foot-deep ditch along the many long levels of the Erie. In 1818 Andrew Bartow's experimentation with the limestone of Onondaga County resulted in the development of a quicklime cement that hardened underwater—a property that made it especially valuable for the canal and many other projects that followed.

When work began on the canal, no engineering school existed in the United States. Engineers either got their training in Europe or, more commonly, simply trained on the job. Many of the first canal engineers learned their trade after joining a canal crew, perhaps most famously John Jervis, who began as an axeman and surveyor's aide, but quickly rose to be a superintending engineer. Jervis's long and successful career after the Erie's completion reveals the value of this practical training, but the great demand for engineers during the canal's construction convinced some that a more reliable source of capable engineers had to be found. Thus the Rensselaer Polytechnic Institute was established in Troy, near the eastern terminus of the canal. Many of the engineers who later joined the canal-building craze in New York and elsewhere in the United States received formal training at RPI. In this way the Erie's construction, the very size and complexity of the project, inspired the development of the civil engineering profession in the United States. Those engineers, of course, continued the work of transforming the landscape in New York and beyond.

At the canal's completion, the state organized a grand celebration along the entire route. On October 26, 1825, the canal boat *Seneca Chief* departed from

Buffalo carrying two kegs of Lake Erie's "pure waters," along with a number of products from around the Great Lakes. Cannon fire announced its departure, and all along the canal and the Hudson, evenly spaced cannons repeated the blast until reports echoed in New York City some three hours and twenty minutes later. On November 2 the *Seneca Chief* reached Albany, greeted by the largest celebration yet. At Albany Basin the canal boat was joined by steamers for the journey down the Hudson, and on the morning of the fourth, the Erie water reached New York Harbor, again greeted by cannon fire. With all the pomp that had surrounded the entire ten-day celebration, Governor Clinton and other dignitaries poured the Erie water into the Atlantic near Sandy Hook. The celebration was called the "Wedding of the Waters," a perfect symbolic gesture to mark the canal's completion. Waters had been joined, and everything in New York would be transformed.

ENGINEERING WATER

The Erie and the many canals that followed were just part of a much grander project under way across New York: the piecemeal reworking of the state's waterscape. Controlling water was an important step in taming the wilderness, in making nature more productive. This engineering of water came in many forms, including the improvement of harbors. As early as 1816 a group of men gathered in the infant city of Buffalo to determine how to ensure economic growth. The city had been platted just north of Buffalo Creek, a small, slow stream that ran parallel to Lake Erie for some distance. This might have served as a fine harbor save for a sandbar that blocked the river's mouth, making it impossible for larger ships to enter. In 1817 the state designated Buffalo as the western terminus of the Erie Canal, ensuring that the sandbar would be removed and other harbor improvements made to accommodate the anticipated flood of goods.

Elsewhere, local residents engaged in projects to improve travel and increase agricultural production. By 1818 a series of locks on the Seneca River allowed boats to pass between the two largest Finger Lakes. Nearby, workers drained as much of the Cayuga marshes as they could, to improve navigation and open up "waste lands" to farming. Throughout the state, natural rivers were cleared of overhanging trees and snags; they were dredged of sandbars and gathered silt. All of this work undoubtedly diminished fish habitat and reduced ecological productivity, but the desired results followed. The altered waterways more efficiently carried boats to markets and floated logs downstream to mills.

In 1825 Theodore Dwight described a nine hundred–foot dam that crossed the upper Hudson near Fort Edward, and a canal along the bank used to allow boats to pass. Early dam building such as this was often undertaken to raise water levels to improve navigation, as well as to increase the head at mill sites. Thousands of small wooden dams backed up water to supply power to thousands of mills scattered across the state. After mid-century, dozens of additional dams raised water levels in streams and lakes to facilitate the floating of logs, especially in the Adirondacks. In the 1850s a dam raised the level of Tupper Lake, and later dams raised the level of the Raquette River farther north, where in the 1870s dead trees drowned by elevated water lined the river for thirty miles, standing as testament to the scale of the intervention on behalf of logging. On many smaller rivers in the North Woods, "flood dams" held back water to be released after logs had been assembled for the ride downstream. Other projects increased the power water could supply, such as "The Tunnel" on Fall Creek in Ithaca, which Solomon Southwick called a "stupendous work of art" in 1835. Built to deliver water to a mill between the first and second falls on Fall Creek, "The Tunnel" was part of the hydraulic infrastructure built to power industry in the gorges around Ithaca.

Of all the works engineered to control water, canals were the most important. But the Erie didn't work alone; by 1860 upstate New York was laced with canals. The Champlain Canal connected Lake Champlain to the Hudson River and the Erie Canal by 1823. The Oswego Canal linked Syracuse and Lake Ontario by 1828, and a year later the Cayuga-Seneca Canal linked the two largest Finger Lakes to the Erie Canal. By 1833 the Chemung Canal linked Elmira with Seneca Lake, and two years later Oneida Lake had its connection to the Erie Canal. In 1837 the Chenango Canal linked the Erie at Utica with the Susquehanna River in Binghamton. The two most difficult canals were completed in the 1850s: the Black River, which headed north out of Rome and climbed into the foothills of the Adirondacks; and the Genesee Valley, which after a long hiatus in construction at Mount Morris connected Rochester south to the Allegheny River at Olean. At its greatest extent the New York canal system connected Lakes Erie, Ontario, Seneca, Cayuga, Oneida, and Champlain and the Hudson, Susquehanna, Allegheny, and Delaware rivers. Nearly every place of any size in New York State was connected to every other by water route.

The economic impact of the canals is difficult to quantify, but even apart from all the goods that traveled along its course, the mere operation of the system brought growth. By the 1840s, thirty thousand New Yorkers worked to keep the Erie Canal functioning. Many of these men handled the 3,400 boats that plied the canal and moved goods to and from the boats—backbreaking and time-consuming work. Men also operated the locks day and night. The thousands of horses that worked the canals needed stables for resting and stable hands to tend them. These horses needed feed, too, and this encouraged farmers to grow oats and hay along the routes. Just as stables attended to the needs of horses, hotels and taverns clustered along the canal to attend to the needs of workers and travelers. And of course warehouses and shops spread along the canals to attend to the goods and those who bought and sold them. Many cities and villages used canals as main streets, with façades facing the water, as in Syracuse and Binghamton, a reflection of the canals' centrality to the urban economy.

Tourists, like Hawthorne, did travel the canals, but the success of the artificial rivers came from the eased transportation of goods, not people. The canals transformed the state's economy by connecting markets and creating opportunities in new lands, including those along the "feeder canals." The Chenango Canal was not nearly as successful as the Erie, but it did boost the economy in its central New York valley in the 1830s. Improved access to markets encouraged the building of mills and small manufactories, and all along the route new hotels and taverns opened. Even small communities, such as Earlville, experienced growth. The completion of the Black River Canal in 1855 allowed Lewis County to diversify its economy. Tanneries sprang up along the Beaver, Moose, and Oswegatchie rivers, often taking advantage of water power to crush the hemlock bark harvested in the Adirondack foothills. Although individual establishments remained small, manufacturing dotted the countryside, and of course along both the Chenango and the Black River canals, farms filled the valleys, sending their surpluses to distant markets via barges.

Combined with new roads, the canals were instrumental in the state's effort to settle the land and bring prosperity to the "waste of creation," as William Cooper had described it. Mid-century maps show these new lines on the landscape, and the new place-names they connected, suggesting how thoroughly wild forests had been pushed back, to the North Woods, the highest parts of the Catskills, and the remotest parts of the Southern Tier. Native Americans, too, continued to cede lands, and reservations shrank over time. In 1838, for instance, the federal government signed the Treaty of Buffalo Creek with the six Iroquois nations (the Tuscarora having joined the original five tribes in the early 1700s), in an attempt to force them westward, out of New York. Considerable complaint and confusion followed the treaty, but it resulted in the termination of the Buffalo Creek Reservation. Nearly fifty thousand acres just west of the growing city of Buffalo became available for sale to settlers, further evidence of the canal's transformative powers in the western part of the state.

The Erie Canal thus served as the linchpin in an extensive state-financed transportation system. Only one major New York canal, the Delaware and Hudson, was the product of the private sector. When completed in 1828, it connected the anthracite coalfields in northeastern Pennsylvania with the Hudson River near Kingston. Although it was much shorter than the Erie, the Delaware and Hudson passed through much more difficult terrain, testing the skill of engineers. In 1841 Washington Irving traveled the route, which entered Pennsylvania at Lackawaxen, and he marveled at the accomplishment. "Altogether it is one of the most daring undertakings I have ever witnessed to carry an artificial river over rocky mountains and up the most savage and almost impractical defiles," he wrote. The canal ushered in significant changes for Kingston, the Rondout Valley, through which the canal passed, and the Delaware Valley, into which it ran. Most obvious, tons of coal made their way to the Hudson; by the 1850s more than a million tons of coal moved over the docks in Kingston every year. Much of the coal headed downstream, to New York City and Brooklyn, where residents burned it for heat and cooking, and growing industries became reliant on it. This good anthracite connection shaped industrial growth in New York Harbor, and it helped ensure that New York would long retain its reputation for having clean air despite industrial development, since anthracite burned with much less smoke than the bituminous coal that fueled industrialization in Pittsburgh, Cincinnati, and Chicago.

AGRICULTURE

As canals spread, landscapes changed dramatically, especially as agricultural production boomed. In this regard the Erie's influence was instantaneous. In his memoir of the canal's construction, published in 1825, Cadwallader Colden remarked on the visible growth. "We see with astonishment the progress already made in populating regions which only yesterday it may be said, were uninhabited," he wrote. "Already the whole Canal line is occupied." Growth was rapid, to be sure, but settlement took time, partly because prospective farmers first had to clear their lands of forests, a long and arduous process. With so many forests falling along the canal route in 1827, traveler Basil Hall commented on the "appearance of bleakness or rawness" surrounding new villages, "whose dreary aspect was much heightened by the black sort of gigantic wall formed of the abrupt edge of the forest, choked up with underwood, now for the first time exposed to the light of the sun." Even in the fields before the black wall of forests, Hall found desolation, "with innumerable great black stumps" and "tall scorched, branchless stems of trees." He was appalled by the "numbers of magnificent trees standing . . . with their throats cut," girdled and left to die upright. Progress, it seems, was a messy and costly business.

Three years later, in 1830, the Englishman John Fowler traveled through upstate, on roads rather than the canal, to report on the agricultural opportunities available in New York. Fowler was not wholly impressed with American agricultural practices, and like Hall, he commented on the generally untidy appearance of New York's farms. Fowler was nevertheless struck by the pace of change. On a stagecoach from New Hartford to Vernon, a trip of thirteen miles, he saw good land and good farms the entire way. Though mostly concerned with farmland, Fowler also took note of the region's woodlands, including "one of the finest specimens of *native forest* I have seen in the country," just east of Chittenango. To Fowler this "*dense mass of forest*" seemed "to bid defiance to the footsteps, ay, even the hands of man; and yet," he continued, "but a few years may elapse ere this wilderness becomes a fertile plain, ere the share of the husbandman passes over its surface, and the abodes of happy industry are raised upon it! So rapid are the strides of improvement and cultivation in this enterprising country." Farther west, Fowler found even finer farms near Geneva and Canandaigua, two communities that had both boomed and grown beautiful in his estimation.

Beyond Canandaigua, Fowler entered the Genesee Valley, which had attracted farmers even before the canal's construction. The soils were rich, and the river itself gave settlers access to Lake Ontario, and hence to Canadian markets. In 1820, 67,000 barrels of flour left Rochester this way, and soon "Genesee Flour" had gained a reputation for high quality, even earning a premium in urban markets. But the region's real growth awaited the completion of the canal to Rochester. Just six years after the canal's opening, the city exported 240,000 barrels of flour. Nor was Rochester the only city loading the region's wheat onto canal barges. Throughout the valley, forests made way for wheat, still a hand-sown and harvested crop in the early 1830s. Farmers mostly grew winter wheat, planted in the fall and harvested in the spring. In the early years fertilizing may have been light, as farmers relied on the natural fertility of the soil, but by the

Figure 7. A diversity of soil types and topography permitted the development of a diversity of agriculture in the nineteenth century. The growth of urban markets and a taste for beer encouraged the development of hops farms in central New York. "Hop Pickers," possibly by Washington G. Smith or Arthur J. Telfer (1880). Smith-Telfer Photographic Collection, New York State Historical Association, Cooperstown, N.Y.

1840s, many farmers augmented their soils with gypsum—sulfate of lime—much of it taken from a quarry in Wheatland.

The success of Genesee Flour inspired further settlement, well south of Rochester. In Wyoming and Allegany counties, settlers began to demand better access to markets, which they would gain through the construction of the Genesee Valley Canal, completed to Mount Morris in 1840. By that time the Genesee Valley was producing more than 300,000 bushels of wheat each year, along with admirable quantities of potatoes, oats, corn, and wool. In the most suitable areas, cultivated fields occupied as much as 75 percent of the land, with farmers leaving woodlots mostly to supply their own cordwood for winter heating. In some areas, including around Geneva, farmers eager to put acres into wheat may have removed too much forest, increasing the value of woodlots and the cost of fuel.

Although change was most rapid and complete in the Genesee region because of its rich soil, over time nearly the entire state witnessed significant change. In the twenty years after the Erie's opening, the western New York counties that constituted the Holland Purchase gained nearly 155,000 residents, more than doubling in population. During these years settlers cleared an additional 850,000 acres in the Holland Purchase—more than 1,300 square miles of land. Changes in agriculture were no less apparent in Kings, Queens, and other downstate counties, as farmers turned away from grain and livestock and toward vegetable production. Rapid growth in New York City and Brooklyn meant ample markets for cabbages, lettuce, spinach, and potatoes, all of which could be carted in daily or sent on ferries to East River markets. At the same time, the cities' growing herds of horses, used mostly for moving goods and people, created great quantities of manure, which could be used as fertilizer on surrounding farms. Land values rose outside cities, and farmers responded with an intensification of production. With the regular addition of fertilizer, suburban farmers no longer needed to leave fields periodically fallow or follow the strict crop rotations increasingly used in other parts of the state.

Urban growth thus doubly influenced New York's agriculture, by providing markets for a growing number of truck farms and by supplying the fertilizer that allowed them to increase production. By 1860, five of the largest vegetable-producing counties in the country were in New York State, and all of them lay just outside sizable cities. Queens County was first on the list. Two others—New York County (Manhattan) and Kings (Brooklyn)—also supplied the growing metropolis, while Albany and Monroe counties supplied vegetables to upstate cities. All of these changes revealed the increasingly integrated nature of New York's economy and environment. Growth in cities begat growth in the hinterlands, as production intensified.

The Erie Canal brought market changes upstate, downstate, and around the nation, as American agricultural production rose dramatically. Beyond New York, Ohio in particular boomed with the improved access to eastern markets. As midwestern grain poured into Buffalo, New York farmers, especially those on marginal land, shifted their own production. In Madison County, for example, early farmers had grown wheat and other grains, but competition from farther west compelled the region to turn toward dairy, fruit, and hops. As Catskill resident Abner Austin reported in 1835, farmers in the Hudson Valley turned away from wheat and other grains, choosing to leave more land in pasture for dairy herds and sheep, or, as Austin noted, simply for harvesting hay for the urban market, where it fed urban horses. "Every considerable farmer has his hay press, & sends all his surplus hay on to market," Austin declared. Even

Figure 8. Although decline began in the late nineteenth century in some agricultural regions, a strong market for hay persisted, largely because of the turn toward dairy farming, but also because of the demand created by huge herds of urban horses. "Hay Wagons on Main Street" by Arthur J. Telfer (1910). Smith-Telfer Photographic Collection, New York State Historical Association, Cooperstown, N.Y.

the rocky and rugged farmlands of Delaware and Sullivan counties sent products to the city, especially butter, shipped down the Hudson through several river ports. By the 1850s, many New York farmers had begun to specialize in dairying, a very labor-intensive agriculture but one that held out the promise of greatest reward in the market. Since women and children could milk cows and churn butter, dairying captured more of the family's labor and allowed greater market participation.

John Burroughs, the well-known nature writer, was born on a Delaware County farm in 1837, "only one generation from the stump in the history of settlement," as he described it. Late in life he reflected fondly on his family's work on their land, from which they produced maple syrup, wool, and dozens of other products. Foremost, however, were the products of dairy cows, especially butter. The large Burroughs family worked together, with the children walking the cows in from the fields, milking them, and washing the many tin pans, but the butter making itself was mostly the job of their mother, who had the stamina to work the churn. The fields were primarily the domain of their father, who had the strength to manage the plow. In the end, twice a year in the 1840s, the Burroughs family took firkins of butter down to Catskill for shipment to the city. "How much of the virtue of the farm went each year in those firkins! Literally the cream of the land," Burroughs reminisced.

New York farmers also increased their sheep flocks, particularly as the demand for woolen uniforms spiked during the Civil War. Together the growing focus on dairy and wool meant that a greater percentage of New York farmland was in meadow by the 1860s than during the grain boom of the 1820s. The Greene County farm of Levi Gilbert can serve as an example of this broad transition. In the decade after 1855, Gilbert increased his herd of cows from two to twenty head and added a flock of 113 sheep. This shift allowed Gilbert to send 2,000 pounds of butter to market, along with 150 pounds of cheese. To support his growing animal herds, Gilbert's farm had seventy-seven acres in meadow, from which he could collect the necessary tons of hay.

SCIENTIFIC FARMING

As the growth of Gilbert's farm suggests, the rural economy boomed after a six-year depression finally relented in 1843. Agricultural prices began a long rise, besting inflation through the antebellum period. Farmers used cash profits to purchase consumer goods such as clocks, mattresses, stoves, hats, books, and even factory-made clothes. Farmers also invested in their own businesses, buying more and better equipment and purchasing fertilizer; powdered gypsum and lime were increasingly added to fields along with manure. Greater use of fertilizer was part of a turn toward "scientific farming," dedicated to increasing production and profit. In a growing agricultural press, which included *The Genesee Farmer* and *The Cultivator,* both published in New York State, farmers read about the latest techniques and equipment. Among the leaders in this movement toward "book farming" was Andrew Jackson Downing, who had inherited his father's Newburgh nursery and trained himself to be a landscape gardener at a time when such a profession did not yet exist in the United States. Downing may have become more famous for his comments on rural aesthetics, but he also contributed greatly to the agricultural press through his 1845 book *The Fruits and Fruit Trees of America* and his journal *The Horticulturalist,* founded the next year and published in Albany. Among other things, the agricultural press helped spread the practice of crop rotation and the abandonment of summer fallow. With crop rotation, farmers shifted fields from corn in some years to nitrogen-fixing beans or peas in others. Perhaps alfalfa or some other hay crop might be added to the rotation, all in an effort to retain soil fertility and heighten productivity.

The turn toward scientific farming could also involve considerable capital investments, even beyond fertilizer and equipment costs. In 1835 John Johnson, who had immigrated from Scotland and purchased a farm near Geneva and the Erie Canal, began to install clay tiles more than two feet under his wet fields, certain that the drains would improve yields, just as they did in Britain. In an 1849 *Cultivator* article, Johnson described the significant increase in productivity his investment had brought. By then he had laid nearly sixteen miles of tile beneath 320 acres, and he estimated his wheat crop had doubled for the effort. Soon other farmers, many from well beyond New York, were calling on Johnson for drainage advice, and the small tile factory Johnson had helped establish in Waterloo strained to meet orders. Soon several other tile factories opened in the area. In the 1850s, burying tiles under damp fields became common, and farmers paid more attention to drainage in general, especially in the relatively level areas along the Great Lakes, where thousands of miles of buried tiles and open ditches helped keep fields dry and productive. In this way, progressive farmers participated in the broader changes in hydrology in upstate New York—changes initiated by the construction of the artificial river. Improved drainage dried out soils, which when plowed were more prone to wind erosion, but any adverse consequences for fertility were more than compensated for by the increasing application of fertilizer. Altogether, scientific farming, along with favorable market conditions, spurred agricultural production, and collectively New Yorkers cleared another 2.1 million acres of land for farm fields in the 1850s.

With scientific farming still in its infancy, many progressive farmers supported the creation of an agricultural college. Formal lobbying for the institution began in 1841, with the formation of the State Agricultural Society. After several false starts, however, the desired college did not materialize until 1865, three years after the federal government had promised land-grant support for an agricultural and technical college in each state. New York's college needed the additional support of Ezra Cornell, who not only donated his Ithaca farm for the school's use but also provided much of the initial endowment. Cornell University began enrolling students in 1867, and soon its students and professors were engaged in any number of experiments to improve the fertility of New

Figure 9. Scientific farming helped expand agriculture across the state as farm families invested in the latest technologies to increase production. "Reaping on Fenimore Farm" by Arthur J. Telfer (1895). Smith-Telfer Photographic Collection, New York State Historical Association, Cooperstown, N.Y.

York's soils and the productivity of its farms. In 1882 the experimental fields in Ithaca were joined by the New York State Agricultural Experiment Station near Geneva, where agricultural scientists conducted practical research in an effort to improve farm incomes. Over decades, and into the present, the research conducted in Ithaca and Geneva transformed New York agriculture, influencing everything from the varieties of apple trees grown to the treatment of soils.

Scientific farming, market production, and the profit motive encouraged farmers to specialize in those products that returned the greatest reward for their labor. Despite growing specialization, however, the labor and land on mid-nineteenth-century New York farms remained diversified. Even midsized farms typically raised a variety of animals, including milch cows, horses, pigs, and chickens. And farm gardens produced potatoes and myriad vegetables. Some farmers collected sap for maple syrup, although cane sugar was so inexpensive that sugar from trees yielded no real profit. Orchards were more profitable, and at least a small stand of apple trees for home consumption grew on most farms.

Farm families sometimes supplemented their income with wood products, such as cordwood, barrel staves, and hemlock bark, if their properties held the right species. Thus woodlots retained value and persisted even in intensely farmed regions. In 1875 the state had over 240,000 farms, with nearly 16 million acres of "improved land," that is, land in pasture or under plow. But those farms also contained nearly 10 million acres of unimproved land, mostly woodlands and wetlands. Thus the continued diversity of production on New York farms also ensured a diverse ecology, even though the land had been stripped of many of its most spectacular species, such as bears, wolves, and panthers, which could not thrive in a mixed landscape of fields and woodlots.

LATE-CENTURY RURAL DECLINE

Improved agricultural technology and market connections meant that some areas could be improved for farming, while others simply couldn't keep pace. And so changes in the agricultural market brought greater wealth to some hard-working farm families but not all. In some parts of the state, farmers increasingly realized that their marginal soils and short growing seasons could not support their families in a way they would like. Perhaps especially in good times, acres that couldn't be made to pay were abandoned, sometimes left as meadow to be hayed twice yearly or even neglected altogether, left to return to forest. Agriculture remains important to the state's economy to this day, but in many ways its importance peaked in the late 1800s. Tellingly, through the mid-nineteenth century, many counties experienced considerable growth in improved acreage but little growth in population. For example, in 1845 Allegany County had roughly forty thousand residents, but over the next thirty years it gained fewer than two thousand more. Over those same years, however, the county's farmers improved an additional 170,000 acres. By itself, expanding agriculture was not enough to support a growing population.

In total, New York farms remained very productive, but some parts of the state began to see an agricultural retreat just after the Civil War. Agriculture receded most rapidly from the Tug Hill Plateau, the Southern Tier, and the foothills of the Adirondacks. By 1885, out-migration from some areas of the Adirondacks cast a pall across the landscape. As the Forest Commission report from that year noted, a traveler through the region would have been struck by the "recurrence of deserted homesteads; in many cases he will encounter whole villages, abandoned and going rapidly to decay as if struck by a blight."

Brookfield Township, Madison County, had become home to a sawmill and a gristmill as early as 1792, as well as a site of migration for Quakers, who settled a ridge that became known as Quaker Hill. By 1870, however, parts of the township felt abandoned, or nearly so. "The atmosphere of the whole location seems pregnant with loneliness," wrote Luna M. Hammond in her early history of Madison County. Brookfield had had nearly 39,000 acres of improved farmland in 1845, supporting a population of 3,600. Thirty years later, the township's 504 farms had just 36,000 improved acres, and Brookfield's population had already begun its long decline. As happened in many rural townships, the population of Brookfield peaked during the rush of settlers, many of whom purchased inexpensive land and cleared it, but found they could not long support a family on it. From Quaker Hill, "one of the highest in this hilly region," Hammond could see "broad grazing farms, dotted with herds of cattle, and now and then an isolated barn," but there were "very few farm houses in view." This was surely a sign that the forests just might return.

Rural decline became more general across upstate New York after 1880, the year when the state's agricultural acreage peaked. After 1880 the total acres dedicated to agriculture declined by about forty thousand acres a year until 1920, when the decline accelerated. Townships with marginal farmland and poor market connections lost population. From 1870 to 1900, sixteen of Chenango County's twenty-one townships lost at least 10 percent of their population, and ten of them lost more than 25 percent. In hilly Schoharie County over those same years, fifteen of sixteen townships lost 10 percent or more, eight of them losing at least 25 percent. Three rural areas in New York retained population in the late 1800s, however. The counties closest to New York City grew as farmers found nearby ready markets for fruits and vegetables, and farming became more intensive. In the townships along the southern shore of Lake Ontario and the eastern shore of Lake Erie, good farmland—rich soil on relatively flat parcels—allowed farmers to compete on the national level. And in the Adirondacks, logging spurred economic growth in some parts of the North Woods, compensating for the decline of agriculture in the region.

Participation in the market had helped make farmers wealthier, but they had also become more vulnerable. By mid-century, rural complaints about transportation costs and fluctuating grain and produce prices spoke to the precarious position of farmers in the American economy. Farming was hard work, and its rewards were modest, especially in comparison to the wealth being generated in cities. To express their growing dissent, New York farmers participated in a national movement, the Patrons of Husbandry, also known as the Grange, first organized in New York in 1868 in Fredonia. The New York State Grange was formed five years later, and soon thereafter 320 local Granges had more than sixteen thousand members. The Grange was in part a broad social movement, through which farmers pressed their political agenda, reminding the nation of the continuing importance of agriculture to the national economy and the centrality of independent farmers to American political culture. The Grange also provided direct economic benefits to members, creating cooperatives, for example, through which farm families could purchase goods at wholesale prices and through which they could buy insurance. In addition, the Grange was a social organization that sponsored picnics, dinners, and educational gatherings. At weekly meetings, members considered farm problems, discussed strategies for crop selection and milking practices, and sometimes listened to visiting agricultural experts. All of this activity was directed toward one broad goal: improving the lives of farm families and ensuring a continuing place for agriculture in New York.

Joining the Grange was one way to address the struggle many farmers engaged in to stay on the land. Most experimented with new crops and livestock breeds, seeking a combination that would produce the income they needed. Some sought employment off the farm, even traveling to cities during the winter months to earn paychecks. Others sold parcels of land or took in summer boarders to earn cash. Although many rural folk gave up on farming, especially young adults who sought their futures in cities and towns, the long struggle to stay on the land came from a deep attachment to place and lifestyle. John Burroughs remembered fondly the days he spent in the fields, even when his task was spreading manure with a pitchfork. "The farm boy always has the whole of nature at his elbow and he is usually aware of it," he wrote. Surely not all farm children developed a love of nature equal to Burroughs's, but undoubtedly most developed a love of the land—a love of their land. Nineteenth-century Americans still believed fervently that farm life instilled virtue in those who lived it. They still spoke easily of the special role farmers—especially settlers— had played in making the nation, in wringing wealth from the wilderness.

URBAN GROWTH

The growth of cities went hand in hand with agricultural growth, and the changes in urban environments were no less noticeable than those in the

Figure 10. Early industrial development remained scattered around the countryside, even beyond the plants that processed agricultural products. "Milk Delivery to International Cheese Plant" by Arthur J. Telfer (1912). Smith–Telfer Photographic Collection, New York State Historical Association, Cooperstown, N.Y.

countryside. Several cities boomed, including Albany and Buffalo, at either end of the Erie Canal, and Rochester and Utica, both of which became the commercial centers of large, productive regions. But the explosion of commerce did more than create a handful of successful cities. As the appearance of so many towns with a "port" suffix or prefix reveals, settlers in dozens of places expected the canal to bring urban growth: at Weedsport, Port Byron, Port Gibson, Fairport, Brockport, and Middleport. Most important there was Lockport, which did not exist in 1820, but five years later this instant city had more than three thousand residents. It also had warehouses, gristmills, hotels, barbershops, tanneries, taverns, tinplate factories, churches, and, according to one observer, "thousands of tree stumps, and people burning and destroying them."

By the time the canal's work crews reached Rochester in 1821, it had just 1,500 residents. Two years later, however, the canal was opened to the Hudson, and growth began in earnest. Tilled acreage more than doubled in the area around the canal's Genesee River crossing, and flour exports from Rochester increased tenfold in a decade. The Genesee Valley became the breadbasket of the state nearly overnight, and Rochester, which stood at the center of the nation's most prosperous agricultural hinterland, naturally became a regional center for milling. By 1830 the city had become one of the nation's many inland boomtowns, with a population approaching ten thousand. Its complex economy included more than just flour mills and merchants, however, for a wide variety of artisans and journeymen set up shop in the young city, making wagons, tools, guns, nails, woolen cloth, and other goods that the region's growing farm population required. John Fowler was astonished by the city he found along the Genesee's banks in 1830: "It is, indeed, scarcely credible that in the period of eighteen short years a place of the present extent and importance of Rochester should have arisen from the wilds of a forest; and, if such evidence were needed, it would alone speak volumes as to the energy and enterprise of a people who, with the obstacles and impediments which they must have had to contend against, have produced such splendid results." Here Fowler sounds like the historian Frederick Jackson Turner, who decades later would praise the role of the frontier in American history. On the frontier, in places like the Genesee Valley and the city of Rochester, Americans both revealed and built their character, a character of "energy and enterprise."

The canal reached Utica in 1820, and the small town of merchants, craftsmen, and shopkeepers grew dramatically. Just four years later a description printed on china made in Utica revealed a confidence that grew along with the city: "Utica, a village in the State of New York, thirty years since a wilderness, now inferior to none in the Eastern Section of the State in Population, Wealth, Commercial enterprise, active industry and civil improvement." Farmers, sawyers, coopers, and any number of small manufacturers brought their products to the waterside. Goods stored in warehouses, pulled through town, and stacked along the canal provided ample evidence of the economic energy of the region. In hopeful cities like Utica, small crafts were especially encouraged, as blacksmiths, carpenters, wheelwrights, and others found ample work meeting the needs of the growing population. Nearby, New York Mills grew on the New England model, as a company town where workers spun cotton in handsome mill complexes. In the early years, even this factory life fit in with rural endeavors. One employee, Abram Camp, received pasturage of his cows as part of his compensation. By 1825 the land around Utica had been well settled, meaning the next generation would largely seek its fortune in town or farther west. Those who came to Utica found a diversifying economy, with garment works and shoe manufacturing prospering by the 1860s.

Albany was an important city long before the building of the Erie Canal, and not just because it had served as the state capital since 1797. A place of commerce for two hundred years, Albany had been nurtured on the trade in furs and lumber. But the canal brought growth of a new magnitude, and it became a thriving commercial city, handling the wheat that filled the holds of Hudson River sloops heading down to New York Harbor, and the goods that flowed back up, headed west. At the other end of the canal, Buffalo grew even more impressively, as it moved goods from lake vessels to canal barges and vice versa. As early as 1836 Ohio's grain production surpassed that of New York, and four years later Buffalo handled 4 million bushels of lake-borne grain. As European demand for wheat increased, the growing stream of wheat taxed the city's infrastructure. By the early 1850s, Buffalo was handling more than 20 million bushels a year. Joseph Dart's 1842 invention of the steam-powered grain elevator made this increased flow possible. It moved more grain with less labor and stored it in less space. Twenty-five years after the opening of the Erie Canal, Buffalo was the largest inland port in the United States, and the ten grain elevators along the city's expanded harbor and ship canal had become tourist attractions. Just as nature and technology flowed together in the water of the canals, in the grain elevators technology and nature came together in the streams of golden wheat that so vividly represented the nation's growing wealth. Here in the elevators, city and country came together, too, evidence of the increasingly integrated national economy and intimately connected national landscapes: the wheat fields of the Old Northwest and the waterfronts of eastern port cities.

Much of Buffalo's prosperity was linked directly to the grain trade, but other products also made their way to the Erie Canal's terminus. In the 1850s timber began arriving at Buffalo, delivered by sailing ships in great quantities—pine from Ontario and Michigan, hardwoods from Ohio and Indiana. By the 1870s, steamships took the timber farther, to Tonawanda, which quickly developed into the second-largest white pine market in the United States, after Chicago. The city also developed a sizable manufacturing sector. Lake ships brought iron ore, and by the 1850s Buffalo had good railroad connections to the Pennsylvania coalfields. The iron industry expanded rapidly, as the city manufactured a wide variety of metal consumer goods. Most prominently, Jewett and Root's Stove Factory occupied five acres near the terminus of the Erie Canal. By 1860 this thriving economy had encouraged a steady growth in population; with 81,000 residents, Buffalo was the tenth-largest city in the nation.

The Delaware and Hudson Canal sparked growth in Kingston, as the old agricultural village evolved into a small city of more than ten thousand people in 1850, just a little over twenty years after the canal's completion. Kingston handled coal, by far the largest commodity to travel on the 108-mile canal, but its invigorated docks also handled lumber and firewood. The canal carried hides shipped up the Hudson, destined for the tanneries of Sullivan County, and of course it carried the leather that returned, on its way to the factories of New York City. The canal and the city's docks also handled bluestone, some of which was cut for the urban market, where it became sidewalk flagging, fireplace mantles, and windowsills, among other things. Limestone and cement, too, became important products of the city and its hinterland, and several sizable manufacturing plants opened near the mouth of Rondout Creek. In this way Kingston's growth was further encouraged by growth elsewhere, especially around New York Harbor, as the mid-Hudson region's cement and stone helped build growing cities. Though still small by today's standards, Kingston and its waterfront neighbor, Rondout, began to acquire troubling urban attributes. The noise of machinery, the crushing and cutting of stone, the whistling steam from engines of all sorts, the sound of heavy metal wheels running across stone streets all filled the bustling port with the din of success. Residents began to complain of smells, the "sickening odors and stenches" of filth collecting in streets, of hides stacked dockside and offal collecting behind abattoirs, all held in the still air of dense development.

The complaints in Kingston were but the beginning. Population growth and industrial development in the state's cities brought a host of environmental changes, which together helped shape evolving urban landscapes. Early commercial cities were densely settled, with a diversity of land uses mingling in tight quarters. A certain amount of segregation existed from the outset: warehouses gathered near docks; prominent banks, hotels, and important civic buildings clustered at the core; and the poorest residents lived on the cheapest land, sometimes on the outskirts or in low-lying, undesirable spots. Still, if the poor and working classes found themselves in less convenient, noisier, and dirtier neighborhoods, the limited geographical size of small cities ensured considerable mixing of the classes. Many middle-class residents—craftsmen and shopkeepers especially—lived at their sites of work, upstairs from storefronts or with workshops in the backyard. As cities grew, however, the expanding middle class increasingly lived in fashionable districts along streets differentiated from others. Over time, deteriorating urban environments—the noise and filth of the streets—would play a critical role in encouraging the development of purely residential sections of cities, where the wealthy could escape the environmental disamenities of economic growth.

NEW YORK CITY'S TENEMENT DISTRICTS
AND CROTON WATER

The population growth and industrialization in upstate cities couldn't match the growth of New York City, where continued economic success compounded environmental problems. Immigrants continuously poured into the crowded districts, filling four- and five-story tenement buildings. By 1830 Manhattan had more than 200,000 residents. Over the next decade, as growth accelerated, the city's tenement districts became infamous for their filth and disorder. Especially on the Lower East Side, impoverished residents had too little space, too little water, and inadequate ventilation. The city failed to keep the streets clean, as did the pigs that foraged through lingering refuse. With no comprehensive water supply system, residents relied on a mixture of cisterns, public and private wells, and companies that sold water carted from outside the city. Most people used little water, either for drinking or for bathing, as it tended to be polluted or expensive. Since the city also had no comprehensive sewer system, most human waste collected in privy vaults, to be periodically pumped into carts and dumped into nearby waterways. Some industries built their own sewer lines, which led directly to one of the rivers. Altogether these were ideal conditions for disease, which New Yorkers perpetually feared, especially in the summer. In 1832, when a cholera epidemic spread to Manhattan, over 100,000 people fled, bringing the city to a standstill. By the time the epidemic subsided, 3,500 people had died in the city.

The epidemic's devastation forced politicians to undertake the long-delayed work of providing ample clean water. Supporters of a new water supply argued that its construction was the most important step the city could take to improve environmental conditions and reduce the incidence of disease. In 1835 the state created a water commission charged with planning the new system, bypassing the sluggish municipal government. The commission in turn hired David Douglass, a retired army engineer trained at West Point, to undertake the design. Since local sources of water were too small, polluted, or brackish,

Douglass looked north to Westchester County, where the Croton River could be dammed and an aqueduct built to carry water by gravity down to the city. Despite opposition in Westchester, the state legislature enabled New York City to take land for the system. Construction was set to begin in 1836. When Douglass proved reluctant to get shovels moving, the water commission replaced him with another engineer, John Jervis, whose brilliant career had taken him from axeman to superintending engineer on the Erie Canal, then to the Delaware and Hudson Canal, the Mohawk and Hudson Railroad, and the Chenango Canal. By the time he joined the effort to bring Croton water to the city, Jervis personified the engineer's importance to the reordering of New York's environment. He had already drawn several significant lines across the state.

Unfortunately, Croton water would come too late to fight the great fire that spread through the city in December 1835. Firefighters had little chance against the wind-driven blaze; their hand-operated pumps produced too little water and not enough pressure. By the time the fire was out, perhaps seven hundred buildings had been destroyed, some of them intentionally blown up in the hope of creating a firebreak. A tenth of the city was in ruins. Although the city's strong economy meant quick recovery and rebuilding, the fire had taught yet another lesson regarding the need for a municipal water supply, and the city grew impatient for Croton water. In June 1842 a small skiff, the *Croton Maid*, embarked on a journey through the enclosed aqueduct from Croton to the Harlem River. Just as the *Seneca Chief*'s journey had announced the completion of the Erie Canal, Jervis's arrival at Harlem aboard the *Croton Maid* announced the successful completion of the forty-one-mile aqueduct that delivered water from a new four hundred–acre lake behind the Croton Dam. On July 4 Croton water began to fill the Murray Hill Reservoir at Forty-second Street, and the new supply spoke to the obvious value of expert-led projects. Over the following decades, the city created a system of water mains to connect customers with the reservoir, and though it took longer than it should have, the city also eventually created a system of sewers to carry away wastewater and sewage. As was the practice of the day, all of the sewers simply discharged into waterways without treating the waste.

A huge celebration marked the arrival of Croton water later that fall. With cannon fire, a long parade down Broadway, and a massive gathering around the new fountain at City Hall Park, the city expressed its joy at the engineering triumph in a celebration reminiscent of the "Wedding of the Waters," and fittingly so. Engineers had made another artificial river, this one an enclosed aqueduct that redirected much of the Croton's flow into lower Manhattan. Similar celebrations marking engineering feats would continue for decades, as New Yorkers acknowledged the application of science as a means of overcoming limits set by nature. New York City evolved into the ultimate engineered landscape, reordered by a grid of streets and watered by a lake nearly fifty miles away. Jervis and the nation's growing number of engineers understood that the control of nature was central to the production of great wealth, both in the city and in the countryside.

FROM CANALS TO RAILROADS

Canals transformed the state's economy and landscape, but they did so under significant limitations. Goods and people traveled no faster than the pace of a walking horse, with heavy freight barges moving just two miles per hour. The canals were engineered streams with controlled feeders and discharges, but even artificial rivers could flood during heavy rains and spring melts. Just as important, canals were seasonal transportation routes, since they froze in the winter. Commerce ceased in the cold months—up to five months each year upstate. This seasonality of the canals reinforced the seasonality of life, especially in the countryside, where crops kept farmers busy in spring and fall, and other work gained attention in the slack times. Cutting firewood was an early spring activity. Winter too had its work, such as quarrying and cutting ice for summer storage. In Kingston the Knickerbocker Ice Company cut and stored eighty thousand tons of Hudson River ice annually in the 1850s. Others used winter snows to sled bark and logs out of the woods, a much easier task than building passable wagon roads on rough terrain. In short, canals maintained the seasonal rhythms of agricultural society. This very seasonality would limit their useful life spans, as railroads, which could function year-round, offered a better transportation option.

Railroads eventually replaced canals as the primary means of moving freight through the state, but the transition was a remarkably long one. Tellingly, the first railroad chartered in New York was the aforementioned Mohawk and Hudson, connecting Albany and Schenectady, a fifteen-mile route completed in 1831. It was designed to supplement the canal, carrying passengers around its steepest section, bypassing twenty-seven locks and saving an entire day's travel. The Mohawk and Hudson revealed how the two technologies—railway and canal—could complement as well as compete with each other. It also revealed the importance of passenger travel to early rail construction. Other early railroads served passengers primarily, including the twenty-one-mile Saratoga and Schenectady Railroad, which delivered passengers to the popular resort via Ballston Spa. In New York City, rails laid in the streets eased the burden on horses pulling cars and proved to be a transition to steam locomotives performing the same task.

In the 1830s the state chartered dozens of railroad companies, which in turn sold stock as a means of funding construction. Many of the planned railroads were never completed, and for others completion could not ensure prosperity. Still, by the 1850s as many as thirty different railroads operated across the state, many of them using names that identified their terminals, such as the Oswego and Syracuse Railroad and the Watertown and Rome Railroad. Although steam locomotives could travel faster than canal boats, and could travel in cold weather (provided the snow could be removed from the tracks), railroads did not immediately outcompete the canals, in part because the state required freight traveling by rail to pay canal fees anyway, and because the multiplicity of companies created hassles for longer shipments. This latter problem diminished after 1853, when the New York Central consolidated several companies to create a continuous system that operated between New York City and Buffalo. Two years earlier the Erie Railroad had also finally completed its line from the Hudson River in Orange County to Lake Erie at Dunkirk. These two expansive railroad systems would be as instrumental in shaping transportation in New York in the second half of the 1800s as canals had been in the first.

Steam transportation ushered in a new industrial order, more removed from the natural rhythms of agricultural life. By mid-century, New Yorkers increasingly obtained power through fossil fuel: coal. Engineers created more and more machines to tap into this stored energy, which in turn propelled economic growth. Just as the consolidation of railroad companies increased their economic and political clout, the increasing power and speed of locomotives changed the value of time. The pace of life quickened, measured increasingly by the hands of the clock rather than the movement of the sun.

Still, the growing importance of rail transportation did not prevent the state from investing in the Erie Canal, even beyond the enlargement that began in 1835 (but wasn't finished until 1862). Eventually the state replaced the Erie with the Barge Canal in the 1910s. Ironically, the enlargement of the Erie, which allowed larger boats to travel on the main canal, posed a problem for the lateral canals, which warranted no improvement and therefore couldn't handle the larger boats. After struggling for years, and costing the state sizable subsidies, the Chenango, Genesee Valley, and Chemung canals were officially abandoned by the legislature in 1877. This provided opportunities for redevelopment in cities and villages, but in many places the canals continued to exist as an eyesore and public health concern owing to the stagnant water. Some sections of the abandoned canals remained in state hands; others were sold. Where development pressures have remained slight, evidence of the former canals is abundant even to this day. Parts of the canal system have persisted because they now serve other purposes; for example, the various reservoirs in Madison County, built to supply water to the Chenango Canal's high point, have been maintained as recreational lakes for central New York residents.

"CHAOS BROUGHT INTO ORDER"

Through the middle decades of the 1800s New Yorkers brought a new order to the landscape. Expansive systems eased transportation, delivered pure water, and carried away wastes. A society dedicated to economic growth had enlisted science in the task, often with great success. New lines crossed the landscape: canals wound gracefully along the levels; railroad tracks pushed somewhat less gracefully across the state. And on farms, miles and miles of fences and drainage ditches spoke to the new order. On the Burroughs farm near Roxbury, John's father, Chauncey, built forty or fifty rods of stone wall each year. John described how his father would pick the rock that surfaced annually with the freezing and thawing and plowing, and how he would place them in straight, sturdy lines at the edges of fields. "Gathered out of the confusion of nature," they were "a bit of chaos brought into order." These walls established boundaries and defined possessions, as Burroughs described, but they were much more than markers of property. "These were the only lines of poetry and prose Father wrote." And, Burroughs noted decades later, "They are still very legible on the face of the landscape and cannot be easily erased from it." By the late twentieth century, however, miles of stone walls—not just those on the Burroughs farm—stood nearly hidden in second-growth forests across the state, poignant reminders of the hard work of making a farm and the ease with which time and nature could reclaim untended fields.

But from the perspective of the mid-nineteenth century, those walls and the other lines on the landscape held a very different meaning. The Erie Canal had helped turn New York into the Empire State, by far the largest of the United

States. New York led the nation in the value of farm products through the 1870 census, and it remained the nation's largest industrial state much longer. By 1900 nearly one of every ten Americans lived in New York State. This growth had significant consequences for the state's environment, with deforestation being the most obvious. New Yorkers couldn't help but express pride in their state's growth, its wealth and progress. Still, progress was not without its perils, and increasingly New Yorkers began to question some of the consequences of the market revolution, both for society and for the environment. In 1883 the New York State Survey's report contributed to the ongoing debate about the consequences of deforestation. Although the report focused on western New York, where surveying was under way, concerns about the Adirondacks were not far from the discussion. As survey director James Gardiner concluded, "While it is thus evident that the destruction of the woods has not modified the mean rainfall, it has materially affected the flow of streams; and this effect has been different on different water-sheds." Ironically, the major topic of immediate concern was the Oak Orchard Swamp and how it might best be drained. North of Batavia, it had a feeder canal running through part of it and was, by the standard thinking of the day, wasted land.

3

We Are Still in Eden

Romanticism, Tourism, and the Power of Culture

In October 1826 Thomas Cole headed into the thick woods around Windham, paper and pencil in hand. He climbed up a mountain using a poorly made road, probably built to haul out bark and wood. At the summit he found "a wide prospect"—the forest having been removed by fire—and surveyed the panorama of the Catskills. He described the scene later in his journal: "Summit rose above summit, mountain rolled away beyond mountain,—a fixed, a stupendous tumult. The prospect was sublime." While at the summit Cole made "a hasty sketch or two," as was his habit in the mountains. On his descent he came upon a log house, where he sought lodging for the night. His hosts served him "a plain supper of cheese, rye-bread and butter," and regaled him with tales of hunting and hardship, of their twenty years in this backwoods valley. Although Cole's love of the Catskills would surely grow to equal that of families like this, who had worked so hard to make a living among the mountains, the artist's experience could hardly have been more different. The "hard-featured, long-bearded, long-legged" people of the settlement surely looked upon Cole and his portfolio as a mystery. For his part, Cole could only imagine how months upon months of swinging an axe might influence his thoughts about the forest.

That simple scene in a Windham log house in 1826 foreshadowed the revolutionary changes that would take place in American culture over subsequent decades. Increasingly Americans would approach the mountains as Cole had that autumn. They would be visitors, their interests in forests driven by their love of nature, not by their need to make a living. They would bring with them their romantic sensibilities, thoughts about God's hand in nature, about the wild landscape's various powers to awe, inspire, frighten, and soothe. By mid-century, tourists would stream out of the nation's growing cities, New York foremost among them, and head into the countryside, bringing with them expectations of beauty and peacefulness. Inspired by art, especially the landscape painting movement that became known as the Hudson River School, and by romantic literature, much of it written by tourists, Americans would develop powerful cultural ideas about benign nature, about the human need to retain contact with wilderness or, at the very least, with natural beauty. These ideas would be at the heart of the earliest efforts to protect natural scenes, especially in New York State, home to so many artists, writers, and tourists, as well as numerous popular tourist destinations. New Yorkers were among the nation's early prominent romantic preservationists, hoping to protect God's handiwork in nature. New Yorkers also led a movement to bring natural scenes into the city itself, where their healing powers might provide a salve to sooth the wounds inflicted by urban living.

THOMAS COLE AND THE HUDSON RIVER SCHOOL

At the time of Cole's journey to Windham, he had lived in New York just a year, but he had already met with great success. He had taken a sketching trip into the Catskills the previous summer and returned to New York City with the drawings that would guide his earliest landscape painting. From his first Catskills adventure Cole created three paintings, including *The Falls of the Kaaterskill* and *Lake with Dead Trees,* landscapes that caught the eye of prominent artist John Trumbull. Trumbull's enthusiastic reaction instantly catapulted Cole into the elite of New York's growing art community. Not insignificantly, so too were the Catskills and the Hudson Highlands catapulted into prominence among American landscape painters. Over the next fifty years, dozens of well-known painters would stream up the Hudson every summer, sketching out the scenes, the prospects, the clefts in the mountains known as cloves, the shapes of mountains, the details of nature—the pieces that would come together on their canvases. Each winter, studio season brought them back to New York City, where the great landscape artists of the age gathered—Asher Durand, Frederic Church, Jasper Cropsey, and John Kensett among them. They used their summer's sketches and knowledge of natural history to paint seemingly realistic landscapes. These artists traveled widely, often to Europe, and their canvases treated a variety of landscapes, including those in the White Mountains and other, more distant American scenes. Still, they became known as the Hudson River School because of the regularity with which New York scenery appeared in their paintings.

Through the mid-1800s, landscape artists from around the country came to New York City to work and, if they were fortunate, to sell their paintings. In the city they joined a remarkable community of talent—literary and artistic—clustered in Greenwich Village. They learned from one another, and learned from the art market as well, which increasingly demanded native scenes, depictions of the wild and romantic landscapes that spoke to America's great natural wealth. So more and more artists made their summer trips up the Hudson, seeking inspiration and sketching suitable subjects. Although the market demanded recognizably American scenes, the art itself reflected European sensibilities. Popular landscape paintings followed remarkably firm rules of composition, set by the work of the seventeenth-century French painter Claude Lorrain. Trees and sometimes mountains or looming clouds framed the scene; a field or body of water ran from the foreground into the middle ground, while mountains rose in the distance, drawing the viewer's eye toward infinity. Along the Hudson—in the Highlands, the Catskills, and the Adirondacks—artists found easily accessible and worthy scenes that contained all the elements necessary for a successful landscape painting.

By 1836 Cole had moved his home permanently to Catskill, in sight of the mountains that he had already made so famous in the world of painting. He made regular sketching trips into the mountains, often up Kaaterskill Clove, where he and his fellow artists frequented boardinghouses and hotels. Although other parts of the Hudson Valley became important destinations for landscape painters, this area around Palenville, Haines Falls, and Tannersville—Kaaterskill Clove, Kaaterskill Falls, and the surrounding region—was crawling with artists every summer. Durand, Cole, and his only true student, Frederic Church, were among the most popular of the Hudson River artists, but dozens of others joined their ranks. Among them were Sanford Gifford, a native of Hudson; James McEntee, who hailed from Rondout, the riverside section of Kingston; and Jasper Cropsey, a Staten Island native who moved to Hastings-on-Hudson after having lived and worked in New York City for many years. Well after Cole's untimely death in 1848, Gifford, McEntee, Cropsey, and many others made regular sojourns into the Catskills, keeping those mountains alive in American art long after their champion had died.

Hudson River art often captured real rural scenes, sometimes with farmers at work, or at least with the results of their work evident, but these pastoral images only served to romanticize rural life. The peaceful scenes so evidently contrasted with the city's chaos. Instructively, the artists who lived and worked in New York City rarely painted urban scenes. Instead, Hudson River art became ubiquitous in the city. Indeed the influence of these images in American culture is difficult to overestimate. They dominated the National Academy of Design for decades. They hung on the walls of wealthy patrons and in public buildings, in galleries and steamships. Hudson River landscapes graced painted china, calendars, and less expensive lithographs. They appeared in myriad publications—books as well as magazines. Even New Yorkers who rarely traveled might think they knew the Shawangunks, or Kaaterskill Clove, or Lake George, so often had they seen them, in so many paintings. Altogether this art set the dominant image of upstate New York as wild, romantic, and recognizably in contrast with the city.

Although Hudson River landscape painters created mostly wild scenes for mostly urban customers, these paintings did more than provide beautiful distractions for urban eyes. They were lessons, each of them, on how to view nature, how to frame a picturesque vista, how to appreciate the power of God by contemplating wild landscapes. Their work was steeped in romanticism and represented the powerful cultural shift away from positing nature as a force to be conquered and toward an appreciation of nature as a critical component of human life. Romanticism lay at the heart of nineteenth-century art, and New York scenery lay at the heart of the landscape paintings themselves.

These landscapes became so central to American culture that they created a lasting impression of the New York landscape. One hundred years later, as author Robert Boyle traveled up and down the Hudson studying all its various scenes, he held in his mind one common theme: "the notion that this is the way the world ought to look." Though not referring directly to Hudson River art, Boyle's phrase nicely summarizes the power of art to inspire a preservationist sentiment. Hudson River landscapes were worth preserving, both framed in museums and scattered across the countryside, because this was the way the world ought to look.

ROMANTIC LITERATURE

Romanticism became the dominant influence in literature as well as painting, as poets and other writers rhapsodized about nature's beauty and power.

Among the most important of New York contributors to this literary move-ment was James Fenimore Cooper, whose "Leatherstocking Tales" romanti-cized frontier life. In 1823, Cooper's novel *The Pioneers* introduced American readers to one of the great characters of nineteenth-century literature—Natty Bumppo, the quintessential frontiersman. Although the book concerns the set-tling of Otsego County, one of its most famous scenes takes place in the Catskills, which Bumppo periodically visits while living alone in the wilderness. Ironi-cally, Bumppo comes to the mountains to overlook civilization, standing at the precipice of the Catskills' eastern wall. From there he can see miles of the Hud-son River and its well-cultivated valley. While recounting his visits, Bumppo speaks what would become one of the most often repeated phrases concerning the Catskills, noting that from this spot he could see "Creation . . . all creation." These words, and the passage that surrounds them, became intimately attached to the spot they describe—a place at first called Pine Orchard and then more commonly the Mountain House Overlook, taking the name of the hotel built at the precipice. This attachment of words to place reveals how critical literature could be in shaping tourists' ideas about nature, about what they would find when they arrived at their destination. This is how romanticism worked its way so deeply into the culture. When tourists came to take in the sites, they often already had words in their head, which they would sometimes repeat aloud upon their arrival.

Among the many romantic writers of mid-century New York was Thomas Cole. Although he was much more influential as a painter, Cole's writings took on special status because of his art. His best-known piece, "Essay on American Scenery," appeared in the *American Monthly Magazine* in early 1836. Here, in typical romantic fashion, he declared "the wilderness is YET a fitting place to speak to God." Although Cole appreciated agricultural scenes, God's "undefiled works" were of special value to him. For Cole, wilderness was where "the mind is cast into the contemplation of eternal things." Like other American artists and the tourists they helped inspire, Cole was steeped in the romantic idea that in nature one could find God. Although surely God was everywhere, in certain places—sublime places—he was most evident. Here, perhaps atop a rugged mountain, overlooking some vast space, or near a riotous cataract, the power of God could be felt in an overwhelming sensation that drove many nineteenth-century tourists to tears. An important aspect of European romanticism, the sublime became central to mid-century American landscape art and literature, especially literature written by and for tourists. The idea of the sublime helped create expectations of an emotional connection, not just with nature but with specific natural places—places to which tourists flocked.

Cole wrote generally about the American landscape in "Essay on American Scenery," but his thoughts continually came back to the Hudson. He wrote lovingly of his river, "The Hudson has its wooded mountains, its rugged precipices, its green undulating shores—a natural majesty, and an unbounded capacity for improvement by art." Cole undertook this improvement—especially in his canvases—but also in his writings, in which he attributed religious importance to natural places. He concludes the essay with a lament that "the ravages of the axe are daily increasing." He then discusses "the road society has to travel," a metaphor for what Americans would eventually call progress. That road might lead to "refinement," Cole notes, "but the traveler who sees the place of rest close at hand, dislikes the road that has so many unnecessary windings," a prescient description of the way increasing travel would require the building of larger, less picturesque roads. Despite his lament, Cole concludes, "We are still in Eden; the wall that shuts us out of the garden is our own ignorance and folly." Cole dedicated his life's work to teaching fellow Americans the value of nature, using art to reveal the persistence of Eden. He would help teach Americans that wild nature was more than "the waste of creation" awaiting the taming hand of man. Here was the central lesson of romanticism in America: wilderness had value *as* wilderness.

Dozens of important romantic authors lived in New York City, many of whom befriended Cooper, the nation's leading novelist. Among these other writers was William Cullen Bryant, a poet turned journalist, who wrote extensively about the natural world. Born in the Berkshire Mountains, Bryant had developed his love of nature long before he moved to New York City to pursue a writing career. He became a respected journalist through his work at the *New York Evening Post*, and eventually he moved to a suburban estate in Roslyn, Long Island, where he occupied that prized middle ground—living an urbane life while simultaneously remaining connected to the countryside. Although he wrote romantic poems throughout his career, one of his early works, "A Forest Hymn," remained among his most influential. It opens with the memorable phrase "The groves were God's first temples." Presenting a very different picture of forests than would the nation's frontiersmen, those who worked so hard to clear the trees to make the fields that sustained America's growth, Bryant worshipped God in nature, in forests where he witnessed "the great miracle that still goes on," the continuous creation of life. Bryant compares God's temples with the churches "our frail hands have raised" and wonders why people should "neglect God's ancient sanctuaries." Altogether, the poem is a fine articulation of the romantic vision of nature—as a place of communion with the Creator, a place worthy of protection.

THE GRAND TOUR AND TOURIST LITERATURE

The romantic arts did not work alone in changing cultural views of nature. As the middle class grew with the economy, and more Americans could afford the time and expense of travel, tourism also grew in popularity. Early tourism took in a wide range of sites, both natural and cultural. By the late 1820s, however, a regularized tour, the American Grand Tour, had developed, as tourists headed to already famed sites, some cultural, such as the hotels of Saratoga Springs, and others natural, most important among them Niagara Falls. The American tour featured New York State partly because the Erie Canal provided a means of travel to Niagara. From Schenectady to Buffalo, packet boats holding as many as thirty passengers, who paid a fixed rate for the voyage and meals, traveled day and night. They could cover about eighty miles every twenty-four hours, a slow pace for travel, especially between interesting sites. The slow pace encouraged the development of multiple side trips—to Trenton Falls, for instance, a substantial cataract north of Utica. In some places the canal itself was worthy of tourists' attention, including the Genesee Aqueduct and the deep cut at Lockport. These places, and many others, became "points of interest," places tourists read about before beginning their journeys. Although well-traveled tourists took in sites outside New York State, including in the Connecticut Valley and the White Mountains, the Empire State lay at the heart of antebellum American tourism.

Tourism and literature worked hand in hand to change the way Americans thought about their nation's landscape, particularly through the growing genre of tourist literature. One early contribution, Theodore Dwight's *Northern Traveller*, published in 1825, chronicled travels to a variety of places that became popular stops on the Grand Tour. Dwight began his trip in New York City, but he said almost nothing of the place, other than to note its importance as the point of embarkation. "As this is the point from which the traveler is supposed to be setting out, it is not considered necessary to attempt a description of the city," he wrote, "nor of any of its places of resort or public institutions." Cities were the places from which tourists departed; they were not primary destinations, at least not for tourists traveling through America.

Dwight's first significant stop was Lebanon Springs, where Shakers had established a large community. After noting the popularity of the Shaker Village among travelers, he concludes, "The village itself presents a scene of great neatness and beauty, as it is situated on a beautiful level, and laid out with the utmost regularity." Next came a trip along the Erie Canal, not yet finished. Dwight observed and described the many locks and aqueducts, and he was especially taken with the combined beauty and utility of the aqueduct over the Genesee River in Rochester, which he called "one of the finest works on the course of the canal." The structure "is borne across the river's channel, on ten arches of hewn stone," he wrote with enthusiasm. "The river dashes rapidly along beneath, while boats, with goods and passengers, glide safely by above."

Over time, travel literature helped guide tourists to culturally significant destinations, and around the state, landscapes gathered new layers of meaning. The literature set expectations for what travelers might find, even what they might feel, when they arrived. By the late 1820s, steamboats had improved travel up the Hudson River, offering shorter, less expensive trips to a variety of destinations. Writing with typical romantic drama, Bayard Taylor, a popular author, described at length the primary route by which American tourists traveled: "there is one river which, from its source to the ocean, unrolls a long chain of landscapes wherein there is no tame feature, but each successive view presents new combinations of beauty and majesty...and its name is, The Hudson." The majestic Hudson, with its Palisades, Highlands, and thriving ports, offered myriad points of interest, and it gathered endless commentary in the tourist press. But the Hudson itself remained primarily a route for accessing three other important places: Saratoga Springs, Niagara Falls, and the Catskill Mountain House.

Saratoga Springs became New York State's first great tourist destination. Inspired by English spas, Americans sought mineral springs closer to home in the early 1800s. Gideon Putnam opened a tavern at Congress Spring in 1802, where he also operated a lumber mill. Over time, Putnam's operation grew, and by the mid-1820s his neoclassical hotel could accommodate more than 150 guests a night and had gained renown for its long, colonnaded piazza, where visitors strolled and mingled through the short summer season. By then several other hotels were offering fine accommodations. Most guests at the larger hotels traveled at least partly for the society in Saratoga, where cards, billiards, and promenading filled the days and formal balls filled the evenings. Of course, the waters too had their attraction, and by the mid-1820s, physicians had begun to extol the springs' mineral content and medicinal value. The waters purportedly eased diseases as various as dyspepsia, jaundice, rheumatism, gout, and "depraved appetite." Saratoga offered a beautiful lake nearby, where some guests engaged in sailing, but for the most part the young village had few scenic amenities, as many early travelers noted. Its fame grew at first through the popularity of its many mineral springs, and later through the addition of tourist attractions such as gambling and horse racing. Beyond the springs, the wilderness setting of Saratoga Springs was of little interest to early-nineteenth-century tourists.

In the early national period Niagara Falls was much harder to reach than Saratoga, but that did not prevent the great cataract from becoming the leading tourist destination in North America. Travelers came from near and far to visit the falls, even before the Erie Canal greatly eased the journey. In a popular book, *Views of Society and Manners in America,* the English traveler Frances Wright described her 1819 trip to Niagara, building readers' expectations as she approached the falls along the river: "You saw and *felt* immediately that it was no river you beheld, but an imprisoned sea." Her description of Niagara is a torrent of words nearly the equal of the falls themselves, complete with "thunder" and "lightning," "pillars of moving emerald," and "a tumbling ocean." Wright declared that at Table Rock, on the Canadian side, you feel yourself "a helpless atom amid these vast and eternal workings of gigantic nature!"

By the 1830s a Niagara visit was almost requisite for the American middle class. For many travelers, writing about the trip also became regularized, even if the jotted words appeared only in lengthy letters to friends or in personal diaries. The young Nathaniel Hawthorne, however, expected his essay, "My Visit to Niagara," to appear in print, which it did in 1835 in *New-England Magazine.* "Never did a pilgrim approach Niagara with deeper appreciation than mine," Hawthorne announced at the outset. The essay wonderfully balanced reportage of his actual feelings with the extraordinary expectations of the falls. He knew this was supposed to be a religious journey, as the term "pilgrim" implied. Niagara did not impress Hawthorne at first, and he was unable to conjure the awe he expected. "Had its own mysterious voice been the first to warn me of its existence, then, indeed, I might have knelt down and worshipped," he wrote. Over the course of the next few days, however, he came to appreciate the falls on their own terms. His journey, both psychological and physical, concluded with an epiphany. While he was boarding a ferry to head back to the American side, Hawthorne looked up at the falls as he descended the stairs and was somehow transported: "The solitude of the old wilderness now reigned over the whole vicinity of the falls. My enjoyment became the more rapturous, because no poet shared it, nor wretch devoid of poetry profaned it; but the spot so famous through the world was all my own!" Hawthorne captured perfectly the challenge of nature tourism: finding individual inspiration in a physical setting so fully transformed by consumption, in a cultural setting so demanding of specific reactions, and, as was particularly the case with Niagara, in a place swarming with crowds.

Even as Niagara Falls reigned as the nation's most famed tourist destination, the Catskill Mountains developed into a worthy rival. In part because of Cole and other painters, but mostly because of their proximity to New York City, the Catskills became one of the nation's earliest mountain destinations. The Catskill Mountain House opened in 1824, offering lodging right at the precipice about which Leatherstocking had rhapsodized just a year earlier in *The Pioneers*. From this spot, and now from the rooms of the hotel, tourists could awake early and catch the sunrise over the Hudson Valley. With the Berkshire Mountains as backdrop to the north and the Hudson Highlands to the south, here was the very embodiment of sublime nature. Humid skies, clouds and fogbanks, light breezes and shifting light all combined to create glorious, moving scenes, captured endlessly in the tourist literature of the day. Indeed some tourist guides did more than describe the accommodations and attractions of the Catskills, using the writings of various famed pens, from Washington Irving and James Fenimore Cooper to Bayard Taylor and N. P. Willis, to impart the romantic mood, the power of sublime nature in the mountains.

In this way, literature published both in New York City and in the Catskills helped sell and define the mountains. In particular, the continual publication of Irving's "Rip Van Winkle," about a man whose long slumber was said to have taken place in the mountains just above Palenville, ensured that one of the Catskills' most famous sons would be born in romantic fiction. Thirty years after writing "Rip Van Winkle," Irving wrote an essay on the Catskills which appeared in *Home Book of the Picturesque*. In typically romantic prose, Irving referred to the mountains as the "great poetical region of our country" and "the fairy region of the Hudson," helping to solidify the reputation he had done so much to create with the story of Rip Van Winkle.

If literature partially shaped the Catskills in the minds of tourists, helping set their expectations of what the mountains should be, tourism itself had a more direct effect on the landscape all around the state. Tourists needed accommodations convenient to popular destinations. There were massive hotels,

such as Congress Hall in Saratoga Springs and the Sans Souci in Ballston Spa,
and numerous smaller taverns and less fashionable hotels. But the effects on
the landscape were much more complete. The state gradually filled with points
of interest, linked by carriage paths and narrow trails, and around these points
developed lore, stories that helped define places like "Fawn's Leap" and "Artists' Rock," both within walking distance of the Catskill Mountain House.
Around Niagara Falls, a complex infrastructure of tourism evolved—stairs,
towers, ticket booths, gates, and fences—which alternately elevated the tourists'
experiences and detracted from them. Visitors took in the falls from multiple
angles—including from the *Maid of the Mist,* which began steaming up the
torrents toward the falling water in 1846. By then the typical visit to Niagara
consisted of a series of requisite stops. Tourists consumed the landscape bit by
bit; "doing the falls" became "a matter of covering all the bases," in the words
of historian John Sears.

Tourism worked changes on landscapes around the state, but like Niagara,
the Catskills were especially altered by the mid-1800s. In 1840 N. P. Willis described the dramatic changes around the Catskill Mountain House: "The cool
winds, the small silver lakes, the falls, the mountain-tops, are all delicious haunts
for the idler-away of the hot months; and, to the credit of our taste, it may be
said they are fully improved—Catskill is a 'resort.'" That resort, which took the
name Kaaterskill Park, consisted of dozens of points of interest, and featured
the Mountain House Overlook, North and South lakes, and Kaaterskill Falls,
which had graced one of Cole's earliest canvases. The top of the falls was a short
hike from the Mountain House, and as at Niagara, a complex infrastructure
evolved to amplify tourists' experiences there. As early as the mid-1820s a dam
across the creek allowed the owner to charge tourists for the pleasure of seeing
the falls with ample water. Eventually a wooden platform attached to the side
of the falls allowed tourists to view the water as it tumbled over the rock's edge.
A staircase gave easier access to the base of the falls, and the Spray House offered refreshments. John Fowler, on his way back from upstate farmland, made
the obligatory stop in 1830, where he was not especially impressed with the
falls—it was no Niagara surely—but he was taken by the vista from the top.
He concluded that the spot was "well worth visiting, if it were only for the view
above the falls, where the eye roves over the finest and most extensive dell I ever
beheld, wooded throughout, and the varied hues of autumn now adding to the
foliage an almost more than vernal richness and beauty." Clearly romantic tourism would continue to inspire change in the mountains—more hotels, more

trails and carriage paths—and these mixed natural and cultural landscapes would remain "well worth visiting," and eventually worth preserving.

Early-nineteenth-century tourism served purposes beyond cultivating the romantic connection to nature. Many travelers sought to improve their health. Spa visits—to Saratoga, Ballston Spa, and Richfield Springs—brought healing waters and rest. For others, simply leaving the city, nearly regardless of destination, could be a means of protecting health, especially by avoiding the ravages of summer epidemics such as yellow fever and malaria. Increasingly over the course of the century tubercular patients headed out of the city, in search of the cool clean air that physicians recommended for healing diseased lungs—or at least for easing the discomfort of that deadly disease.

Other tourists were most concerned with social status, and traveled largely to see and be seen at fashionable places. Travelers also sought personal connections to the nation's history. Theodore Dwight's 1825 descriptions certainly make it clear that history was part of the attraction to upstate New York. He discussed both Revolutionary War sites and Oneida Indian locations. He gave a long description of the Battle of Saratoga, and he described in detail the French and Indian War in the Mohawk Valley. A decade later Nathaniel Hawthorne stopped at Ticonderoga on his way back to Massachusetts from Niagara, a stop he described at length in "Old Ticonderoga: A Picture of the Past," published in 1836. Here Hawthorne writes as romantically about the old fort as he had the falls: "Tall trees have grown upon its ramparts, since the last garrison marched out, to return no more, or only at some dreamer's summons, gliding from the twilight past to vanish among realities." From the beginnings of tourism in the state, then, historic landscapes, buildings, and battlefields were also places worthy of seeing and preserving.

TOURISM UNDER STEAM

As the century progressed, tourists more frequently traveled by steam, with regularly scheduled steamboats plying the Hudson and railroads connecting more and more locations. In 1833 the state's second railroad joined Schenectady to Ballston Spa and Saratoga Springs, an indication of how important early rail investors considered tourism. Over the next fifty years New Yorkers built rail lines all over their state, connecting all sizable cities and a good number of small towns. Ever-improving steam locomotion decreased the cost of travel, while the growing rail infrastructure greatly increased tourist access to all corners of the state.

Under steam, tourism mushroomed. Not all rail lines served primarily to deliver passengers to vacation spots, but as most railroad companies struggled for profitability, they all advertised actual and potential tourist destinations along their routes. Some lines passed by or through very popular tourist regions. The West Shore, for example, featured the Catskills in its many publications. By the 1870s the Ontario & Western, which ran through the less popular Sullivan County region, advertised summer homes and boardinghouses along its route nonetheless. The New York Central advertised Saratoga and the Adirondacks, and of course Niagara Falls. This too was the destination for many travelers on the Erie Railroad, which took a southerly route through New York, near Watkins Glen and past Chautauqua Lake, both of which had become popular destinations. The Erie, in competition with both the New York Central to the north and the Pennsylvania Railroad to the south, noted that Pennsylvania had "no lakes of prominence," while New York had "on and near the line of the Erie Railway alone, no less than ten lakes." In sum, selling tourism—and specific tourist destinations—had become a critical component of the rail industry by the 1870s.

As travel became less expensive and more convenient, tourists could take shorter trips or travel greater distances, and they could more easily reach more destinations. Even the distant Thousand Islands became a fashionable resort in the 1870s, after George Pullman, who had made his fortune building posh railroad sleeping cars, purchased an island and built a summer home. The publicity generated by Pullman's arrival in 1871 helped create the "Rush of 1872," when hotels were overflowing and residents took in paying guests. That summer President Ulysses S. Grant visited Pullman for eight days, affording even more publicity to this newly attractive resort area. The rush encouraged the building of the Thousand Island House, a large hotel in Alexandria Bay that accommodated about six hundred guests. Soon other wealthy families purchased islands, making the small town of Alexandria Bay a better-known destination, though the area's great distance from New York City ensured that the tourist trade would serve a fairly local crowd, including summer home owners from Watertown and Ogdensburg. Still, by the end of the century, urbanites were making the long trip via railroad and staying in stylish Victorian hotels such as the Crossman in Alexandria Bay.

The Crossman Hotel was part of an extensive tourist landscape built in the second half of the nineteenth century to accommodate the burgeoning numbers of vacationers. Great hotels sprang up around the state, including the Mohonk Mountain House in the Shawangunks, the Hotel Kaaterskill in the Catskills, and Paul Smith's in the Adirondacks. The Long Island Railroad brought urban tourists by the thousands to beaches along the ocean. The Hamptons flourished, with second homes for weekenders and hotels for the less committed. Developers dreamed of a tourists' paradise in Montauk, near the very tip of Long Island and yet so accessible to the city by rail. At the other end of the island, in Brooklyn, Coney Island brimmed with amusements for day trippers, who steamed out of Manhattan at first by ferry, and later more commonly by train and trolley. By the end of the century, tourism had shaped wide swaths of the state's economy, culture, and landscape. The grand Victorian hotels, souvenir shops, and ice cream parlors all reminded rural residents of the unseen city at the other end of the rail lines.

Not all tourists headed to grand hotels for five-course meals, orchestras playing on the lawn, and evenings on the veranda. Some were bound for more rustic retreats, often boardinghouses run by farmers. Much less expensive than large hotels, boardinghouses offered even working-class families a chance to escape the city's summer heat. Since most boardinghouses were set on active farms, they also offered fresh, nutritious food, featuring milk, eggs, and fruit. Many urban residents relished the opportunity to relax in an agricultural setting. Wagon rides through the countryside to modest attractions such as small waterfalls or mountaintop overlooks could occupy tourists seeking a break from city life as long as finances allowed. New York City's Jews were particularly eager participants in late-nineteenth-century tourism. Although most had modest incomes, they saved through the busy winter working season, especially in the garment industry, and then found humble accommodations in the country, usually close to the city, especially in the southern Catskills, an area that eventually gained the derisive nickname the "Borscht Belt." By the end of the century, mass Jewish participation in summer vacations revealed how broad the tourist culture had become, even if many working-class New York families could afford only the occasional trip to Coney Island or a week in the Catskills.

Tourism had multiple environmental consequences, even beyond the obvious infrastructure built and maintained to accommodate and please visitors, in part because tourism stamped new meanings on the landscape. Tourist destinations served two populations, local people and visitors, and in many places fulltime rural residents resented the degree to which the tourist economy impinged on their ability to control their own communities. Throughout the state, tourists became important voices for preservation, hoping to save the landscapes—both natural and cultural—that they had come to know through repeated visits.

Places worthy of seeing were also places worthy of preservation. Indeed tourism helped set the preservation agenda over the course of the next century, as both cultural and natural tourist destinations became integral to the way New Yorkers understood their state. By the end of the century, tourism had solidified New Yorkers' attachment to the state's landscape, and many had woven it into their personal identity. To mar these places—from the falls of Niagara to the battlefield at Saratoga and the beaches of eastern Long Island—would compromise New Yorkers' sense of themselves.

Romantic sensibilities elevated the role of landscape in nineteenth-century culture, both in recreation and in commemoration. Although New York witnessed no Civil War battles, the state gradually filled with memorials to that epic struggle. In a process that gathered momentum in the 1880s and 1890s, New York's communities built memorials to sacrifice into the landscape, often in the heart of villages and cities. Obelisks and statues depicting soldiers at attention or on horseback increasingly occupied town squares, public parks, and landscaped cemeteries. New York City's Riverside Park, designed by Frederick Law Olmsted in the 1870s, gained two noteworthy memorials to the war. In 1897 the public celebrated the completion of Grant's Tomb, a grand, solemn neoclassical edifice dedicated to remembrance. Two years later Governor Theodore Roosevelt laid the cornerstone for a similarly grand Soldiers' and Sailors' Monument farther south in the park. These memorials helped elevate the spaces they occupied, as other memorials did around the state, granting even more value to those places and ensuring their preservation.

SUBURBAN AESTHETICS

With the help of steam transportation, romanticism played a central role in guiding tourists to certain destinations and informing their reactions when they arrived. The combination of romanticism and steam transportation played a similar role closer to home, shaping wealthy New Yorkers' choices of where and how to live. Increasingly, affluent New Yorkers kept their distance from the city, wary of urban life, with its congestion and disease. As New York City grew rapidly, its suburban hinterland filled with great country estates. Although some of these properties were on Long Island, including William Cullen Bryant's, many of them clustered along the Hudson. "There is a suburban look and character about all the villages on the Hudson which seems out of place among such scenery," wrote N. P. Willis in 1840. "They are suburbs; in fact, steam has destroyed the distance between them and the city." Over the next several decades, great homes would fill the Hudson Valley. The nation's cultural elite occupied many of them, including Frederic Church, who built his exotic Olana across the river from Cole's former Catskill home in 1872. The nation's economic elite also occupied great homes along the Hudson, including James Roosevelt, who made his fortune in the railroad industry and purchased a Hyde Park estate called Springwood in 1866.

Fittingly, a new aesthetic developed among these villas, in part inspired by Andrew Jackson Downing, the landscape gardener from Newburgh who used his journal *The Horticulturalist* to encourage scientific farming. Downing also cultivated a suburban sensibility. "In the United States," he wrote, "nature and domestic life are better than society and the manners of towns. Hence all sensible men gladly escape, earlier or later, and partially or wholly, from the turmoil of cities." And when they did, Downing was happy to design their country homes, complete with expansive landscaped yards, using an aesthetic he described in detail in *The Architecture of Country Houses,* published in 1850.

Beyond his work and his writings, Downing's lasting influence came through the work of his partner, Calvert Vaux, who moved to Newburgh to work with Downing in 1850. Vaux went on to design country homes in the Hudson Valley and to pen his own influential volume, *Villas and Cottages,* published in 1857. For both Vaux and Downing, the Hudson itself played a central role in their imaginings of a picturesque suburban ideal. As Downing wrote, wherever "the wildness or grandeur of nature triumphs strongly over cultivated landscape," and "especially where river or lake and hill country are combined," that is where "the highly picturesque country house or villa is instinctively felt to harmonize with or belong to the landscape." Downing specifically noted that these conditions existed beyond the Hudson Valley, but his ideal had been formulated there.

CENTRAL PARK

New York's economic elite did not abandon the city altogether, of course; even most of those who built country estates maintained a town home, from which they could remain connected to the economic and cultural life of the city. And so they remained connected to the urban environment as well, and they expressed concern about a variety of environmental problems facing the burgeoning city. Middle-class and wealthy New Yorkers were especially troubled by filth and disease, and the ways in which these issues plagued expanding working-class neighborhoods. Deeply influenced by romanticism, New York's elites sought ways of bringing nature into the city, as a means of improving both the aesthetics of the urban environment and the morality of the urban masses. Americans nearly everywhere had allotted only meager public space in their small but growing cities. New York City had only Battery Park at the southern tip of Manhattan, a patch of green in front of City Hall, and scattered squares to break up the streetscape. In the early 1800s, residents could and would simply walk or ride out into the countryside for escape and diversion, making publicly owned and maintained green space in the city less necessary. By the mid-nineteenth century, however, New York and Brooklyn had grown so large that easy escape from these two cities had become nearly impossible, especially for the expanding working class.

In response, New York's cultural elite initiated efforts to create natural patches in the urban landscape. Samuel Ruggles recognized the value of open space, and in 1831, as he began to develop a farm north of the city, he set aside land and called it Gramercy Park, which became the center of his very successful development. Gramercy remained a private park, however, reserved for residents of the immediate area. But Gramercy Park's success, both economic and aesthetic, helped inspire grander thinking among other New Yorkers, including William Cullen Bryant, who became an advocate of building a large park in New York City in the 1840s. Bryant knew that New York would face myriad problems if its burgeoning population were confined to Battery and City Hall parks, or, even worse, if the city's 500,000 residents were forced to spend their free hours in the relentlessly crowded streets. Supporters claimed that building a large new park would improve citizens' health and morality, and benefit the reputation of the city, which suffered in comparison to the great European cities in part because it contained no great public space. As those who worried most about the conditions of the poor pointed out, however, a large park located miles up island from the most crowded neighborhoods would not solve the city's most pressing problems. Thus the park became largely a project of the city's elite, who were eager to develop some grand space where they might retreat from the pace and noise of the crowds.

New Yorkers debated where the new park should be built, but the cost of land at the southern end of Manhattan ensured that any large park could be developed only well north of the densest neighborhoods. In 1853 the state gave the city permission to take land for Central Park. Frederick Law Olmsted and

Calvert Vaux won the design contest that followed in 1857. Their "Greensward Plan" contained a great variety of landscapes to help break up the monotony of Manhattan's streets, but in particular it featured a large open sheep's meadow that would give visitors the greatest sense of distance within the park. The larger purpose, both of the meadow and of the park as a whole, was to make "the visitor feel as if he had got far away from town," as Olmsted later wrote. This effect would take considerable labor. By the time Olmsted and Vaux had finished their work, they had completely remade the landscape inside the park. A formal mall lined with benches provided space for promenades and people-watching. A ramble laced with meandering footpaths provided a piece of wild forest in which to get lost. Even the structures in the park, many of them designed by Vaux, helped create an idealized rural landscape. The park's many bridges and small buildings reflected Vaux's romanticism, the rustic and picturesque sensibilities encouraged by his mentor Andrew Jackson Downing. The design also included a vegetative screen separating the park from the rest of the city, heightening the sense of removal to the countryside. Crosstown traffic traversed the park on sunken drives, minimizing the disruption. Altogether the completed park was a fully constructed landscape, with new lakes and rock outcroppings, plantings and vistas, all of them created to match the vision of Olmstead and Vaux.

The partners hoped to create a place of respite from the city, for relaxation and contemplation. As Olmsted wrote during construction of the park, its purpose was "not simply to give the people of the city an opportunity for getting fresh air and exercise." Nor was it merely a "place of amusement or for the gratification of curiosity or for gaining knowledge." The park was not to be a place for sport or competition. Instead, Olmsted wrote, "The main object and justification is simply to produce a certain influence in the minds of people and through this to make life in the city healthier and happier. The character of this influence is a poetic one and it is to be produced by means of scenes, through observation of which the mind may be more or less lifted out of moods and habits into which it is, under the ordinary conditions of life in the city, likely to fall." In other words, the park's landscape should impart to urban minds the sensation of being in the country, in nature, for at the heart of Central Park lay the romantic notion that nature would heal weary city dwellers.

From the very beginning the park plan gained little support from the working classes, especially the 1,600 residents displaced by the purchase of the land—Irish and German immigrants and a small black community called Seneca Village. When workers put the finishing touches on Central Park in 1864,

Figure 11. Central Park brought aspects of the countryside into the city, following romantic notions of the healing force of nature. Sheep on the green, Central Park, New York City (n.d.). New York State Archives, Albany.

the 843-acre retreat was still quite a distance from the masses gathered in the neighborhoods of lower Manhattan. Over time, however, building Central Park would prove to be not only the most important development decision in the city's history but also, as the park inspired so many other large urban parks, one of the most important events in environmental history. Eventually cities from Boston to San Francisco would have their own expansive landscaped parks, shaping development and recreation, and leaving lasting romantic features on the nation's urban landscape.

After Central Park's great success, Olmsted and Vaux continued to work across the state and the country. Most famously, the partners designed Brooklyn's Prospect Park in the 1860s. With a mixed landscape reminiscent of Central Park, it featured the "Long Meadow" and gracefully curving carriage paths, which combined to create a sense of rural expansiveness. Even as work in Brooklyn progressed, Olmsted traveled to Buffalo in 1868 to begin planning that city's park system. He envisioned three different kinds of parks in three different parts of Buffalo, connected by a system of parkways. The first park to be built, now called Delaware Park, included a 150-acre meadow and a deer paddock, following Olmsted's theory about the desirability of bringing a bit of the countryside into the city. Although Olmsted created parks around the country, he returned to New York State in the 1880s to design Rochester's park system. There he again connected three different types of parks with parkways and created a large meadow park, called Genesee Valley Park.

NIAGARA FALLS STATE RESERVATION

Even as Olmsted designed dozens of urban parks, he engaged in other important works, perhaps most famously the effort to restore the natural beauty of Niagara Falls. Through the first half of the 1800s, the land around the falls had become crowded with private parks, amusements, and sideshows—all part of the great tourist landscape that evolved to serve thousands of visitors every year. Perhaps even worse, industry had developed along the riverfront, as mills took advantage of the water power. Niagara had become so cluttered and unattractive that tourism suffered. Tourists still came, of course, but they stayed only briefly, taking in the falls and, often, expressing dismay at the condition of the area. In 1869 Olmsted and Vaux joined William Dorsheimer, a prominent Buffalo lawyer, in an effort to liberate the falls from the cultural clutter and return the area around it to a more natural state. Their call for the public purchase of land along the river met with a slow response. By 1878 Frederic Church had joined the crusade. Church's magnificent painting of the falls, completed in 1857, had forever connected the artist with that place and, significantly, helped create the dominant image of the falls among late-nineteenth-century tourists. The painting also gave Church special influence in the debates that followed.

In 1880 the New York State Survey issued a report on the "Preservation of the Scenery of Niagara Falls," which made the case for state purchase of lands and the restoration of the scenery to "its original character." Published with the report were notes from Olmsted and an appeal to Governor Alonzo Cornell, both of which supported the creation of a state reservation at the falls. Although seven hundred prominent Americans had signed the appeal, including dozens of powerful politicians, Cornell thought the expenditure of taxes for purposes of protecting scenery frivolous. State protection of the falls had to await the inauguration of a new governor, Grover Cleveland, who signed the bill creating the reservation in 1883.

The state spent nearly $1.5 million to purchase land through eminent domain, to remove obtrusive structures, and to landscape the shoreline, Bath Island, and Goat Island under the direction of Olmsted and Vaux. In July 1885 the reservation opened to great fanfare, with thirty thousand visitors taking in the falls without having to pay admission. The *New York Times* described the creation of the reservation as "a distinct step forward in civilization." In a speech on the occasion, Dorsheimer appropriately compared the celebrations at Niagara with those that had attended the creation of the Erie Canal. Both projects involved the expansion of state authority and the use of state power in the interest of the people. Both were also important moments in environmental history, moments when the state used its power to shape landscapes to meet the expectations of citizens. At Niagara Reservation, for the first time in the nation's history, the government purchased land for aesthetic purposes.

The Niagara Reservation was not New York State's first purchase in the interest of preservation. That distinction belongs to Hasbrouck House, in Newburgh, which had served as George Washington's headquarters from the spring of 1782 through the following summer. In 1849 New York created the nation's first state-owned historic site to protect the home and keep it open to the public. Together Hasbrouck House and the Niagara Reservation reveal how preservation of natural and cultural heritage overlapped, particularly through tourism. New York State contained many important places, some created by nature, others by culture, and most by a combination of both. At Hasbrouck House, New Yorkers could recount how the Hudson and its Highlands had lain at the center of the Patriots' endeavor. At Niagara, tourists could view one of the great works of God while wandering through one of the great works of the nation's most prominent landscape architects. After the turn of the century, in 1909, New York added another preserve to protect a mixed natural and cultural landscape. Saratoga Springs Reservation protected that tourist destination's most precious natural resource—its spring waters—while simultaneously protecting the state's century-old spa heritage and its ongoing tourist industry.

THE NORTH WOODS

It isn't surprising that many of New York's early preservation efforts took place along the beaten paths of the Grand Tour, but the state's largest preservation project occurred well north of most tourists' routes. As late as the 1840s, New York's North Woods remained largely unvisited, unsettled, and unknown.

The first recorded hike up the state's highest mountain, not yet named Marcy, awaited the year 1837, when geologist Ebenezer Emmons ascended with a guide. He proposed to name the mountains he overlooked the "Adirondacks." Even as the Catskills developed into the nation's first great mountain resort region, and Niagara became burdened by tourism's trappings, the North Woods remained surprisingly distant. In the words of historian Philip Terrie, this distance assured that the Adirondacks would be "fundamentally different from the rest of New York."

At mid-century, however, the tourist culture began to take notice of the Adirondacks, especially as a growing number of travelers sought out more rustic vacations in the types of wilderness areas that the North Woods offered in abundance. In 1849 Joel T. Headley published what would become a remarkably influential book: *The Adirondack; or, Life in the Woods.* Headley, a minister, praised the mountain wilderness, contrasting it directly with the city. Rural vacations to resorts like Saratoga were one thing, Headley noted; trips into the wilderness were another altogether. Headley's romantic language offered a stark contrast with that of settlers, still battling thick forests with their axes. "I love the freedom of the wilderness and the absence of conventional forms there," he wrote. Only tourists could find freedom in wilderness; settlers found endless work. Headley also praised the healthfulness of the wilderness, claiming, "I love it, and I know it is better for me than the thronged city, aye, better for soul and body both." His most stirring passage, where he revealed most clearly the attraction of the wilderness, described his emotions as he stood atop Mount Marcy, overlooking a forest broken only by a few clearings:

> My head swam in the wondrous vision; and I seemed lifted up above the earth, and shown all its mountains and forests and lakes at once. But the impression of the whole, it is impossible to convey—nay, I am myself hardly conscious what it is. It seems as if I had seen vagueness, terror, sublimity, strength, and beauty, all embodied, so that I had a new and more definite knowledge of them. God appears to have wrought in these old mountains with His highest power, and designed to leave a symbol of His omnipotence. Man is nothing here, his very shouts die on his lips.

All this and it was in New York, too, a fact that Headley found worthy of repeating. How could such an astounding wilderness remain so close to the nation's metropolis?

Mount Marcy brought out Headley's emotions, but other places were more important to his book, including Martin's Hotel, an outpost on Lower Saranac

Figure 12. In the late nineteenth century, a rush of tourists headed into the wilds of the Adirondacks for romantic wilderness adventures. Cranberry Lake in the Adirondacks. Postcard (ca. 1900). Author's collection.

Lake that served as a jumping-off point for wilderness adventurers like Headley. Here travelers could stuff themselves with trout and venison and stories of adventure. They could also hire the guides who were essential to exploring the North Woods. Martin's was the launching point for other famed wilderness adventures, including that of Ralph Waldo Emerson, who joined other members of the Cambridge, Massachusetts, elite, including Louis Agassiz, James Russell Lowell, and William Stillman, at Follensby Pond. For two weeks in the summer of 1858 these men, with their guides and their canoes, lived out their romantic adventure, communing with nature, feeling the isolation, playing at being primitives. Stillman, who most completely described the trip, hinted that the wilderness might make these highly cultured men less civilized; this was the danger posed by wilderness to touring elites, quite different from the dangers that settlers faced.

The Cambridge expedition became an important chapter in Adirondack romantic lore, but the literature it created was not as influential as that published by William H. H. Murray in 1869. A Boston minister, Murray added a best-seller to the growing list of wilderness travel writing: *Adventures in the Wilderness; or, Camp-Life in the Adirondacks.* Murray wrote "to encourage manly exercise in

Figure 13. Tourism altered the environment in many ways, most obviously by dotting the landscape with large hotels, even in the deep woods of the Adirondacks. The Sagamore, Long Lake, in the Adirondacks. Postcard (ca. 1900). Author's collection.

the open air, and familiarity with Nature in her wildest and grandest aspects." Like Headley before him, Murray found in the wilds "free life by field and flood," and an environment "eminently adapted to restore impaired health." The balsam and pine gave the air "curative qualities," Murray thought, and in the woods God was everywhere. Murray's book became so popular, and the rush to the Adirondacks became so overwhelming in the 1870s, that the press referred to the arriving tourists as "Murray's Fools." Popular writer Charles Dudley Warner also contributed to the growing wilderness literature, publishing a series of essays concerning his Adirondack adventures. *In the Wilderness* described a chain of challenges Warner claimed he faced in the deep woods, including a confrontation with a bear (which he killed) and a long battle with a trout (which he ate). True or not, these were stories of mastery, of man struggling to survive away from the comforts of civilization.

For men like Warner, wild adventure was a way to feel one's manliness and build character. This was certainly the opinion of another, more famous wilderness adventurer: Theodore Roosevelt. Wilderness tramping was not about dominance, however, even for Roosevelt, famous for his prolific hunting trips. His approach to nature also included an ever present appreciation of both the trials and the beauty presented by trackless wild lands. Roosevelt often described his enthusiasm for nature in very masculine terms, steeped in struggle and adventure, but he was not immune to the romanticism of the age. While in the Adirondacks during the summer of 1877, Roosevelt partook in a failed evening deer hunt. "Wearied by our unsuccess," he wrote,

> we at last turned homeward when suddenly the quiet was broken by the song of a hermit thrush; louder and clearer it sang from the depths of the grim and rugged woods, until the sweet, sad music seemed to fill the very air and to conquer for a moment the gloom of the night....Perhaps the song would have proved less sweet in the daytime, but uttered as it was, with such surroundings, sounding so strange and so beautiful amid these grand but desolate wilds, I shall never forget it.

This was the power of romanticism—the love of nature that connected travelers to places—even places they visited only once.

THE FOREST PRESERVE

Even as romantic tourism was changing the meaning of the North Woods for many New Yorkers, the Adirondacks were also becoming home to increasing numbers of settlers, many of whom worked in the growing timber industry. Not surprisingly, concern for the preservation of the North Woods grew along with the export of wood products. The state's debate about the preservation of forestlands arose after the publication of George Perkins Marsh's *Man and Nature; or, Physical Geography as Modified by Human Action* in 1864. Instantly influential, Marsh's book argued that human actions had and would continue to exact a heavy toll on nature, claiming that deforestation had even played a role in the decline of great European civilizations. Marsh noted that "poetical" views on preservation had already sparked some discussion of preserving the North Woods. "It is desirable that some large and easily accessible region of American soil should remain, as far as possible, in its primitive condition, at once a museum for the instruction of the student, a garden for the recreation of the love of nature, and an asylum where indigenous tree, and humble plant that loves the shade, and fish and fowl and four-footed beast may dwell and perpetuate their kind," Marsh wrote. But Marsh was much less influenced by romantic thinking than by his understanding of what would become the science of ecology. He connected deforestation with diminished water flow, and he specifically warned against the destruction of the Adirondack forest, just then beginning to see

Figure 14. Adirondack logging accelerated in the late 1800s, rapidly altering the North Woods and arousing concern around the state. In 1867 a dam raised the level of Cranberry Lake, drowning trees and facilitating the floating of logs. Drowned forest; dead stumps and trunks—the result of raiding the water level (1913). New York State Archives, Albany.

considerable logging. "The felling of the Adirondack woods would ultimately involve for Northern and Central New York consequences similar to those which have resulted from the laying bare of the southern and western declivities of the French Alps," Marsh warned. Without forests, erosion would silt the Hudson, while temperatures would become more erratic and the mountains drier. Thus, Marsh argued, the "collateral advantages of the preservation of these forests would be far greater" than those of nature recreation and study.

Marsh's work sparked a growing concern about deforestation and the possibility of diminished water flow in some of the state's major rivers, especially the Hudson. Others noted that northern waters were critical to the state's canal system, which still carried freight inexpensively from Albany to Buffalo despite the growing importance of railroads. This commercial argument for forest preservation gained political support, especially in New York City. A drought in 1883 left the upper Hudson perilously low, adding a sense of urgency to the debate. With the backing of the New York Chamber of Commerce, the state legislature finally took action. The following year, the legislature created a temporary Forestry Commission to investigate conditions in the state's mountain ranges. Led by well-known Harvard forester Charles S. Sargent, the commission directed most of its efforts toward the Adirondacks, but its members also toured the Catskills. In its 1885 report to the state assembly, the commission recommended the creation of a forest preserve in the northern mountains and proposed a bill that would prohibit the sale or lease of state lands in enumerated counties. Interestingly, the commission did not advise the creation of a preserve in the Catskills, since those mountains had already seen considerable logging and because they contained "no streams of more than local influence." The commission failed to foresee that the Catskills would eventually become the largest source of New York City's water supply.

The commission's report persuaded the state legislature to act quickly, and it created the Forest Preserve later that year—six years before Congress passed legislation allowing the president of the United States to set aside federal forest reserves. New York's preservation act listed counties in which state-owned forests would remain in the public domain and therefore be "forever kept as wild forest lands," a phrase that became one of the most repeated in New York history. A new three-person State Forest Commission, appointed by the governor, would oversee the management of the preserve. Although the state's focus had been on the Adirondacks all along, state lands in three Catskills counties—Greene, Ulster, and Sullivan—also were added to the Forest Preserve at the insistence of Ulster County's representatives. At its creation in 1885, the Forest Preserve included 681,000 acres in the Adirondacks and just under 34,000 in the Catskills. In 1894 the popularity of the preserve became evident when New Yorkers added the "wild forever" stipulation to the state constitution, which now barred logging on state lands in Forest Preserve counties.

Creating the Forest Preserve and adding the protective phrases to the state's constitution marked only the beginning of preservation in New York's mountain forests. In 1902 concerned citizens, mostly downstate residents with recreational interests in the mountains, created the Association for the Protection of the Adirondacks, for the purpose of preserving "the Adirondack forests, waters, game and fish, and the maintenance of healthful conditions in the Adirondack region." The association helped keep the Adirondacks in the press and maintained pressure on the legislature to pass protective measures and add acreage to the preserve through purchase. By 1904 the state owned over 1.4 million acres in the Adirondacks and 104,524 acres in the Catskills. Much of this forestland covered higher elevations, land that was least valuable to loggers and potentially most valuable in protecting headwaters.

In 1911, while surveying the accomplishments of New York State, the forester Bernhard Fernow claimed that for the first time in North America "the idea of State forestry, management of State lands on forestry principles," had taken hold. "A new doctrine of State functions had gained the day." Clearly the Forest Preserve represented a significant leap forward in establishing government authority over the environment, a trend that would continue through the next century, but state ownership and regulation of the forests brought only incomplete protection of the North Woods. Market changes, especially the turn to wood pulp for papermaking, set off a wave of logging in the north. No longer did loggers take just the valued white pine, since even small trees could be cut and fed to the growing paper industry. The Forest Preserve brought protection to great swaths of land, but logging only quickened in the Adirondacks around the turn of the century. In 1898 International Paper consolidated the holdings of several smaller companies, increasing the industry's efficiency and thus the pressure on the forests. Two years later New York State accounted for more than a third of the nation's pulp mills, many of them ringing the Adirondacks. Logs poured out of the mountains, run down rivers to mills or, increasingly, shipped out on railroad lines punched deeper into the woods.

Slash left behind became fodder for fires, which increased in frequency and intensity. A succession of dry years led to a series of horrible fires, some of which raced through thousands of acres. In June 1903 raging Adirondack fires became front-page news in New York City. Small armies of men fought numerous fires—around Long Lake, Indian Lake, and North Creek. Ashes fell on Saratoga fifty miles away. And down in the city, the fires gave New Yorkers a "yellow day," as acrid smoke drifted over the metropolis. If reading about the distant fires hadn't convinced New Yorkers that something was terribly wrong in the North Woods, perhaps the smell of burning wood might. The smoke of the city's factories and the smoke of the countryside mingled above New York Harbor, proof of the supremacy of economics and the limited ability of romanticism to blunt the power of capitalism to remake the landscape.

In the same year as the terrible fires, the Association for the Protection of the Adirondacks published *A Plea for the Adirondack and Catskill Parks,* which offered several reasons for continued state purchases in the North Woods, with a special emphasis on the Adirondacks as a recreation site. In the Catskills, too,

Figure 15. Logs flowed out of the Adirondacks, especially down the Hudson, pictured here at Fort Edward. Logjam above the D&H Railroad bridge (1913). New York State Archives, Albany.

the group urged, the state should own many times the acres it did to "assure a desirable and convenient summer resort for the vast and increasing population of New York City and the Hudson Valley." Of even more interest, the association argued that the Catskills "have become invested with a wealth of legendary and historical association which gives them a peculiar and exclusive charm." Throughout history the Catskills had been filled with "Myth and Legend," including that of Rip Van Winkle. In sum, "the Catskills preserve the memorials of a people's origin and should be cherished as a potent inspiration to the student of history, as well as to the poet, the painter and writer." The region, the pamphlet concluded, "has a peculiar claim upon the community for its preservation, favored, as it is, by historic and patriotic association and enriched by romantic traditions and legendary lore reaching back into the dim morning twilight of the Nation's life." In addition to Cole and Church, Kensett and Cropsey, all of whom are cited in the plea, the association noted that the Catskills "may be said to have given the State a Literature." The argument revealed how closely New York's identity had been linked to landscape through culture—landscape painting and literature as well as tourists' experiences.

Even before the Association for the Protection of the Adirondacks issued its plea, however, the influence of romanticism had begun to fade. Hudson River art had lost favor, and was even earning ridicule. Romantic writing now seemed overwrought and unrealistic. But even if a new realism was taking hold in the new century, romantic notions of nature never disappeared. Indeed, just as Central Park still set the standard for American urban parks, so too would romanticism underlie evolving environmental politics. Romantic literature and art, combined with tourism, had created a new way of knowing nature, and the state as a whole. Places all around New York State took on new layers of meaning through the entangling stories romantic culture told about nature. Increasingly, New Yorkers identified the Empire State with the landscape it contained: mountains, lakes, rivers, expansive forests, as well as spas, hotels, and historic homes. These were places worth knowing—and protecting.

4

Tainted and Unwholesome Atmospheres

*Urban Environments,
Government, and Reform*

On May 24, 1883, a procession of dignitaries made its way past immense, cheering crowds along Broadway, as hundreds of American flags waved in the clear day's cool breeze. The procession, complete with soldiers and musicians, ended at City Hall Park, where President Chester A. Arthur, New York State governor Grover Cleveland, New York City mayor Seth Low, and dozens of other notables climbed from their carriages and made the short walk to the Brooklyn Bridge. There a ceremony announced the completion of the first structure connecting New York, the largest city in the nation, and its neighbor Brooklyn, the third largest. The crowds cheered the president, the brightest of the assembled stars, but they had really gathered to cheer the bridge itself, an architectural and technological wonder. Its towers now dominated the skylines of both cities; its span promised to reshape travel and growth in New York Harbor. The presence of the president and so many American flags announced that this moment was a triumph not just for New York but for the nation as a whole. As with the celebrations marking the completion of the Erie Canal in 1825 and the Croton Aqueduct in 1842, on this day New Yorkers cheered the ability of Americans to overcome the obstacles set by nature. The Brooklyn Bridge instantly became a symbol of urban promise, economic growth, and the seemingly limitless possibilities of modern technology. It was a symbol of the age.

The next day, when the bridge opened to the general public, tens of thousands of Brooklyn residents streamed into New York, paying a penny each to walk across the span. In Manhattan the crowds became backed up as the elevated railroad deposited customers nearly at the foot of the bridge, and lines of horse cars dropped off thousands more. Some had clearly come for the chance to take in the views, the panorama of the city, and to experience the bridge. Others were taking the first of many trips to work via the span, which would, as promised, impel even more growth in Brooklyn. Though just across the East River from lower Manhattan, Brooklyn had grown relatively slowly, even after regular steam ferry service began in 1814. In 1830 it still had just over fifteen thousand residents, and most of Kings County remained farmland. But the exponential growth of New York City, and rising land costs in Manhattan, resulted in longer commutes to work, including ferry rides from Brooklyn. As more and more ferries plied the East River, more and more Manhattan workers made the daily trip from decidedly less crowded, less polluted Brooklyn neighborhoods. By the time the bridge opened in 1883, Brooklyn was a sizable city, approaching 600,000 residents, and it had developed its own industries and port facilities.

URBAN POPULATIONS

The Brooklyn Bridge was the most spectacular addition to New York's growing transportation system, which allowed urbanites to live farther from work and propelled the city's influence deeper into the countryside. Railroads brought middle-class workers to and from distant suburbs. Elevated trains moved others to and from city enclaves far from the crushing crowds of lower Manhattan. Many escaped, mostly those with comfortable means, but as much as transportation enabled some people to travel longer distances to work, it also ironically heightened congestion at the city's core. The Lower East Side, just north of the new bridge, had become infamous for its density, and overcrowding had become one of the city's most dire problems. The transportation revolution encouraged a concentration of businesses in a place New Yorkers increasingly called "downtown," a term later used throughout the United States to describe the peculiar kind of sorting that occurred in American cities. In contrast, "uptown" referred to the quieter, more residential sections of Manhattan. Every morning hundreds of thousands of workers streamed down the avenues, and every evening they made the reverse trip, marking what had become the two rush hours that characterized the modern American city.

Through the nineteenth century, Manhattan's population continued to soar. In 1880 New York had become the first American city to exceed a million residents. Just twenty years later it would be the first to exceed 2 million. Brooklyn, too, doubled in size over those years, and by the time it became part of the consolidated New York City in 1898, it also housed more than a million residents. Shortly after the 1910 census, the five boroughs of New York exceeded 5 million residents altogether. But New York City wasn't just growing; its economy was changing. Continued industrialization drove the rapid population growth, especially in Manhattan and Brooklyn. By 1910 the city was home to 26,000 manufacturing plants employing 680,000 people. Growth, density, and industrial development posed numerous environmental challenges to New Yorkers. Public health suffered in filthy tenement districts, as tuberculosis and other communicable diseases spread seemingly unchecked. Pure air became precious, as in some neighborhoods the foul odors of industries and stables mingled with the smells of congested, unwashed humanity. Municipal officials struggled to supply basic environmental services, like keeping the streets clean and carting away garbage. Supplying adequate housing for the working poor became a chronic struggle.

Although New York City experienced these problems more acutely than other places, it was not the only city in the state to suffer the environmental consequences of rapid industrialization and demographic growth. By 1910 more than 60 percent of the state's population lived in cities with more than 100,000 residents. Even as some rural counties lost population, including Madison, Delaware, and Otsego, the state as a whole grew by nearly 25 percent in the first decade of the twentieth century alone. Nearly all of this growth occurred in the state's four largest cities. After New York City, which accounted for more than half the state's population, Buffalo approached 425,000 people, Rochester neared 220,000, and Syracuse topped 137,000. Altogether Buffalo, Rochester, and Syracuse had added nearly 300,000 residents in the twenty years leading up to the 1910 census. As in New York City, their growth was driven by expanding manufacturing sectors, in which 3,600 factories employed nearly 130,000 workers.

The municipal response to urban environmental problems in the late 1800s was halting and incomplete, but by the first decade of the twentieth century, many Americans expressed a new faith in government and a willingness to rely on publicly employed experts in fields as disparate as public health, engineering, and planning. New Yorkers participated eagerly in public interest groups, some of which undertook direct action, attempting to make improvements through their own efforts. But reformers also increasingly lobbied for more effective government action. These progressive reformers recognized the failure of the free market to supply adequate affordable housing and to keep urban populations healthy, and they turned to municipal and state government to find and implement solutions. As a result, interventionist municipal governments passed a wide variety of environmental regulations, from anti-smoke laws to building codes, designed to keep residents safer and healthier. Cities used eminent domain to take and demolish troubled properties, sometimes replacing them with parks and playgrounds. They built public baths and invested huge sums of money in improving water supplies and sewage systems. By the end of this reform era, municipal governments had gained much greater control over the urban environment, significantly restricting the unregulated market. This was especially evident in the wide implementation of zoning laws that gave cities remarkable control over land use decisions. This long wave of progressive reforms left cities much altered, though still obviously imperfect. In short, the absolute necessity of developing solutions to environmental problems led directly to the expansion of government authority. In an industrial, urban state, laissez-faire governance simply could not suffice.

THE URBAN TRANSPORTATION REVOLUTION

Reform activism intensified in the late 1800s, but rapid change in urban environments had begun much earlier. New York City's growth in the decades surrounding the Civil War was astonishing, in part because of increased immigration from Europe. The city added over 300,000 people in the 1850s alone. Many of these immigrants were Irish and poor, and their presence in the city played a role in changing middle-class perceptions of urban space, adding a sense of foreignness and danger which compounded many Americans' fear of urbanization. Other than Central Park, well removed from the poorest neighborhoods, the city had very little public space, save for city streets and occasional squares. Most of the city was composed of mixed-use neighborhoods, where manufacturing, retail, and residential buildings occupied the same blocks. Indeed, many buildings served multiple purposes: groceries or saloons on the ground floor and residences above, for example. Workplaces and residences also mixed in tenements themselves, since many working poor brought piecework into their apartments—sewing garments, for example, in their cramped rooms and returning them to their employers for payment.

Rapid growth posed tremendous challenges for the city. Housing was inadequate throughout the nineteenth century. Sanitation was poor, and for decades it did not significantly improve. Public health actually worsened throughout much of the century, and with the spread of contagious diseases such as consumption (tuberculosis) and typhus, mortality rates in the city increased in the 1850s. (Mortality rates did not significantly improve until much later in the century, when reforms began to take hold.) Physical change came quickly, leaving parts of New York City unrecognizable to those who had been away for even a short period. Factories and warehouses filled an increasing number of blocks, and larger tenement buildings replaced smaller ones. In 1856, after the demolition of a prominent Broadway hotel—an edifice that had stood just a dozen years—a *Harper's Monthly* editor lamented that a "man born in New York forty years ago finds nothing, absolutely nothing, of the New York he knew. If he chances to stumble upon a few old houses not yet leveled, he is fortunate. But the landmarks, the objects which marked the city to him, as a city, are gone."

To sustain their growth, industrial cities required a transportation revolution, not unlike the revolution in the countryside initiated by canals and sustained by railroads. In the city, horses were an integral part of the evolving industrial infrastructure. Though often portrayed as rural remnants in industrial cities, horses were in fact absolutely essential to urban growth. In the 1830s, omnibuses began to transform New York's urban transportation. Essentially horse-drawn covered wagons with bench seats, the omnibuses introduced regular routes and schedules, allowing middle-class residents the option of commuting farther to work. In New York City, omnibuses moved up and down the avenues, converging on City Hall Park near the heart of downtown, and allowing growth in both the residential areas to the north and the developing business district south of City Hall. Gradually horse-drawn cars made use of tracks laid into city streets, which reduced friction, increased speed, and decreased the number of horses needed to pull each car. Since they allowed passengers to travel faster for less money, these horsecars encouraged even more growth beyond the city's core. Of course, horses did more than pull people through the city; they were also essential for moving goods. By 1900, altogether 130,000 horses worked in Manhattan, and most of them lived there, too, many of them in huge multistory stables where as many as a thousand horses were housed together.

Horses worked in tandem with steam technology in the transportation revolution. The New York & Harlem Railroad, for example, began as a streetcar company, running horse-drawn cars from Pine Street to Fourteenth Street by 1832. By 1839 the company was pulling passenger cars from City Hall to Harlem, about nine miles away. To speed the long trip, the company employed a steam engine north of Twenty-seventh Street, but horses continued to pull the cars along the rails through the most densely populated portion of the city. Steam locomotives were so unpopular in the city—in part because they were loud, smelly, and smoky, and emitted dangerous sparks, and in part because they occasionally exploded—that in 1844 the city banned them below Thirty-second Street. In 1856 the exclusion zone was pushed north to Forty-second Street. Although it was not always obeyed, the ban ensured that horses would continue to move most passengers south of midtown. More important, horses, working with steam locomotives, helped spread the city well beyond its dense core. In 1855 an estimated seventy-thousand people commuted to downtown, some by ferry but most by steam railway and horsecar.

Congestion was compounded by the multiple uses of streets. They were the primary means of moving material, although ferries also transported goods to and from docks around Manhattan, Brooklyn, New Jersey, and Long Island. Streets were often crowded with horse-drawn wagons, carts, and drays, as well as pedestrians. Streets were also important recreational spaces, particularly for children with few other options. Since most women would not (or could not) frequent saloons, where men spent much of their limited recreational time, women used streets as community space, conversing with friends and neighbors on stoops. There were also peddlers offering any number of goods, from ice to produce; there were scavengers, ragpickers, and prostitutes, all trying to make a living on the streets. Newsboys shouted from their favorite corners. Homeless people did their best to find work and shelter. Increasingly, middle-class reformers grew wary of city streets and the people and behavior they saw there, and concern for the mixed crowds and activities changed thinking about the city generally. Eventually the mere presence of certain people could debase particular places, and vice versa. Just as romantic tourism added layers of meaning to places in the countryside, immigration and concentrated poverty added new layers of meaning to city streets. In short, as the city grew, it filled with increasingly problematic places.

In the 1860s worsening traffic persuaded the state to allow the development of steam-driven elevated railroads, yet another step in the transportation revolution. At first stationary plants pulled the trains by cable, but as companies built longer lines they required the use of steam locomotives, called dummies. This in turn required another change in the law. By the late 1870s, elevated railroads had gained enough political and legal support for new lines to be built up and down Manhattan. More than any other place in the world, New York City allowed companies to build massive, obtrusive, and lengthy elevated lines above city streets. By 1880 elevated railroads ran up and down Second, Third, Sixth, and Ninth avenues, along with the Fourth Avenue line, which ran north of Forty-second Street.

Although they were extremely popular with commuters—giving a total of 180 million rides in 1890—they were scorned by many of those who lived near them. Lawsuits claimed that elevated railroads diminished property values and scared horses, among other things, though in dismissing one 1876 lawsuit the judge declared, essentially, that the horses would get used to the noise. The nuisances were many and obvious, however. The elevated structures darkened and obstructed the streets, and passing trains at the level of second stories were extremely noisy. Locomotives' stacks issued smoke and cinders, while passing trains dripped lubricating oil down onto the street; altogether the lines were a remarkable intrusion on urban neighborhoods, built for the convenience of those who passed through at the expense of those who lived there. In this way, elevated railroads encouraged dispersal by making city neighborhoods less attractive as well as providing the means by which people could move away. In the late 1800s, state and municipal authorities assumed that moving around the metropolis was much more important than staying put, an assumption that would drive public policy for more than a hundred years.

New York City built the state's only elevated lines, but steam railroads altered every city. Locomotives pulling narrow-gauge and standard-gauge trains helped turn dense walking cities into dense commuting cities. Wealthier residents increasingly lived outside the city, in distant suburbs. But this sorting by income did not make the heart of the city any less important to growing metropolises, since railroads needed to put their terminals as close to ports and docks as they could. Railroads also encouraged growth, as commerce and industry continued to mix in urban landscapes. In 1853 Erastus Corning drew together disparate lines to make the New York Central Railroad, connecting New York City with Albany, Utica, Syracuse, Rochester, and Buffalo, and giving yet another economic boost to upstate New York. New economic activity centered on the rail depots. In Buffalo, the New York Central occupied a huge yard between the docks and the city, where grain was moved from lake ships or elevators to long lines of train cars. In Albany, both commercial and industrial life focused on Steamboat Square and several blocks to the north, along the Hudson, where steamboats and railroads came together. Within two blocks of the river one could find coal yards, foundries, machine shops, warehouses, hotels, boardinghouses and other residences, and, significantly, the terminus of the Albany and Susquehanna Railroad, as well as the busy New York Central

Figure 16. Among the most intrusive of transportation technologies, elevated railroads cast shadows over streets, spewed soot into buildings, and brought additional noise and chaos to the dense neighborhoods of Manhattan. This late-nineteenth-century image captures the great diversity of transportation that coexisted in the crowded city, including trolleys and horse-drawn wagons. J. Loeffler, elevated railroad, Bowery, N.Y. (1895). Picture Collection, New York Public Library, Astor, Lenox and Tilden Foundations.

Station. The streets here teemed with life, with draymen and teamsters moving goods to and from trains and steamboats.

Railroads were more than an impetus for industrial growth. They were a symbol of industrial technology. Companies forced their lines through city neighborhoods, often over existing streets. At first, little-used lines carried small engines pulling short trains. Over time, especially after the Civil War, engines grew in size, as did train lengths and the frequency of trips. The noise of steam engines and the sheer weight of the trains moving across imperfect tracks all added to the din so often invoked to describe the industrial city. One Albany newspaper sympathized with residents who lived near the tracks and "the unearthly shriek of the steam whistle," which it called "an appalling nuisance." Smoke and cinders from passing trains left entire neighborhoods dusted in soot and at constant risk of fires. Worst of all, the trains themselves were deadly, not just to workers and passengers but to pedestrians who failed to yield. By the 1880s, trains killed more than two hundred people a year in New York State and injured hundreds of others. One *Buffalo Courier* editorial, titled "The Last Rail-road Slaughter," lamented two recent wrecks in the city, one of which killed a thirteen-year-old boy. The editorial declared that unless the public demanded change, residents "must expect to be occasionally smashed, scalded or burned to death."

Disaffected city residents did engage in long struggles to remove tracks from street grades, in Buffalo and around the state. These changes brought benefits to both railroads and residents, as separate railroad grades and new bypasses reduced conflicts with residents and improved traffic flow. Regulations protecting residents came slowly, as politicians were loath to upset powerful railroad companies and their customers, but eventually cities cleared their streets of dangerous trains, bringing tangible improvement to the urban environment.

Other rail systems also laced city streets by the early 1900s, changing the way urban residents lived their lives. In the early 1890s, streetcars began converting from horse power to electric power, stringing overhead lines along their routes. Although the new technology brought fear of electrification and fire, electricity had significant advantages. Electric trolleys could move faster than horse-drawn cars, allowing even working-class commuters to travel farther to work and homebuilders to create great expanses of housing well beyond urban centers. Brooklyn became famous for its many trolley lines; even its baseball team took the name Dodgers because residents there needed to be on the alert for approaching cars. But all large New York cities gained trolley lines, some of which evolved into remarkably comprehensive systems. Even much smaller cities developed extensive lines, such as Utica's Belt Line, which connected communities miles from downtown. Saratoga Springs had lines that linked downtown hotels with the racetrack, Saratoga Lake, and Geyser Springs, all major tourist attractions. By the end of 1893, the state contained forty-seven electrified street railroads, and the age of the trolley was only just under way.

Trolley systems proved to be so efficient that some covered great distances, competing even with steam railroads. An electrified line connected Buffalo with Niagara Falls, for example, providing service to communities along the way, including Tonawanda and the farming community of LaSalle. By the 1920s, trolley lines had transformed the way many New Yorkers traveled, in places as different as Brooklyn, Westchester County, and Ithaca, all of which had popular

Figure 17. Trolleys helped transform the urban landscape, allowing longer commutes by more workers. They also pushed surprisingly far into the countryside, as in this case in central New York. "Road Bed Cut for Trolley, Herkimer County," by Arthur J. Telfer (1904). Smith-Telfer Photographic Collection, New York State Historical Association, Cooperstown, N.Y.

lines. The regular routes of trolleys encouraged growth along their lines, and flexible stops allowed travelers to hop on and off the cars wherever it was convenient. Trolleys, like steam railroads, helped reshape residential and work patterns, allowing longer commutes—greater separation of work and home—and more expansive urban and suburban development. Like steam railroads, trolley lines pulled urban culture into the countryside, further mixing landscapes of fields, forests, and residences.

TENEMENT DISTRICTS

Even as cities expanded outward, only the most fortunate New Yorkers commuted from leafy suburbs. Most workers lived in the tight, dark quarters of tenement districts—slums—which came to represent the human cost of industrialization. In New York City, the arrival of Croton water in 1842 was not as revolutionary as some had hoped it would be. Many buildings were slow to connect to the new supply, especially in the poorer neighborhoods. Even those buildings that did tap in needed considerable plumbing changes—new pipes, sinks, tubs—to make the water useful to residents. Not surprisingly, these improvements came slowly to the tenement districts, and many people continued their daily trips to the street to get water from hydrants. In addition, Croton water couldn't begin to solve all the problems of tenement crowding. New York City had created a Board of Health in 1804, and city inspectors could investigate nuisances, but the city did little to regulate the urban environment. Well into the nineteenth century, overcrowded city lots harbored people, domesticated animals (especially pigs), and contagious diseases.

Although effective reform came very slowly, attention to the plight of the poor persisted. Tenement districts became havens for disease and crime, solidifying the connections many New Yorkers drew between filthy environments, poor health, and impure morality. In 1844 physician John H. Griscom undertook the first municipal study of the tenement districts. Published as *The Sanitary Condition of the Laboring Population of New York,* Griscom's report confirmed the connection between urban living and the spread of disease. The report reflected the prevailing miasma theory of contagion, which emphasized "the congregation of animal and vegetable matters, with their constant effluvia," and the "absence of free circulation." Like other public health officials, Griscom believed that disease spread through the foul smells and vapors created by standing water and putrefying garbage. After touring the city's tenements, he concluded, "Our people, especially the more destitute, have been allowed to live out their brief lives in tainted and unwholesome atmospheres, and be subject to the silent and invisible encroachments of the destructive agencies from every direction." He described rooms with no ventilation at all, tiny bedrooms built under staircases, buildings soiled with "the effluvia of vermin," stained by "the blood of unmentionable insects," and covered in "dirt of all indescribable colours." Griscom argued that investments in sanitation improvements and the education of the laboring poor would pay for themselves through better public health. It was an argument that he and many reformers who followed would have to make for decades.

In 1849 the most feared epidemic disease struck New York: cholera. Victims experienced intense vomiting and diarrhea, and death could be violent and swift owing to rapid dehydration. Fatality rates of 20 percent or more were not uncommon. The excruciating symptoms, high death rate, and poor understanding of how the disease was transmitted led to panic when reports of its arrival spread throughout the country. Although many residents fled Manhattan quickly, the 1849 epidemic took five thousand lives in New York City. In Buffalo it took nearly nine hundred lives, with an obviously disproportionate fatality rate among the city's poor, especially the Irish who lived in the First Ward, down by the Buffalo River and the canals. These deaths, and thousands of others in cities around the nation, reveal the failure of cities to provide basic environmental services, since the disease was caused by bacteria spread through human wastes. Indeed, as sewer systems and water supplies improved over the second half of the 1800s, the actual threat of cholera subsided, even though fear of this terrible disease continued to drive reformers, who demanded cleaner streets, improved drainage, and tighter regulation of the city's housing.

In 1864 New York City reformers frustrated with corrupt and inefficient municipal government undertook their own study of the tenement problem, forming the Council on Hygiene. In Hell's Kitchen, on the West Side around Thirty-eighth Street, the council found poorly built apartment buildings mingled with nuisances such as slaughterhouses, stables, a distillery, and a varnish factory. The air in such neighborhoods was polluted by "putrefying masses of animal and vegetable matter, together with dead animals," and by "poisonous exhalations from manufactories of various kinds." The better neighborhoods isolated themselves from such nuisances, keeping noxious industries and livestock at a safe distance. Through the course of the nineteenth century, reformers came to think of this separation of living quarters from industrial land uses as critical to improving urban neighborhoods, and the regulation of urban animals became an important component in the effort to improve public health.

As New Yorkers read reports of the ravages of cholera in Europe in early 1866, the state created the Metropolitan Board of Health, which possessed broad powers to regulate and police the environments of Manhattan and Brooklyn. Although quickly made improvements could not prevent the spread of cholera in New York, only six hundred New Yorkers died in the epidemic, a significant decline in comparison to 1849. This success had a lasting effect on public health in New York City and cities across the country that followed the New York model and empowered inspectors to police urban sanitary conditions. The metropolitan board itself was relatively short lived, replaced in 1870 by a municipal Department of Health. This back-and-forth regarding public health authority was part of the political struggle between Republicans, who controlled the statehouse, and Democrats, guided by the famously corrupt Tammany Hall, who controlled the city. Regrettably, continuing corruption at the municipal level impeded effective policing of the urban environment, and public health continued to suffer. "The summer will soon be upon us," the *New York Times* lamented in 1874, "with its long train of diseases, pursuing the unfortunates in the tenement-houses; typhoid fever, dysentery, and cholera infantum will soon make their dreaded appearance in the crowded quarters of the poor."

Municipal health officials and city inspectors did make some advances against disease, especially through the improvement of the urban environment. They banned pigs from city streets, regulated notoriously unhealthy dairies inside city limits, and stepped up oversight of street cleaning and garbage removal. But improvements in public health would be only incremental until advances in medical science, especially in bacteriology, increased the understanding of how diseases spread and could be contained. Meanwhile, urban crowding persisted, even grew, and so too did tuberculosis and other crowd diseases. Immigrants, especially from Ireland and Germany, continued to pour into Manhattan's tenement districts, even as those who could afford to do so moved out. In the second half of the 1800s, New York City contained some of the most densely settled places on earth, with certain wards containing as many as seven hundred people per acre—in a city where most buildings did not exceed five stories.

Croton water could help save "the great unwashed" of the tenement districts, or at least get them clean, but the paucity of plumbing proved to be an intractable problem. The washing, it appeared, would have to take place outside the tenements themselves. In 1870 the city built two bathhouses in support of the effort, one on the East River at the foot of Fifth Street and the other on the Hudson at the end of Charles Street. On Mondays, Wednesdays, and Fridays, women could bathe for free, and gain the use of a towel for three cents. The rest of the week, men and boys made use of the facilities. And hundreds did every day throughout the summer. By 1878 the city was operating six public baths, all of them along the East River and the Hudson, affording access to the salt waters of these much-used and unsanitary waterways. In 1891 the New York Association for Improving the Condition of the Poor, an organization whose very name reveals the close connection between social and environmental reform, opened a new kind of public bathhouse. Located on Centre Market Place in the middle of a densely populated tenement district, the People's Bath gave residents with no bathing facilities in their own apartments—that is, most of the neighborhood—the opportunity to pay a nickel for the use of pure Croton water, soap, and a towel. Unlike the city's bathhouses, the People's Bath was open year-round, and it featured clean country water piped in from outside the city.

So many New Yorkers made use of the People's Bath that the value of public baths became evident, and in 1895 the state passed a law requiring cities of more than fifty thousand residents to open and operate as many public baths as local boards of health thought were required. Two years later Buffalo opened the first free public bathhouse in the densest part of the city, near Terrace Park. Residents could make use of the hot and cold water, free soap and towels, and even have their clothes washed as they bathed. Four years later Buffalo opened a second public bath, and in 1901 altogether it provided more than 230,000 baths. In that year New York City operated three public baths, a number that was wholly inadequate for the large numbers of New Yorkers without tubs in their own homes.

Throughout the second half of the 1800s, improving public health remained a central goal of environmental reform, a goal that was especially evident in the work of the Ladies Health Protective Association, organized in 1884 by a dozen women living in the Beekman Hill neighborhood of midtown Manhattan who shared a concern for the vile odors emanating from a manure handler along the East River. The manure heaps were eventually removed, and the women gradually expanded their concerns to the entire slaughterhouse district near their homes, including the tenements fouled by sickening smells and backed-up sewage. Led by Mathilde Wendt and Mary Trautmann, the association contacted business owners directly with their complaints, and if the nuisances persisted, they organized demonstrations at the offending location, inviting the press to witness their lay inspections. The *New York Times* followed the women to an East Side plant and quoted one activist, who carefully explained why they were there. "Our object is to get rid of the offensive odors that rise in invisible clouds from the gas houses and are blown directly into our homes." The women also gained considerable publicity when they brought their complaints to the Board of Health. Successes followed, as they battled the odors emanating from fat renderers, gasworks, and other noxious industries.

Despite these victories against individual nuisances, the Ladies Health Protective Association was circumscribed by the gender expectations of the era. Women could properly complain about issues affecting their own homes, and even the homes of other families, but they had limited access to authority. At public meetings, for example, often the association's leaders allowed men to speak for them, and women did not expect to fill the government positions from which their activism might have more immediate effects, such as the Board of Health. Despite these limitations, women had the moral authority to keep cleanliness, odor, and public health issues in the press, and eventually they played a role in forcing broader reforms on the urban environment. Indeed their success was such that they inspired similar groups to form in other cities, igniting a movement that became known as "municipal housekeeping," a term that made clear the gendered nature of their work but also revealed the strong connection these activists had to their cities, both inside their homes and out. All around the state and the nation, middle-class women's municipal housekeeping initiated critical environmental improvement over the next several decades.

Middle-class women played a lesser role in the movement to improve the conditions in tenement districts, in part because the reform required the creation of extensive new building codes, which were developed in the male sphere of politics. In the second half of the 1800s, a series of tenement laws, some passed at the state level, held out hope of improvement. These well-meaning laws were largely ineffectual, however, either because they were so vague as to be easily skirted or because even when clearly expressed, they were poorly enforced. Some laws did nevertheless have a significant impact. An 1860 New York City law required fire escapes, at least for new buildings; two years later, as deadly fires persisted in older buildings, the city required fire escapes for all buildings with more than eight apartments. Another law in 1879 required a window to admit outside air in every room, an ordinance that ushered in the infamous dumbbell tenement, designed to maximize floor space while following the letter of the law. Air shafts between buildings allowed very little light into most rooms, and even less fresh air, especially on the lower floors. Garbage collected at the bottom of the shafts, foul smells permeated the air, and too often fires raced up the openings, quickly engulfing entire buildings.

In 1890 Jacob Riis, a journalist who used his experience on the police beat to familiarize himself with the living conditions in New York City's poorest neighborhoods, became the nation's most important voice for housing reform with the publication of *How the Other Half Lives*, a long essay that exposed conditions in the various immigrant neighborhoods. A series of photographs that accompanied the essay illustrated how dire conditions actually were. Some of Riis's most powerful prose described the effect of summer's heat, which forced families outside, onto tenement roofs and fire escapes, and into the streets. Diseases became more virulent in the hottest months, and death visited too many families. Readers must have visualized the "sleepless mothers" Riis described

Figure 18. New York City's tenement districts were failed environments. Captured by the flash photography of Jacob Riis, the squalor of the Lower East Side's housing sparked reform. "Lodgers in a Crowded Bayard Street Tenement—Five Cents a Spot" (ca. 1890). Museum of the City of New York, Jacob A. Riis Collection.

walking "the streets in the gray of the early dawn, trying to stir a cooling breeze to fan the brow of the sick baby." Although he was hardly the first to write extensively about the evils of the tenement districts, Riis was the most effective, and *How the Other Half Lives* became one of the most important books of the nineteenth century. His work helped focus attention on failed urban environments, making clear that improving people's lives would require improving the places where they lived.

In partial response to Riis and other reformers, in 1901 the state passed a comprehensive Tenement House Law, covering everything from stairwells and fire escapes to lighting, ventilation, and plumbing. In total the code was forty pages long, with 165 sections, revealing how intimately involved in regulating the urban environment the state had become. The law's length and specificity also showed how dramatic the market's failure had been. In booming cities with continuously arriving newcomers, property owners had too little market incentive to keep their tenants safe. While the law could not instantly improve the lives of the city's poor, it was a start. At the very least it codified society's expectations of how Americans ought to live.

Like other reformers, Riis was not concerned with housing alone. He wrote extensively on New York's slums, including a very persuasive article in favor of securing playgrounds for all city schools, published in 1894. Riis proposed creating these playgrounds through the use of the Small Parks Law, which granted the city condemnation powers in lower Manhattan for the creation of parks. "Let enough land be condemned around every public school in the city that is not already isolated, to make a very small park that shall at once be a playground for the children, and a breathing-spot for the over-worked mothers with their babies," he wrote. Riis was a proponent of parks as well as playgrounds, and he lobbied for the creation of a series of parks on the islands in the East River, as well as smaller parks within crowded neighborhoods. He was among those who praised the creation of a park at Mulberry Bend, the notorious Italian section of Five Points, where the city took a number of properties through eminent domain and demolished them in 1895. In the process, the city displaced more than two thousand residents, but it also reduced crime and disorder in Five Points. The demolition of Mulberry Bend was so successful that it became a favored technique in urban reform. Piece by piece the most troublesome urban neighborhoods would see reform through removal, the clearing of substandard housing to make way for parks and roads (and eventually highways), as well as better housing.

Manhattan experienced environmental problems much more intensely than other New York cities. Buffalo, the state's second-largest city, grew rapidly around the turn of the century, attracting Italian and Polish immigrants particularly. The newcomers clustered in immigrant neighborhoods, Italians between downtown and Lake Erie, and Poles on the East Side. The Polish district contained mostly two-story frame houses, and even though many families could share one home, the presence of yards meant that ventilation and light were not problems the way they were in dense Manhattan neighborhoods. Buffalo also had well-paved streets, which among other things allowed working-class men to commute by bicycle—a popular means of transportation in the 1890s. The Italian neighborhood faced more problems, with families crowded into converted hotels and warehouses as well as tenement buildings in an area called the Flats. This low-lying neighborhood was surrounded by polluted waters, including those of the Buffalo River, which received most of the city's untreated sewage. Nearly all Buffalo residents were adversely affected by untreated sewage, however. Until a new water supply intake in Lake Erie was completed in 1910, waste regularly entered the city's water supply through the old intake on the Niagara River. Still, Buffalo's environmental problems paled in comparison to those in Manhattan. This was also the case in other upstate cities. In both Rochester and Syracuse, tenement buildings were rare, and most working-class residents lived in modest homes. In Syracuse, two-family homes were particularly popular as economical residences. Both cities had surpassed 100,000 residents by 1900, but neither experienced the problems of crowding, filth, and disease that plagued New York City.

Although conditions were much better in upstate cities, they did inspire reforms. Buffalo, for example, hired an activist health commissioner, Dr. Ernest Wende, in 1892. Wende professionalized the Health Department, using his knowledge of bacteriology in the effort to improve human health in the city and decrease the death rate. Wende campaigned to eliminate all wells and privy vaults in Buffalo, and it was his activism that persuaded the city to invest in the new water intake in Lake Erie. He also worked for the passage of a strict tenement law, intended to prevent the development of dense neighborhoods like those that plagued Manhattan. Buffalo also expanded its environmental reform to include the creation and operation of municipal playgrounds. The first opened in Terrace Park in 1901, and within three years the city was operating six playgrounds, where children could play basketball, run on cinder tracks, or play on swings and in sandboxes. In its 1903 study of Buffalo's new playgrounds, the Charity Organization Society reported that the new facilities had improved conditions throughout the neighborhoods in which they were built. Shooting craps, not permitted on the playgrounds, had nearly disappeared in their vicinity. The society went so far as to claim that large numbers of boys had quit smoking since they knew it would interfere with their athletic competitions. The society's report, along with the city's maintenance of the playgrounds, revealed how important reformers thought improved environments were to the moral development of the city's children, and thus how important these advances were to the future of the city.

COAL SMOKE

Tenement districts clearly contained myriad environmental hazards, but some were spread more evenly across all areas of the city. The state's industrial cities suffered under a thickening pall of coal smoke in the late 1800s. Soot, the result of incompletely burned coal, covered industrial America like a dark, acidic blanket. It spoiled goods on store shelves, soiled furniture and drapes. Soot killed trees and prevented the growth of flowers. It exacerbated lung ailments, including many of urban America's leading killers such as tuberculosis and pneumonia, and, physicians claimed, it worsened the depression and malaise suffered by many residents of smoke-shrouded cities. But despite periodic calls for smoke abatement, cities could not clear their skies, at least not without jeopardizing economic growth, since coal was so fundamental to industrial cities.

Significantly, although New York State had the largest industrial economy in the nation, none of the state's cities would have made a list of the country's most polluted, largely because several New York cities relied primarily on the cleanest-burning coal, Pennsylvania's anthracite. Beyond the relatively clean fuel, several other factors kept New York City's air comparatively clean despite the fact that it was the nation's largest industrial city. Gotham's industry was labor intensive—its garment sweatshops most famously—but not necessarily energy intensive. In addition, offshore winds tended to keep the air moving above the city, preventing the kind of palls that shrouded cities like Pittsburgh and Cincinnati. Buffalo also had better air quality than most other industrial cities its size, largely because of geographic factors. Most of Buffalo's heavy industry grew up south and north of the residential section of the city. Prevailing winds came off Lake Erie, pushing the smoke over less populated regions. Indeed Buffalo's primary strategy for controlling smoke involved keeping industry south of Genesee Street and north of Black Rock. Other New York cities produced smoke, but not in quantities that posed serious health concerns. In a lengthy pamphlet titled "Report upon Smoke Abatement," issued in 1907, the Syracuse Chamber of Commerce focused on technological remedies and on lobbying for a cooperative approach between government and polluters. The Chamber did concede that even in smaller cities like Syracuse, smoke posed economic and aesthetic problems. Still, eager to head off strict regulation of smoke production, the Chamber argued that vigorous enforcement of an anti-smoke law would not work, but it would certainly impinge on the rights of businesses.

Even though New York's cities were less polluted than the nation's worst, by 1910 the largest had passed anti-smoke laws, expanding municipal authority to monitor smokestacks and issue fines for dense smoke. The Rochester ordinance was typical. Passed in 1906, the law declared it "unlawful to suffer or permit the escape of smoke from any fire not in motion or fire banked or in a state of rest, or from any burning or active fire through a stationary stack, flue or chimney."

Figure 19. Upstate cities such as Syracuse experienced fewer problems associated with housing than did New York City, but continued growth did lead to air pollution concerns. Erie Canal at Salina Street, Syracuse. Detroit Photographic Company (1904). Library of Congress.

The lawfulness of smoke would be judged according to a scale of grayness, with only dark grays constituting a violation, and only then if the smoke emission lasted more than five minutes. Shortly after the ordinance came into force, the Macauley-Fien Milling Company issued dense smoke from its flour mill, earning a $25 fine. Rather than pay the fine, the company sued, arguing that the ordinance was an illegal infringement on property rights, and, as it turned out, initiating a four-year legal process. In the end, a New York Court of Appeals decision declared the ordinance a proper use of the city's power to secure the "peace and health" and the "safety and welfare" of the city's residents. The court argued, "In a city or closely populated community where persons and property cannot be removed from the effects of the disagreeable contamination it not only pollutes the air that must be breathed, but it mars the appearance, destroys the cleanliness, and affects the value of the property within the circle upon which such substances from the smoke so fall." The Rochester opinion was an important step in solidifying municipal authority to regulate

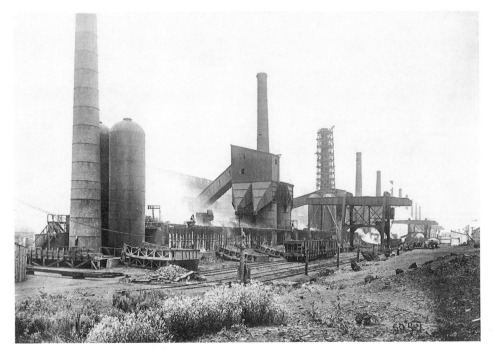

Figure 20. Industrialization intensified in the late 1800s and early 1900s, including the construction of the massive Lackawanna Steel Mill south of Buffalo, which created jobs and smoke. Coke Oven no. 1, under construction (1903–4). Steel Plant Museum, Lackawanna, New York.

environmental quality, part of a broader expansion of governmental authority in industrial cities. Nevertheless, the authority to regulate air pollution did not translate into the ability to secure better air quality, and coal smoke lingered over industrial cities well into the twentieth century.

WATER POLLUTION

The battle against coal smoke took an odd turn in 1895, when Dr. Cyrus Edison, a former health officer from New York City, claimed that smoke from the Long Island Railroad's Long Island City rail yard served as a deodorant, covering the foul smells emanating from industries along nearby Newtown Creek. Edison's comments, made at the behest of the railroad, were little more than a failed attempt to excuse the use of soft coal despite the municipal law barring it. Still, Edison could hardly have been more accurate in his description of the foul odors produced by the large complex of industry along the creek that separated Queens from Brooklyn. As early as 1877 the *Brooklyn Eagle* had decried "The Stenches and Impurities of Newtown Creek." At that point the paper placed primary blame on two fertilizer factories for poisonous filth that had caused fish kills and driven life from the tidal stream, but oil refineries, too, attracted negative attention. The problems only deepened, and in 1881 Newtown Creek became the focus of a *Harper's Weekly* exposé. Over the course of three weeks, *Harper's* emphasized the connection between industrial stenches and poor health among residents in the area. Sludge acid, a by-product of refining and one of the ingredients in the fertilizer made along the creek, gained special attention. Refiners dumped unneeded sludge acid into the creek, contributing to the once heavily fished area's ecological collapse. In 1886 the New York State Fisheries Commission confirmed that Newtown Creek could no longer support fish life.

Several noxious industries expanded along the creek, including fat-rendering plants and glue works, but the worst by far was the Standard Oil refinery that arose at Hunter's Point, where the creek met the East River. The political power of Standard Oil prevented effective regulation, and so the region around the creek remained terribly polluted. A similar ecological wasteland developed along the Kill Van Kull, between Staten Island and New Jersey, where another Standard Oil facility polluted and destroyed valuable oyster beds. Not all industries had the political clout to deflect public outcry, however. In 1892 New York State outlawed fat rendering and bone boiling in all incorporated areas. Still, despite public protest and periodic interest from the media, the industrial zones surrounding cities remained largely unregulated and terribly polluting well into the twentieth century.

In addition to industrial waste, sewage, garbage, and other refuse entered waterways. Even cities with buried sewer lines had no treatment facilities at the end, so outfalls simply entered surface water somewhere near town. By the early twentieth century, hundreds of thousands of gallons of untreated waste flowed into the waters around Manhattan daily, polluting famous oyster beds and diminishing recreational opportunities. Waterways became favored dumps for all types of waste, since disposal in water was free and easy. As early as 1857 the state banned the dumping of solid waste into New York Harbor, and later laws forced the city to dump its refuse farther out at sea, decreasing the chance of its floating onto beaches. Over the long term, however, ocean dumping posed serious ecological threats to the region's resources, and even into the twentieth century, filling marshes and other wetlands with ashes and street sweepings remained official policy. Later ecological studies indicated just how damaging these policies could be, as formerly productive wetlands were replaced by ash and other waste, and aquatic ecosystems struggled to overcome the effects of oil slicks, acid wastes, and rising bacterial counts.

PROGRESSIVE ERA REFORMS

Efforts to diminish air and water pollution had limited results, but in other areas, turn-of-the-century reformers had much greater success. Building on earlier reform movements, middle-class and wealthy urbanites launched a wide variety of efforts to regulate and improve urban spaces in the first two decades of the twentieth century. In what became known as the Progressive Era owing to the wave of reformism that spread throughout the nation, reformers emphasized the need to improve residents' health and the city's physical beauty, which together would uplift urban residents and thereby improve their moral condition. Many of these reformers hoped that their cities would better reflect the wealth of the nation. Reformers worked to improve housing (including the tenement reform discussed earlier), clean the streets, provide public art, plant street trees, build playgrounds, and any number of other improvements that altogether meant the remaking of the urban environment. In one small example, reformers in New York City gathered together in 1897 to form the Tree Planting Association to encourage the planting of shade trees along the streets of greater New York, "especially in the poorer and more crowded quarters of the municipality," according to the association's secretary, Charles Lamb. New York City was the center of the world's largest economy, and the city's elite hoped to create a more civilized cityscape.

Significant improvement began with the 1894 election of reform mayor William Strong, who in turn appointed George E. Waring Jr. to head the Department of Street Cleaning. After his short career in scientific farming, Waring had become a sewage engineer, completing systems in Ogdensburg and Saratoga Springs, among other places. "There is no surer index of the degree of civilization of a community," he declared, "than the manner in which it treats its organic wastes." In New York City, Waring brought military precision and proselytizing zeal to his work, and his professionalization of the department became symbolic of a new energy in municipal reform. Waring greatly improved the condition of the streets as well as the processing of wastes. Residents separated refuse into three categories: ash, garbage (organic material), and rubbish, which included recyclable materials such as paper, rags, and glass. Waring's men used ash and unsalvageable refuse as landfill, especially at Rikers Island, which expanded steadily until dumping ended there in 1938. Using a system first introduced in Buffalo in 1896, Waring's men processed garbage to recover grease and fertilizer, among other saleable items. The recovery of marketable materials from the waste stream helped Waring pay for his growing department, impressing political leaders. Residents were much more impressed with the city's cleanliness, however. Death rates declined significantly after 1895, led by improvements in child mortality. The transformation of the streets was so apparent that the Department of Street Cleaning became a model for the nation, and Waring's success encouraged an increasing faith in government to solve the nation's problems. One housing reformer, Richard Watson Gilder, went so far as to declare, "If we clean the streets of the Republic we can accomplish other cleanings that have in the past seemed hopeless of accomplishment."

At the turn of the century, a collection of improvements in city life came together under a new term: City Beautiful. Although best known for an infatuation with neoclassical architecture and the creation of grand civic spaces, the City Beautiful movement had broader goals. In 1899 Rochester journalist Charles Mulford Robinson became the leading voice for City Beautiful, and two years later he published the movement's most complete expression, *The Improvement of Towns and Cities*. Robinson, and the City Beautiful movement as a whole, lobbied for improved street fixtures, more street trees, more effective smoke abatement, and the installation of municipal art, including prominent sculptures. Across the country new organizations took up the campaign, including the Society for Beautifying Buffalo, which hoped to remove unsightly billboards and otherwise improve the city's appearance in preparation for the Pan-American Exposition of 1901. Soon supporters of City Beautiful began to think more comprehensively, embedding their ideas in the language of planning. A beautiful city had to be efficient, too, and significant improvements couldn't be made piecemeal. Broader, more attractive streets, residential areas with ample public space, and downtowns with grand civic centers all had to be planned. And they were. The influence of the City Beautiful movement was more than an expression of the era's intense civic engagement; it was an expression of the growing faith in government to regulate the urban environment. More fundamentally, it revealed how important the environment was to reformers, who understood that human behavior and development are deeply influenced by human surroundings. Efficient, healthful, and beautiful environments make civilized and

moral citizens, Progressive reformers thought. And in the end, making better citizens by making better cities was the primary goal of the City Beautiful
movement.

More attractive streetscapes may have provided considerable uplift, but the
majority of urban residents still toiled under difficult conditions. If middle-class
reformers like Robinson needed a reminder of how hard workers' lives could
be, in 1911 a horrible fire, sparked by a discarded cigarette in a shirtwaist factory, claimed 146 lives. With no exterior fire escapes and the door to the roof
locked, employees were trapped by flames. Many of the victims, most of them
girls and young women, died when they leaped from the top floors of the ten-
story building; they lay dead on the sidewalk and in Greene Street as firemen
attended to the flames and a crowd gathered around. Among those who watched
the tragedy unfold was Frances Perkins, who was so struck by the scene that
she became a lifelong advocate of workers' rights, eventually serving as secretary
of labor in Franklin Roosevelt's administration. The fire did more than inspire
Perkins, of course. The deaths at the Triangle Waist Company revealed how dire
conditions in Manhattan's many sweatshops could be. The state engaged in an
extensive study of factory conditions, and a series of laws designed to prevent
future tragedies required changes in buildings, such as better fire escapes, and
changes in behavior, too, such as mandatory fire drills. These were surely small
steps in improving the industrial landscape, but they were important reminders
that for many people the most urgently needed environmental reforms are often
at the workplace.

Regulation of the urban environment took a great leap forward in 1916, when
New York City passed the nation's first comprehensive zoning law. Developed
in response to growing concern about congestion in the city's core and the pressures exerted along Fifth Avenue as manufacturing lofts encroached on fashionable retail establishments, the zoning ordinance allowed municipal authorities
to control land use in the entire city by designating some areas residential and
others commercial. The ordinance also allowed the city to limit building heights
and to regulate the percentage of land that could be built on, in essence requiring yards in certain areas. Perhaps the most visible result of the zoning law
came from limitations on the percentage of lot area that could contain towering
buildings, a response to concerns about air and light reaching the streets in the
city's most congested neighborhoods. The new rules led to the development of
New York's distinctive skyscrapers, which feature gradual step-backs from the

sidewalk toward thin, elegant towers, perhaps best represented in the Chrysler and Empire State buildings.

While these skyscrapers remain the most visible reminders of the 1916 law, they represent just a small part of its accomplishment. Comprehensive zoning became a fundamental planning tool, allowing city officials to rationalize growth and protect residential areas from the encroachment of industry and commerce. Zoning ordinances constituted a remarkable expansion of the police power in municipalities, justified as critical to the protection of health and safety, even though the actual results of the law had more to do with bringing order and predictability out of the chaos of urban growth. After 1916 the regulation of the urban environment through zoning became nearly universal in the United States, as cities across the country followed New York's example.

LEAVING THE CITY

All of these efforts to improve urban environments could not bear fruit fast enough, and so the city remained a relatively unhealthful place, especially during the hot summer months. Many urban residents escaped to the country. In the latter half of the 1800s, as we have seen, summer vacations became increasingly popular, as middle-class families left the city for weeks at a time. Some families vacationed in the Catskills or other healthful environments for up to two months, with fathers commuting by train to spend the workweek in the city. Even working-class families sacrificed to get their children into the country for a few weeks, most famously New York City's large Jewish population, which increasingly patronized modestly priced vacation spots in Sullivan County, often renting small bungalows with few amenities.

Although a surprisingly large percentage of New Yorkers could afford a vacation trip, many could not, a fact that weighed not just on families trapped in the sweltering city but also on middle-class reformers who fretted about the health and morality of "street arabs," children who spent their summers wandering the city looking for entertainment and mischief. Getting these kids out of the city, even just for day trips, became a lively issue for reformers. Following a suggestion made by a local physician, in 1872 the *New York Times* led the campaign for a "Fresh Air Fund" to purchase country excursions for poor children and their mothers. Other newspapers followed suit, including the *Brooklyn Union* and the *Troy Times*, both of which sponsored day trips.

The theory behind the Fresh Air Fund was that simply getting out of the city could do children some good, a theory that also famously drove Charles Loring Brace and his Children's Aid Society, founded in 1853, to send thousands of orphaned and homeless children into the countryside, where they worked on farms, living with good country families. Apparently getting out of the city was literally a cure for the ailments of some children who couldn't be removed from the city permanently. In 1876 the *New York Times* claimed that one infant had been cured of cholera simply by being removed to the Catskills. Benefit might also be seen from taking children on boat trips out into the salt air, because "the oxygenated air or the ozone of the sea or the mountains acts in an extraordinary manner on this fearful malady—beyond anything which either food or medicine can accomplish." Charities offered picnic excursions to parks outside the city; other lucky city residents took brief trips to the Sisters of St. Mary's Seaside Home for Children in Far Rockaway. Altogether these charitable efforts could take only a small percentage of poor children out of the city, but they reflected the era's powerful association of city living with unhealthfulness and immorality, an association that would have significant implications for the way American cities and suburbs would grow. Despite the myriad efforts to improve cities, many New Yorkers understood that the only complete solution to the problems of the urban environment was to leave the city.

UTOPIAN VISIONS

Increasingly, wealthy New Yorkers left the city nightly, retreating to residential suburbs, which had sprung up along railroads running north through Westchester County and into Connecticut, west through New Jersey, and east along the route of the Long Island Railroad. With the opening of Grand Central Station in 1871, Westchester gained the most convenient connections for commuters, unrivaled until the completion of Pennsylvania Station in 1910. Not surprisingly, then, New York's wealthiest suburbanites headed north, as did Jay Gould and John D. Rockefeller, both of whom built "castles" worthy of their amassed fortunes. Westchester became a residential haven not just for the super-rich, however, as upper-middle-class New Yorkers built fine homes on spacious lots near the Scarsdale station and many other rail stops. Unlike the city's street grid, suburban roads curved through the topography, and landscaped front yards lent a rural air. The architecture of these outlying areas eventually reflected the available space, as sprawling Tudor homes with great pitched roofs and Queen Annes with sweeping porches helped create a new suburban aesthetic. Suburban living was superior to city life in several ways, most of them environmental. The air was purer, and smelled of grass and flowering trees. The nights were quieter; the streets were clean and free of congestion, and of course they were bereft of the poor as well. This, the growing middle class increasingly argued, was the proper environment for raising children.

Environmental factors were critical selling points for new suburban communities. In 1882 a real estate developer began selling lots in a distant section of Queens, which garnered the new name Ozone Park. That year a *New York Times* advertisement promised: "Free from Malaria. Ground high and healthy." The new neighborhood also promised relatively easy commutes into the city, though at first residents would have to take the train from nearby Flatbush. As the name suggests, the real attraction of Ozone Park was its air quality. Ironically, given the post–World War II development of ozone smog, in the late 1800s "ozone" had become shorthand for healthful air, and in the nineteenth century, country air had more ozone to offer. Another advertisement in 1886 encouraged prospective buyers to "enjoy the life giving atmosphere of Ozone Park."

Progressive ideas about the city translated into more attractive suburban developments in the early twentieth century. Influenced by the garden city concept articulated by British author Ebenezer Howard in 1898, American planners began to envision nearly complete suburban developments, with retail, recreation, and residential components. New York State became home to the first American garden city, Forest Hills Gardens, planned by Frederick Law Olmsted Jr., who had followed his father into the landscape architecture field. On 142 acres in Queens, alongside the Long Island Railroad, Olmsted designed a model suburban town with financial backing from the Russell Sage Foundation. He hoped to create a planned town that didn't feel planned, whose roads felt organic, natural, unlike the grid that covered most of the city. An emphasis on greenery and flowers, confirmed even in the place name, would also create a contrast between this community and the city. With the opening of Penn Station and the tunnel under the East River in 1910, Forest Hills Gardens was just fifteen minutes away from midtown. By 1912 sales of lots were well under way, and advertisements promised "country air and country life within striking distance of the active centers of New York."

In many ways Forest Hills Gardens was innovative, but it was hardly radical. All involved knew that it would serve as a model for future suburban development only if it played by the market's rules. For this reason the development had to make money. In most ways Forest Hills Gardens succeeded tremendously, but as a moneymaking enterprise it did not. The great initial expense of the land and the cost of aesthetic amenities and public green space all worked against success. Still, Forest Hills Gardens was just the first of many efforts to bring urban planning concepts and Progressive ideas about community and environment to suburban development. In the mid-1920s the City Housing Corporation, a limited dividend company organized by wealthy Progressives, designed, built, and sold a model community called Sunnyside Gardens, also in Queens alongside the Long Island Railroad tracks. Here City Housing Corporation built modestly sized but clean and efficient homes for working people and their families. Most of the six-room houses surrounded a courtyard, where children could play safely, away from the street. Every room had windows for ventilation; every bathroom had sanitary tile floors. Every aspect of the community was designed to promote health and safety among the families. And nearly every aspect contrasted directly with what the slums of Manhattan offered the working poor.

Sunnyside Gardens notwithstanding, most early-twentieth-century suburban development catered to a strictly middle-class clientele. The creation of these "bourgeois utopias," as one historian has called them, represents one of the great movements of people in American history, from the chaotic and filthy environments of cities to the greener pastures of suburbia. But not all utopian visions required escape from the city. In 1892 William T. Love came to Niagara Falls dreaming of a model city built around clean, cheap water power supplied by the Niagara River. Love advertised his scheme, centered on a long canal that would divert water from the river and pass it around the small city of Niagara Falls and over artificial falls, where it would generate considerable power. His model city would contain at least 200,000 residents, but it would be spacious, with ample parks; it would not suffer from the overcrowding that plagued other cities. The plain above the canal would hold thousands of homes, owned by the workers themselves; the skies above the city would be blue, with none of the coal smoke that shrouded other cities.

Love's dream attracted state support, in the form of permission to acquire land and divert water. It attracted investors, too, enough to begin digging east of the city in 1894. By 1896, however, the economy had soured, investors had bolted, and Love's company went bankrupt, leaving just a few hundred yards of Love's canal, seemingly useless. By the time the property was sold at auction in 1920, it had long since become little more than an odd geographical feature, a linear manmade lake surrounded by mounds of earth. For children living in nearby neighborhoods of the expanding city of Niagara Falls, it was ideal for swimming in and biking around. Eventually it would find another use, as the city's chemical industry sought new locations for waste disposal; Love's abandoned canal would seem ideal for that.

Even as Love began to turn his dream into a ditch, Niagara Falls inspired another, even more elaborate utopian vision, though this one developed no further than detailed expression in an 1894 book, *The Human Drift*. Here King Gillette, not yet the inventor of the safety razor, imagined a great metropolis spreading from Niagara Falls to Rochester. Water power from the falls would allow Americans of all classes to live contentedly in this one massive, orderly city. Like Love, Gillette imagined the unlimited power of nature harnessed at Niagara, turned into electricity, which in turn would replace most human labor. The fruits of nature's power would be distributed equally in the form of leisure and a clean, healthful environment, everyone living in identical apartments arranged in massive but airy buildings. Like others from this era, Gillette's utopian vision prized order and equality above all else, surely a sign of the chaos, filth, and inequality of the nation's industrial cities.

That Niagara Falls would inspire these two utopian visions tells us much about people's faith in the power of the falls to transform society through electricity. The ultimate modern technology, electricity was both seemingly magical and fundamentally scientific. It held a certain danger and required engineering at every level, but it promised to remake the economy. Most important to utopian visionaries, it was clean, and by using it, cities could be clean too. The 1901 Pan-American Exposition in Buffalo showcased a wide variety of industrial developments, as did all world's fairs, but it featured electricity. Generated at Niagara Falls in the world's largest power plant, the electricity flowed over wires to the fairgrounds around Delaware Park, where it illuminated buildings and powered machinery and held out great promise for the future. The Electric Tower, illuminated by thousands of bulbs, stood at the fair's center and was, in the words of Walter Hines Page of the *Atlantic Monthly*, an "epiphanous achievement, a masterpiece of human skill, a monument to the genius of man." It was also a monument to the power of nature harnessed by engineers and made to work.

Beyond fairgrounds, electricity first worked its magic in city centers. In New York City, Broadway was so bright at night, mostly from illuminated advertisements, that it took the name "Great White Way," a designation that would soon

spread to the brightest streets in other American cities. But the piecemeal installation of electricity combined with its primarily commercial uses revealed how
untamed the market still was. After years of reform, of expanding regulations
and empowering municipal and state governments, the market still determined
who got electricity and for what purposes. Along Broadway at Madison Square,
H. J. Heinz hung a forty-five-foot-long pickle, illuminated with green light
bulbs, to advertise his "57 Varieties," just across the street from the grand new
monument celebrating the American victory against Spain—the very type of
monument City Beautiful advocates admired. People did protest the grotesque
commercialism of the pickle, but it remained, if only as long as the building
from which it hung. In 1901 both building and pickle were removed to make
way for a larger building, yet another sign of the market's persistent power.

By the early 1900s downtown had gained a romantic aura all its own. Wealth
was evident in the clothes of the men and women on the streets, in the goods
displayed in department store windows. This was true in all sizable cities in the
state. Electric lights made downtown the brightest part of the city, helping to
redefine nighttime in metropolitan America. Perhaps more than anything else,
the towers that leaped up from its streets reflected the centrality of downtown
to the economy. Skyscrapers had become the symbol of urban New York, from
Buffalo to Manhattan. In 1914 the ornate terracotta of the Woolworth Building, the tallest in the world, shone in the daylight; at night it glowed, flooded
by electric light.

Clearly engineers and the market were still hard at work, continuously remaking New York's environment. The electrical system that spread through
the city and into the countryside was just one of the many engineered systems
built across the landscape. Explosive growth in New York City, especially after
the 1898 consolidation, required the creation or improvement of several systems, all engineered to allow even further growth. Too much congestion on city
streets and continued complaints about elevated railroads led to the creation of
a new underground transportation system, a subway. In 1904 the Interborough
Rapid Transit Company opened its line from Brooklyn through downtown to
Times Square; by 1925 the city had gained six hundred miles of subways. (In
the outer boroughs the trains traveled above ground.) These lines allowed suburban development to expand, especially in Brooklyn, Queens, and the Bronx.
By 1925 more than 2 million people commuted into Manhattan, about half of
them coming by subway from these three boroughs. This new subway system,

like previous components of the transportation revolution, focused on downtown, which was serviced by twenty subway stations.

Initially private companies built and operated the subways, reflecting continued suspicion about the efficiency and trustworthiness of municipal government in New York. But the city resisted private ownership of the water supply, another system that had to grow. For fifty years the city had expanded the Croton system by adding new reservoirs, but by 1900 it had taken essentially all of Croton's water. Thus the city had to seek out other sources of acceptable water. Engineers and politicians debated several options, but by 1903 the city had settled on Esopus Creek in the central Catskills, where the building of a massive reservoir, the Ashokan, displaced two thousand people and initiated the transformation of the mountains into a watershed—the city's watershed. Building the Catskills system—and eventually the Delaware system—required the state to grant the city powers of eminent domain in the mountain counties for the taking of thousands of acres for reservoirs on the Schoharie, Rondout, and Neversink rivers and both branches of the Delaware. To protect the city's new supply, the city and state also gained expanded police power to regulate the entire watershed area. By the end of the Progressive Era, city residents could still debate whether government authority and efficacy had grown too slowly to diminish the adverse effects of rapid growth and industrial development, but residents of the Catskills surely understood that urban growth had led to increased government authority, even in the countryside, well away from crowded city streets. And during the next several decades, government authority over the countryside would only increase.

5

A Sound Conservation Program

Theodore Roosevelt, Franklin Roosevelt, and the Power of Individuals

Late in the summer of 1901 Theodore Roosevelt and his family took a train up to the Adirondacks, where they hoped to enjoy a brief vacation. They arrived at Tahawus Club on a Wednesday evening, where they would stay for just a few days. The club was nestled alongside Lake Sanford, thirty-five miles from the nearest railhead and telegraph line, and within hiking distance of Mount Marcy, which Roosevelt was expecting to climb for the first time in his life. Roosevelt was a terrifically energetic man, of course, and an unusually active outdoorsman, well known for his adventures in nature. So this was in many ways a perfectly ordinary trip—the type of wilderness vacation that was becoming popular among wealthier Americans. Indeed Roosevelt personified the wilderness cult, the growing infatuation with the great outdoors. But then again, there were extraordinary circumstances surrounding this particular trip. Roosevelt was vice president at the time he set out to climb Mount Marcy, and President William McKinley had been shot just five days before at the Pan-American Exposition in Buffalo. Assuming that McKinley was out of danger, Roosevelt put himself out of touch. After Roosevelt had reached his goal and begun his hike back toward the camp, telegraph messages relaying that McKinley's condition had turned grave, carried by fast horses over rough roads, caught up with Roosevelt at Lake Tear-of-the-Clouds, the small mountain lake that gives birth to the Hudson River. After a hair-raising ride by buckboard out of the mountains, Roosevelt arrived at the North Creek train station, where he learned he would soon be sworn in as president of the United States. McKinley had died in Buffalo.

This moment tells us a great deal about Roosevelt. His desire to be in the wild was so strong that even with the president struggling to recover from an assassin's bullet, Roosevelt headed for the mountains. Roosevelt, who had served briefly as New York's governor, had a particularly strong desire to climb Marcy, his state's highest peak. It was an accomplishment that would be critical to his identity as a New Yorker. That Roosevelt learned of his impending presidency there in North Creek, at the base of New York's high peaks, adds a fitting touch of romance to an otherwise depressing scene, for McKinley's death meant that the nation's premier conservation advocate had ascended to the nation's highest office.

The conservation movement had begun long before Roosevelt entered the White House and had already accomplished much, especially in setting aside national forests, but it gained far broader support once Roosevelt assumed his position at the "bully pulpit." Roosevelt's rise to the presidency also marks the arrival of New York's leadership in conservation around the nation, a leadership that lasted until the onset of World War II, through Franklin Roosevelt's New Deal. People claimed different meanings and goals for conservation, but generally supporters believed in the need for government to regulate natural resources—especially timber, game, water, and energy—in an effort to encourage efficient use in both the short and the long term. Although thousands of New Yorkers became dedicated conservationists, four individuals in particular—Theodore Roosevelt, Bob Marshall, Robert Moses, and Franklin Roosevelt—played critical roles in the nation's conservation politics through their writings, their work in New York, and their efforts beyond the borders of the Empire State. During the long conservation era, forty years all together, the movement reveals the power of individuals to shape environmental policy and the environment itself.

THEODORE ROOSEVELT

Theodore Roosevelt had much in common with his distant cousin Franklin. They were raised in large homes, comfortable and well staffed. They had all the benefits of great wealth, including an elite education and extensive travel. Both developed strong reform politics and an interest in public service. Although Theodore was a Republican and Franklin a Democrat, both were progressives, and both had faith in the ability of government to improve the lives of citizens and the nation's environment. Both held the office of New York governor, and of course both served as president. And when they did, they both brought a strong conservation ethos to their administrations.

Theodore and Franklin had their differences, too. Theodore became a famed wilderness adventurer; he personified masculine strength and daring. Franklin, by contrast, was stricken with polio and was confined to a wheelchair for most of his adult life. Franklin's love of the outdoors was no less intense because of his affliction, but he approached the forest differently, both literally and figuratively. He was much less romantic than Theodore and more practical in his appreciation of the woods. Theodore was from the city, born and raised in Manhattan; Franklin grew up in the country on a lovely estate called Springwood, overlooking the Hudson River in Hyde Park. Both men preferred the country, however, and as adults both lived within reach of New York City but fully in the country, Franklin at his childhood home and Theodore at Sagamore Hill, the 155-acre Oyster Bay estate he purchased in 1880.

Differences notwithstanding, the traits Theodore and Franklin Roosevelt shared were more important to their influence on environmental history. Both believed strongly that government and individuals must protect natural resources to ensure their longevity. At times this meant more efficient management; at others it meant preservation. They believed in the value of scientific study and the necessity of basing environmental policy on expert knowledge. Both were students of nature themselves. They used their personal experiences in nature to shape their environmental politics, and both elevated the goals of conservation while in office. Together the Roosevelts protected and restored millions of acres of forest around the country, increased recreational opportunities for vacationing Americans, and helped shape a national culture of nature appreciation. And of course they began all this good work in New York State.

Although much of Theodore's childhood was spent in the nation's largest city, his personality and interests were deeply influenced by his many trips away from Manhattan. He traveled extensively with his parents, both abroad and in the United States, his favorite retreats being those to which the family returned repeatedly, especially the Adirondacks and Oyster Bay. In these places Roosevelt nurtured his interest in nature, adding specimens to his own natural history museum. He was most keenly interested in birds, which he studied and collected—with a gun—as often as he could. In the summer of 1874, for example, the teenaged Roosevelt shot a passenger pigeon on Long Island.

He skinned it and added it to his collection. Passenger pigeons had already diminished dramatically in number, especially in New York, but undoubtedly Roosevelt had no inkling that the species, once numbering in the billions, would be extinct just forty years later.

Theodore aspired to be a scientist, and he wrote extensively of his observations and collections, the bulk of which he eventually donated to the Smithsonian and the American Museum of Natural History. After graduating from Harvard, he returned to New York to become a lawyer and politician, though his interest in natural history never subsided. In fact, Roosevelt was an avid reader of natural history and became an accomplished author in that area, too. His first publication, in 1877, was *The Summer Birds of the Adirondacks in Franklin County, N. Y.*, a list of ninety-seven species he and a friend had spotted, mostly around the St. Regis Lakes. This work nicely blended his two early loves: birds and wild New York. He became a more serious author with the publication of three books describing his adventures in the West, beginning in 1884.

Roosevelt loved the open spaces of the Dakotas, and he hunted throughout the plains and various western mountain ranges, but even with all his travels he remained connected to New York. Indeed, although it may seem that Roosevelt's love of nature developed despite his upbringing in Manhattan, it may have developed largely because of it. No doubt family influences were great, especially from his father, one of the founders of the American Museum of Natural History, who did much to teach him nature appreciation, and his eccentric uncle Robert Barnwell Roosevelt, an avid fisherman and hunter, who lived next door to Theodore when he was a child. Actually, throughout Roosevelt's lifetime Manhattan was home to and a gathering place for many of the nation's most avid advocates of nature appreciation and conservation. For instance, Roosevelt knew Frank M. Chapman, raised in northern New Jersey, who became the nation's foremost ornithologist while working at the American Museum of Natural History, and Henry Fairfield Osborn, a geologist who also held a position at the museum. Roosevelt was acquainted with many other conservation-minded New Yorkers, including Madison Grant, who among other things joined Osborn in founding the Save the Redwoods League and helped found the Bronx Zoo, and the zoologist C. Hart Merriam, who had published important works on the mammals of the Adirondacks and undertook critical research for the U.S. Biological Survey.

In 1888 Roosevelt gathered together some of New York's conservation-minded men to create the Boone and Crocket Club. All of the members were wealthy men of high social standing, including Albert Bierstadt, the famed German American painter who had long made his home in New York. Among the most noteworthy members was George Bird Grinnell, a Brooklyn native and the editor of *Forest and Stream,* a leading sportsmen's magazine. Since its founding in 1873, *Forest and Stream* had become an active voice for proper sporting etiquette and wildlife conservation. Indeed Grinnell's magazine was just one example of a growing sportsmen's literature that would play a central role in spreading a conservationist ethic among the nation's wealthy hunters and anglers. Roosevelt served as the Boone and Crocket Club's first president, and through it and with Grinnell's help, he became a leading voice in wildlife conservation issues. The club was a national organization with broad interests, but with so many members living in New York, including its two most important members, state issues inevitably reached the club's agenda. In 1897, for example, the club's lobbying was instrumental in forcing changes in New York's game laws, which henceforth prohibited the use of jacklights and hounds in hunting deer.

Roosevelt cut his political teeth in the New York Assembly in 1882, and while his career would take several twists, he came back to Manhattan to serve two years as New York City's police commissioner, joining George Waring in the administration of reform mayor William Strong in 1895. As commissioner, Roosevelt held a seat on the Board of Health, and he took frequent tours of tenement districts, often with the reporter and reformer Jacob Riis, to see what might be done to improve conditions. "It is one thing to listen in perfunctory fashion to tales of overcrowded tenements," Roosevelt wrote years later, "and it is quite another actually to see what that overcrowding means, some hot summer night, by even a single inspection during the hours of darkness." Roosevelt's reform politics were strengthened by his experience in city government, where he worked to weed out corruption through the professionalization of municipal employees, but the urban environment did not become one of his major concerns. Indeed, Roosevelt and an increasing number of wealthy Americans thought of the urban environment as permanently and tragically flawed. He believed that an outdoor life built character. "The country is the place for children, and if not the country, a city small enough so that one can get out into the country," he wrote.

After his famous foray to fight in the Spanish-American War, Roosevelt was elected governor of New York in 1898, a post he held for two years. He later claimed, "All that later I strove for in the Nation in connection with Conservation was foreshadowed by what I strove to obtain for New York State when I was Governor." If Roosevelt was able to accomplish little of significance in his short tenure in Albany, his administration did in many ways prefigure his presidency. His rhetoric revealed all the hallmarks of Progressive philosophy, especially a faith in expertise and a reliance on scientific study. In his annual address to the legislature in 1900 he noted, "A careful study of the resources and condition of the forests on State land must be made." He also revealed his understanding of the importance of natural resources management: "The subject of forest preservation is of the utmost importance to the State. The Adirondacks and Catskills should be great parks kept in perpetuity for the benefit and enjoyment of our people." Although the management of state lands was still limited to preventing and fighting fires, regulating hunting, and preventing poaching, Roosevelt professionalized the state's forest wardens, hiring more knowledgeable and efficient men, a reform reminiscent of his work as police commissioner. Not surprisingly, he also sought better hunting regulations. He favored building reservoirs, where they wouldn't destroy forests, but only after scientific study.

By the time Roosevelt entered the White House, he had traveled extensively; he had ranched in the Dakotas, served as a soldier in Cuba, and hunted everywhere he could. His experiences in all these other places helped fuel his love of nature and the wild, but Roosevelt knew his New York home best. His Long Island property, Sagamore Hill, afforded grand views of Oyster Bay to the west and Cold Spring Harbor to the east. Roosevelt had intimate knowledge of his estate, the lawns and gardens, wheat fields, and woodlands. He worked his land, knew the stables and the barn. "At Sagamore Hill," he wrote in his autobiography, "we love a great many things—birds and trees and books, and all things beautiful, and horses and rifles and children and hard work and the joy of life." Roosevelt made time for nature while president, even keeping in his head impressive details of natural history. In *Camping and Tramping with Roosevelt*, John Burroughs described a long hike around Sagamore Hill, during which Roosevelt displayed his "extraordinary powers of observation." Roosevelt's love of nature, Burroughs discerned, was "at once scientific and thoroughly human." Roosevelt wanted both to know and to feel nature.

Roosevelt's conservation interests took him well beyond the state's boundaries, and his accomplishments as president were continental in scope. In seven years he set aside more land for protection, in national forests and national parks, than all of his predecessors combined. Roosevelt also created the first national bird preserve, in Florida, initiating a new category of federally protected land, which became the National Wildlife Refuge System. By the end of his presidency Roosevelt had created fifty-three bird and game refuges. He also made excellent use of the Antiquities Act, passed in 1906 to give the federal government the ability to set aside important natural or cultural lands as national monuments. Roosevelt created sixteen of these, including the Grand Canyon National Monument.

Significantly, none of this conservation work focused on New York, which gained neither national forests nor national parks during Roosevelt's administration. Roosevelt and Chief Forester Gifford Pinchot did, however, elevate the national discourse on conservation. They transformed the American political culture, expanding government's authority in the conservation of natural resources, thereby legitimizing activist government in the protection of what they perceived to be the public good. As his administration came to a close, Roosevelt introduced the results of a broad study of the nation's natural resources, reiterating the need for strong government leadership in conservation and the need to think beyond individual profit. "We should do all in our power to develop and protect individual liberty, individual initiative," he urged, "but subject always to the need of preserving and promoting the general good. When necessary, the private right must yield, under due process of law and with proper compensation, to the welfare of the commonwealth." This idea— serving the commonwealth—lay at the heart of Roosevelt's conservation policy and his life's work.

THE PALISADES

By the first decade of the 1900s, conservation had become a broad national movement to husband natural resources, in which Roosevelt was the central figure. His hand was not always visible within the movement, but often it was. For example, in the late 1800s many prominent New Yorkers became concerned about quarrying on the Hudson shore opposite Manhattan. New Jersey quarrymen were blasting away at the beautiful Palisades. After years of activism that had led to little progress, Roosevelt's 1898 election gave concerned citizens an important ally in New York's governor's office. Roosevelt created a study group to work in concert with New Jersey to find a solution. A year later he signed a law that created a ten-person park commission, with five members from each state, empowered to raise money, purchase land (even through eminent domain), and operate a public park. George Perkins, a financier whose Wave Hill home overlooked the Palisades from the Bronx, became the first president of the Palisades Interstate Park Commission. The well-connected and energetic Perkins spent years lobbying for government funding and private donations, the first of which came from J. P. Morgan, who gave the money necessary to purchase the offending New Jersey quarry. When the quarrying moved north, into New York, so too did the Palisades Interstate Park Commission's activities. By the end of 1910 the commission had acquired significant parklands in New York, in part owing to the interest of John D. Rockefeller, whose Westchester property overlooked the Hudson Highlands, now threatened by quarrying. More important, the park gained its largest block of land to date from the estate of Edward H. Harriman, who had assembled an extensive holding in the Highlands.

The Palisades Interstate Park preserved views along the Hudson, but it also served a recreational purpose. A 1924 park survey summarized of the facilities in the Harriman and Bear Mountain sections of the park: "Roads, paths, trails, lakes, docks, beaches, water and sanitary systems, playgrounds, picnic groves, boats, pavilions, shelters, camps and ices houses have been built, and restaurants, lunch rooms and steamer and automobile transportation provided." Visitors could take a steamer up from the city, dock at Bear Mountain landing, spend the evening at Bear Mountain Inn, see the elk herd brought in from Yellowstone and kept in an enclosure, or perhaps catch a glimpse of a beaver, brought in from the Adirondacks but not kept enclosed. This was truly park development. An effective park had to be much more than protected property; it had to be altered in significant ways to enhance utility. In this manner culture shaped the landscape, even on preserved lands. The list of changes reveals the commission's assumption that the Palisades Interstate Park would serve both the romantic and recreational needs of park visitors.

While unique in its interstate composition, the Palisades story was indicative of this conservation era. Interested parties included the extremely wealthy; concerns included aesthetics and the preservation of forests. The campaign to save the Palisades and the Hudson Highlands also contained a historical component, given that region's importance to the nation's history and especially its role in the Revolutionary War. Most important, the solution to the problems in the Palisades was government acquisition and control. Even Harriman, who died before he could donate his estate himself, thought the Palisades Interstate Park Commission worthy of controlling land he had managed for more than twenty years. Just as the reform movement in the city expanded government authority

to blunt the power of the market, regulating natural resource consumption required the expansion of government authority in the countryside, particularly
through government land purchases.

REFORESTATION AND LAND ACQUISITION

Several themes ran through the long conservation movement, most of which
reached back into the late 1800s, before Roosevelt became a political force.
The oldest of these themes was rationalizing the management of the nation's
forests. Progressive conservationists believed that only experts could solve the
problems of the nation, including problems on the land. Thus the growth of
the forestry profession might best represent the character of the conservation
movement. In an effort to support forest science, the state created a college of
forestry at Cornell University in 1898 and hired Bernhard Fernow to develop
an undergraduate program. Fernow, who resigned as director of the federal
Division of Forestry to take the Cornell position, acquired a demonstration
forest in the Adirondacks and created a curriculum within the Department of
Natural Resources at Cornell. After state support for the new college ended in
1903, Cornell's Liberty Hyde Bailey worked to create a new forestry department within the College of Agriculture, a task he accomplished in 1910. The
next year the state created the New York State College of Forestry at Syracuse
University. From that point on, the presence of these two schools ensured that
New York would be a national leader in forestry education and in the developing science of forestry.

Although state control of forest lands muted the market's power, for the most
part modern forestry was designed to improve market outcomes for the timber
industry. "The forester, who is first of all an economist, insists that each acre of
land should be put to its most profitable and best permanent use," wrote Frederick Moon and Harold Belyea in the College of Forestry's *Bulletin*, a quarterly
outreach publication. Moon and Belyea, both professors of forest engineering,
clearly believed in finding the "one right way" to manage the land, and they,
along with others at the college, hoped that through experiment stations and
outreach programs, the experts would be able to educate private landowners,
teaching them to improve their forested lands and reap proper benefits from
them. With modern forestry, no longer was the state exclusively concerned
with preventing fires and catching poachers. Henceforth, state foresters also
addressed disease control, soil conditions, and species selection for cutting and

Falls of the Kaaterskill, 1826, by Thomas Cole (1801–1848), oil on canvas. Property of the Westervelt Collection and displayed in the Westervelt-Warner Museum of American Art in Tuscaloosa, Ala.

Above: As described in chapter 1, Native Americans shaped the landscapes they occupied in many ways, but European Americans tended to think of native peoples as part of nature. In *Falls of the Kaaterskill,* one of Cole's earliest landscapes, the native figure represents wild nature, not human culture. *Next page:* In Cole's more pastoral scenes, such as *View of the Schoharie,* the artist casts a romantic vision of rural life. The relaxed figure surely understands the power of nature, as he leans against a blasted tree, but the pleasant valley below suggests a bright future for Esperance. Similarly, Thomas Chambers includes the disturbed remains of Fort Putnam in the foreground of his *View of Cold Spring,* but they cannot long distract viewers from the prosperous village across the Hudson. *Next page, opposite:* As discussed in chapter 2, industry dotted rural New York. These two paintings remind us of New Yorkers' heavy investment in technology, even in the countryside, and document the important role of horse power.

View of the Schoharie, 1826, by Thomas Cole (1801–1848), oil on canvas, H30¾ × W40¾ in., N0359.1955. Fenimore Art Museum, Cooperstown, N.Y. Photograph by Richard Walker.

View of Cold Spring and Mount Taurus from Fort Putnam, ca. 1845–1855, by Thomas Chambers (ca. 1808–After 1866), oil on canvas, H34⅛ × W49½ in., N0011.1999. Fenimore Art Museum, Cooperstown, N.Y. Photograph by Richard Walker.

View on the Erie Canal, 1829, by John William Hill (1812–1879). Engraving. I. N. Phelps Stokes Collection, Miriam and Ira D. Wallach Division of Art, Prints, and Photographs, The New York Public Library, Astor, Lenox and Tilden Foundations.

Cider Making on Long Island, ca. 1865–1875, by William M. Davis (1829–1920), oil on canvas, H17$^{1/8}$ × W27$^{1/2}$ in., N0368.1955. Fenimore Art Museum, Cooperstown, N.Y.

Chenango River, New York, 1858, by Jasper Francis Cropsey (1823–1900), oil on canvas, 73.40. Memorial Art Gallery of the University of Rochester, Marion Stratton Gould Fund.

Lake George, 1869, by John Frederick Kensett (1816–1872). Consignment: COA0084791. Oil on canvas, H44⅛ × W66⅜ in. (112.1 × 168.6 cm). Bequest of Maria DeWitt Jesup from the collection of her husband, Morris K. Jesup, 1914 (15.30.61). Image copyright © The Metropolitan Museum of Art/Art Resource, N.Y.

Hudson River School landscapes portray nature in a realistic but romantic style, convincing many viewers that the paintings are accurate depictions of actual places. Some talented artists, including John Kensett, surely did capture the splendor of New York's landscape, in this case Lake George, one of the most beautiful lakes in the world. On some canvases, however, artists took considerable liberty with their subjects, a process described in chapter 3. Here Jasper Cropsey has exaggerated the mountains along the Chenango River, adding drama and sublimity to an otherwise prosaic rural landscape.

October in the Catskills, 1880, by Sanford Robinson Gifford (1823–1880). Consignment: COA0084791. Oil on canvas, H36 5/16 × W29 3/16 in. (92.23 × 74.14 cm). Gift of Mr. and Mrs. J. Douglas Pardee, Mr. and Mrs. John McGreevey, and Mr. and Mrs. Charles C. Shoemaker (M.77.141). Los Angeles County Museum of Art, Los Angeles, U.S.A. Digital Image © 2009 Museum Associates/LACMA/Art Resource, N.Y.

Many of Sanford Gifford's landscapes feature the misty glow that often bathes the Catskills, and with this use of light he helped develop the luminist style of painting. His romantic paintings contributed to New York's reputation for sublime wild landscapes worthy of preservation.

Lower Manhattan (View Down Broad Street), 1907, by Childe Hassam (1859–1935). Oil on canvas. Lent by Willard Straight Hall, Gift of Leonard K. Elmhirst, Class of 1921. Photography courtesy of the Herbert F. Johnson Museum of Art, Cornell University.

Above: In the early twentieth century, Manhattan's skyline was in constant motion—upward. Hassam painted a bright, impressionist vision of the canyons created by the new buildings. The dwarfed pedestrians and carriages beneath the New York Stock Exchange suggest the seemingly endless power of capitalism to reshape urban landscapes. *Opposite:* Four years later, George Bellows also captured the energy of Manhattan, but his Ashcan School style emphasized the city's problems. *New York* features the chaos that troubled Progressive Era reformers, as discussed in chapter 4. In contrast, Ralston Crawford's abstract style captures the essence of modernism. Buffalo was the birthplace of the grain elevator, and even during the Great Depression, the elevators' presence on the waterfront spoke to the city's identity.

New York, 1911, by George Bellows (1882–1925). Oil on canvas. Collection of Mr. and Mrs. Mellon. Image courtesy of the Board of Trustees, National Gallery of Art, Washington.

Buffalo Grain Elevators, 1937, by Ralston Crawford (1906–1978). Consignment: COA0084791 Oil on canvas, H40¼ × W50¼ in. (102.1 × 127.6 cm). Smithsonian American Art Museum, Washington, D.C., U.S.A. Photo courtesy of Smithsonian American Art Museum, Washington, D.C. / Art Resource, N.Y.

New York, Night, 1929, by Georgia
O'Keeffe. Oil on canvas, H40¹/₈ ×
W19¹/₈ in. Sheldon Museum of Art,
University of Nebraska-Lincoln,
NAA-Thomas C. Woods Memorial.
Photo © Sheldon Museum of Art.
© 2010 Georgia O'Keeffe Museum/
Artists Rights Society (ARS), New
York.

Before she became famous for painting the Southwest desert, Georgia O'Keeffe captured the romance
of 1920s New York City. Her *New York, Night* reveals how completely electricity changed the meaning
of night in the city, casting the metropolis in a warm glow. From her apartment, looking up Lexington
Avenue, O'Keeffe took in an almost entirely manmade vista, but her painting naturalizes the buildings
and the streets. Even on the Upper East Side, nature blended with culture to create new landscapes.

reforestation. For many conservationists, proper use of natural resources meant simultaneously increasing private profits and attending to the commonweal.

Government also concerned itself with improving access to nature. In this effort voters passed a state bond issue in 1916, which provided the largest amount of funding for land purchase up to that point. The bond allotted $2.5 million to the Palisades Interstate Park and $7.5 million to the purchase of land in the Forest Preserve counties, where the state still owned just under half of the land. By 1927, when the fund was exhausted, the state had acquired nearly 294,000 acres for the preserves, at an average price of $22 an acre. The vast majority of the purchases were in the Adirondacks, especially in the High Peaks area of Essex County.

At the same time, the state expanded a reforestation program, begun in earnest with the passage of a 1908 law that allowed the state to sell saplings to private property owners at cost. Just a year later, state nurseries had already sold more than a million trees for planting; by the 1920s the state regularly sold more than 4 million trees per year. And of course the state planted trees on its own land, especially in the forest preserves. In the first two decades of the 1900s, the state had planted just under 30 million trees using best practices as determined by professional foresters. All of this reforestation work brought a slight but noticeable shift in the balance of tree species, away from slow-growing hardwoods and toward the pines and spruces favored by foresters.

WILDLIFE

Theodore Roosevelt understood that protected forestlands were most valuable when they were home to diverse wildlife—from big game to songbirds. In the late 1800s, conservationists, led by Roosevelt and the Boone and Crockett Club, lobbied for state protection of game species, including deer, waterfowl, and trout, species that hunters and anglers avidly sought. The state acted, passing game laws that restricted market hunting and preserved the quality of sport hunting, engaged in largely by wealthy urban residents. By 1895 hunters could take only two deer per year, for example. Laws also prohibited behavior such as the use of dogs in hunting and nets in fishing. Although in theory these laws ensured the survival of desirable species, they sparked considerable controversy in communities that had long relied on hunting and fishing to supplement diets or incomes. Christopher Goodsell of Old Forge complained that the state was passing laws for "the benefit of the cities alone," and that poorer rural

residents suffered. Indeed, early foresters were essentially game wardens, policing rural communities to protect game from poachers, even if those poachers
were only trying to put food on their tables. After being arrested for poaching
a deer in 1897, Alvah Dunning said, "I dunno what we're a-coming to in this
free country." As Dunning well understood, conservation law favored certain
interests, and they weren't his. When the state regulated natural resources, not
everyone benefited equally.

Not all species warranted protection. A less well known aspect of these wildlife conservation programs was the "Campaign against Vermin" operated by the
Conservation Commission. The state maintained a list of undesirable species
and paid bounties to hunters who killed them. In the second half of 1918 the
state killed over a thousand predatory animals, including coyotes, in the interest
of improving hunting. The following year every hunting license exhorted hunters to "Enlist in the Campaign against Vermin," and "Shoot all you can of foxes,
cats hunting protected birds, harmful hawks, red squirrels and other enemies
of useful wild life." The list of vermin included bobcats, lynx, woodchucks,
porcupines, and weasels, as well as many bird species, such as great horned
owls, snowy owls, sharp-shinned hawks, goshawks, and crows. Though not on
the "vermin" list, beaver could also be a nuisance, at least in the Adirondacks,
where in the 1920s the state allowed property owners to trap beaver that had
erected destructive dams, as long as they sent the pelts to the state. The state
justified the removal of beaver by noting that the water behind the dams destroyed timber.

The Campaign against Vermin became a particular focus for state conservation officials in the early 1920s. By 1920, up to five thousand animals were being
killed each year with its encouragement, and the Conservation Commission
concluded that "an incalculable saving has accrued to the farmer and the sports-
man from the destruction of these animals." Throughout the 1920s the list of
vermin species shrank, as did the number of animals killed under the program,
and by the 1930s the program disappeared. The Campaign against Vermin
serves as a reminder that conservation was not primarily concerned with protecting wild nature. It was a utilitarian and market-oriented movement, focused
on natural resources rather than natural systems. In the conservation era the infant science of ecology had yet to influence public policy significantly, and few
people spoke out in favor of protecting entire ecosystems, predators and all.

The state campaigned against vermin in an effort to protect desirable animals, including the songbirds that had become the favored species of New York

birders. Among these birders was a young man named Roger Tory Peterson, born in Jamestown in 1908. Like Roosevelt, Peterson grew up studying birds. Unlike Roosevelt, however, Peterson was not encouraged in this passion by his parents. Rather he seems to have been influenced by his childhood surroundings, Chautauqua Lake and the woods around it. In addition to birding, the young Peterson made a hobby of painting, and he became so skilled that after high school he took a job painting lacquered furniture in Jamestown.

In 1925, six years after Roosevelt's death at Oyster Bay, Peterson attended an American Ornithological Union meeting at the American Museum of Natural History, where he made connections and saw the advantages of city living. He soon left Jamestown to attend art school in Manhattan, where he also joined a birding group. Peterson and his fellow birders took frequent excursions to city parks to find and study as many species as they could. He eventually joined the National Audubon Society and wrote for *Bird Lore,* an Audubon publication. The critical event in his life came in 1934, when he published *A Field Guide to Birds,* after having been encouraged to do so during a birding trip along the Hudson. That guide, and the many that followed, gave Peterson considerable fame and great influence in the world of conservation. Indeed the influence of Peterson's guides, still extremely popular today, is impossible to quantify. Surely they played a significant role in the spread of birding around the world in the twentieth century; and because, as Peterson himself pointed out, birders almost always became conservationists, as had Roosevelt, the guides undoubtedly bolstered the movement to protect birds and the habitats that support them. Through his guides and other writings, Peterson became one of most influential New Yorkers in American environmental history, his life's work serving as evidence of the power individuals have to shape the world in which they live, even outside of politics.

WATER POLLUTION

Though not generally included as part of the conservation movement, water pollution control was an important issue in the early 1900s. In fact the discussion of water pollution conformed to common conservationist themes, focusing on the profitable use of resources and the provision of recreational opportunities. State law regulated the discharge of several specified wastes, including dyestuffs, coal tar, and effluent from creameries and tanneries. The law required that pollutants not harm fish, meaning that to prosecute offenders successfully, the state had to prove that particular discharges caused biological harm. In especially grievous cases, however, state employees simply introduced minnows to polluted water and waited for them to die. Although urban water quality was especially poor, the state Conservation Commission focused largely on rural streams and rivers in the hope of protecting fish stocks. Enforcement, which centered on creameries and cheese factories in the mid-1920s, was not stringent, however, and only a few dozen violators faced fines each year. Prosecutions were most likely pursued only where anglers complained about diminished stream quality.

One urban water pollution issue did gain considerable attention: the fouling of oyster beds. New York Harbor and other salt waters around the city were important sources of oysters, and Manhattan restaurants were famed for their fresh shellfish. By the late 1800s, untreated sewage and industrial pollution had damaged the "setting grounds" where oysters grew. In 1912 the Conservation Commission announced that contamination had destroyed thousands of acres of shellfish beds. Jamaica Bay, for example, received 40 million gallons of raw sewage a day, which certainly had a negative impact on the bay's oyster population. The commission also estimated that fifty thousand acres along the lower Hudson had been rendered unsuitable for shellfish by industrial waste. Although the state recognized that contaminated oysters posed a public health threat, the commission's concerns were driven largely by the oystering industry's economic value. In 1913 the commission proposed the extensive study of shellfish beds, not to determine which polluters should be stopped, but to determine which shellfish remained healthful. Under the proposal the state would issue a "certificate of sanitary condition" to bolster public confidence in local oysters. When certification was not enough, the state promoted a process by which harvested oysters could be bathed in a chlorine solution for "purification," with one such chlorinating plant having been built in Inwood, along Jamaica Bay. Not surprisingly, since water pollution control remained ineffective, especially around the city, oyster beds continued to collapse, other fish species declined, and recreational opportunities diminished.

RECREATION

Over the first three decades of the twentieth century, conservation evolved to keep pace with cultural changes. The most significant of these changes involved the growing role of the automobile in American life. In the 1920s, expanding automobile ownership, highway building, and leisure time combined to encourage New Yorkers to move around their state as never before. Conservationists, working both in and outside government, emphasized improving recreational access to nature, at first mostly through the building of parks, but increasingly through the construction of parkways and other roads that helped bring tourists to their destinations.

The construction of the Bronx River Parkway, between 1913 and 1923, reveals how conservationists integrated automobiles into modern planning. The Bronx River flowed out of central Westchester County, south through its namesake borough, and past the Botanical Gardens and the Bronx Zoo. Supporters of these two cultural gems conceived of the parkway as a means of protecting the small river's water quality. With state funding, and the power of eminent domain, a park grew up along the length of the river, which was reengineered at points to accommodate the parkway and recreational facilities. The success of the Bronx River Parkway, particularly its limited-access design—the first use of this feature in the United States—instantly inspired the construction of similar roadways. Soon Westchester County was laced with roadways associated with waterways, including the Sprain Brook, Hutchinson River, and Saw Mill River parkways. In theory these highways served multiple functions, although over time the goals of traffic management overwhelmed those of recreation and improved water quality.

In the years after World War I outdoor camping, too, became more popular, with many families adopting the equipment and skills soldiers had used in the field. A steady increase in automobile travel and the popularity of wilderness vacations placed great pressure on recreational facilities. The state continued its efforts to expand the park system and greatly increased the construction of new facilities. In 1920 the Conservation Department inaugurated the effort to develop the Forest Preserve for recreation. By the end of the decade, the Adirondacks and Catskills contained more than twenty campgrounds. In 1929 nearly 130,000 people camped at state campsites in the Adirondacks alone, including more than 17,000 who stayed at the Fish Creek Pond facilities, which had expanded several times since opening in 1920.

Together cars and camping liberated vacationers from railroad schedules and large hotels, opening up the landscape to exploration. With automobiles, vacations could take on new characteristics: they could be quick and flexible, and could cover considerable territory. Although state policies encouraged tourism, the private sector was much more central to this cultural shift. Entrepreneurs in every corner of the state hoped to capture the attention—and at least part of the spending—of these auto tourists. A flurry of new roadmaps pointed the way, marked with all types of tourist destinations. In 1921 Harry Melone authored one of the state's many new tourist publications, *Souvenir of the Finger Lakes Region,* which neatly summarized the area's great attractions, including the roads themselves: "Four hundred miles of good hard macadam, down Indian trails, over rugged promontories, through wooded dales cool in the summer sun and barbaric in the riotous colors of autumn, lead the motorist into the heart of this wonder land, where there are no mosquitoes, black flies or other insects which detract from so many summer resorts."

Though still reliant on agriculture, as the pamphlet's many photographs confirmed, the Finger Lakes offered an attractive mix of hunting, fishing, and boating, which at least some residents hoped would help transform the region into a tourist destination. Not to be outdone, in 1926 businessmen along U.S. Route 20 founded the Cherry Valley Turnpike Association, designed to market the region through which that road ran. A twenty-five-page booklet praised central New York's natural beauty as well as its cultural heritage. Its cover illustration, a map running from the Hudson west to Syracuse, featured images of Rip Van Winkle, Natty Bumppo, the great Mohawk chief Joseph Brant, and, largest of all, George Washington, who visited Cherry Valley in 1783. The map mingled all variety of material, from depictions of historical events, such at the mythical invention of baseball in Cooperstown, to the location of extant institutions like Colgate University. Mixed throughout, however, were images of natural attractions: Chittenango Falls State Park, the sulfur springs of Richfield Springs, a jumping trout, an eight-point buck, a beaver, and migrating ducks. Altogether the Turnpike Association's map, like Melone's *Souvenir of the Finger Lakes Region,* portended the great changes that would soon be sweeping over the state. Henceforth New Yorkers would make much greater use of the state lands, and frequent the places in between, and the state's landscape would be littered with tourist attractions, both natural and historical.

For many tourists the roads themselves became an attraction, especially those that passed through beautiful scenery, such as the Adirondacks and Catskills, where some routes took on special designations to lure tourists, such as the Rip Van Winkle Trail. In some cases the state constructed highways specifically for tourist enjoyment. Storm King Highway, for example, was surveyed across the face of that mountain, perched above the Hudson River, as early as 1903. When finally completed in 1922, the highway gave tourists the ability to drive directly across this stunning feature and to pause at a scenic overlook, where motorists could see the Highlands from a new perspective. In that same year construction began on Bear Mountain Bridge, another link in the growing tourist infrastructure. Even more dramatic, in 1927 voters approved an amendment to the state constitution allowing the construction of Veterans Memorial Highway up the side of Whiteface Mountain outside Lake Placid. The highway was supported by groups of veterans, who hoped to build a spectacular memorial to New Yorkers who had given their lives in World War I, and by local businessmen eager to boost the region's tourism. Fittingly, Governor Franklin Roosevelt, for whom increased accessibility became an important goal in natural resource management, was on hand for the groundbreaking ceremony in the fall of 1929. Workers finished the highway in 1935, bringing motorists to within three hundred vertical feet of the summit and giving all types of tourists access to stunning vistas.

Although increasing tourism reflected broad cultural changes, some individuals played critical roles in shaping the tourist experience. Among the most influential was Benton MacKaye of Massachusetts, who developed a regional plan for camping and hiking in 1921. MacKaye proposed building a trail stretching along the Appalachians from Maine to Georgia, an idea that helped inspire activism throughout the East, including New York. With publicity provided by Raymond Torrey, the *New York Evening Post*'s "Outings" columnist, hiking enthusiasts worked through the recently created New York–New Jersey Trail Conference to build the first stretch of the Appalachian Trail inside Bear Mountain and Harriman state parks. Torrey and William Welch, who managed Harriman Park, rounded up volunteers and completed the first sixteen miles of the trail, from the Hudson to the Ramapo River, by the fall of 1923. MacKaye, Torrey, and other supporters hoped that city dwellers would use the trail as an escape from their busy, overworked lives.

Trail building continued through the 1920s and 1930s, but supporters of outdoor recreation knew that expanding opportunities required the expansion of government landownership. The New York State Association, a reform organization led by Democrats, lobbied for both park expansion and comprehensive park planning in response to increasing demand and projected urban growth. City parks simply could not fill the needs of urban residents, as the great popularity of the Palisades Park revealed. In 1924 the association's Committee on State Parks nicely summarized this new era of park building by focusing on urban demand: "The modern park must provide good roads, lakes, facilities for large outings and where possible camps and other facilities which make a park accessible and attractive to people who come from considerable distances."

That "good roads" should come first on this list indicates just how much cars had changed outdoor recreation in New York.

WILDERNESS, THE AUTOMOBILE, AND BOB MARSHALL

Purchasing more land and building new facilities could alleviate part of the pressure on state lands caused by improved mobility and access, but some New Yorkers began to worry about another consequence of bringing automobiles deep into the forests: the permanent destruction of wilderness values. Among those who expressed alarm was Bob Marshall, who had taken to the woods in more ways than one. Born in New York City, he had spent his childhood summers on Lower Saranac Lake, at his family's summer home. In 1918, at seventeen, Marshall began a systematic attempt to climb all forty-six Adirondack peaks over four thousand feet, and with his companions he became the first to do so.

Marshall knew that he wanted to spend his life in the woods, not in the city, and so he studied to become a forester. In 1922 he summered on Cranberry Lake with his fellow sophomores at the New York State College of Forestry. From the camp Marshall took a series of weekend hikes, his favorite taking him into the Five Ponds area. "It was so pleasant," he wrote in his journal, "as we lay down to reflect, that we were in the heart of a tract of virgin timber about forty miles square, absolutely unmarred by man. And yet we could not help regretting that there should be so very few of such tracts left, due to the almost criminal lack of foresight of our legislatures of the nineteenth century." It was this very sentiment that drove Marshall's efforts to preserve wilderness. Marshall earned a doctorate from Johns Hopkins University, and he became a prolific and influential writer. His career in the United States Forest Service and his interests in the wide open spaces took him well beyond New York. And as was the case with Theodore Roosevelt, Marshall's accomplishments also went well beyond his home state. Marshall inspired others with his enthusiasm for the wild. In 1935 he became a founding member of the Wilderness Society, along with Benton MacKaye. Unfortunately, Marshall died very young, in 1939, leaving much of his inherited fortune to the Wilderness Society.

Even as Marshall expressed alarm at the shrinking of wilderness in the West, others felt the intrusion of automobiles and motorboats in New York. After failing to defeat the 1927 constitutional amendment permitting the construction of the Whiteface Mountain highway through Forest Preserve lands, preservationists found themselves in a constant struggle to limit road building in the Adirondacks. As he engaged in a multifront battle to preserve wilderness in the North Woods, Samuel Ordway, president of the Association for the Protection of the Adirondacks, summarized that organization's position: "Our feeling is that the wild forest idea as stated in the constitution is inconsistent with the building of new roads generally, and particularly inconsistent with the building of automobile roads." In the early 1930s the association lobbied to stop several road projects in the Adirondacks, including a proposed road that would have connected Long Lake with Big Moose by taking a route north of Raquette Lake across miles of uninhabited forest lands. Although the state built or improved several Adirondack roads in the 1930s, this was not one of them.

ALFRED SMITH AND ROBERT MOSES

Activists like Bob Marshall and Benton MacKaye helped shape environmental politics and even shaped the environment, but in the 1920s their efforts could not match those of state government officials, especially Governor Alfred Smith and one of his appointees, Robert Moses. Unlike Theodore Roosevelt, Smith was no outdoorsman. Born on the Lower East Side of Manhattan, Smith was the consummate New York politician, part of the Democratic Party's Tammany machine. Smith became a successful four-term governor, though he is perhaps best known for his loss to Herbert Hoover in the 1928 presidential election. Conservation may not have been among Smith's greatest concerns when he arrived in Albany as governor in 1923, but the movement continued to have great influence on state policies. In announcing an upcoming "Conservation Week," a tradition that began under the impetus of New York City's Women's Club Federation in 1922, Smith encouraged all of the state's educational agencies to engage the public on environmental issues. In a declaration that neatly summed up the conservation ethos of the Progressive Era, Smith claimed, "To protect our forests from fire and disease, our streams from pollution, our wild life against extermination, our sources of water power from exploitation and alienation, is not only a function of government but an obligation of every citizen, and it is a work in which every one can have an active part."

Through the 1920s the Smith administration accelerated reforestation efforts and otherwise perpetuated the conservation philosophy that Theodore Roosevelt had brought to the office two decades earlier. But Smith may be best remembered for giving Robert Moses his first break in state government.

Although his only official post when he arrived in Albany was secretary of the New York State Association, Moses gained considerable power during the decade. Eventually he came to hold several important positions simultaneously. He headed the Long Island Parks Commission and the New York State Power Commission, while serving as Smith's secretary of state and holding several other posts in New York City.

Moses probably would not make anyone's list of important conservationists, but he was a strong advocate for recreation and the preservation of open space, especially in metropolitan regions. In the early 1920s Moses traveled extensively around Long Island, mapping out a new parks system in his head. In the preceding decade New York City had added nearly a million people to its total, which would soon reach 6 million. Moses understood that those people needed access to recreational space outside the city. At the time, however, the state provided very few parks, aside from the popular Palisades Interstate Park, which attracted 4 million visitors in 1922. Most state parks surrounded historic sites, including Revolutionary War battlefields, and they offered few amenities or activities. In 1921 the state purchased what would become the Allegany State Park, the largest state acquisition in western New York since William Letchworth gifted a thousand acres along the Genesee River in 1907, but its remote location limited its promise as a popular recreation site for the state's urban population—except for those who lived in Buffalo. In 1923, with Moses's encouragement, the state began the development of a unified state park system, designed to preserve both scenic and historic sites as well as provide recreation to the state's growing population. Three years later the new Parks Division became part of the Conservation Department, an administrative change that reflected the growing importance of parks and park planning, especially as the state anticipated the needs of auto-liberated vacationers and weekenders from cities.

Recreation planning gained additional advocates when the Russell Sage Foundation sponsored the creation of a regional plan for New York City and its "environs." The plan, completed in 1929, predicted continued rapid growth in the metropolis and emphasized the need to set aside open space in new parks and to create limited-access highways for automobiles. While the plan's major goals reflected broad initiatives already under way, its most lasting impact probably came through the growing acceptance of regional planning generally, especially as promoted by the Regional Plan Association, created in 1929 to carry out the recommendations printed that year under the title *Regional Plan of New York and Its Environs.* In the late 1920s and early 1930s dozens of counties, towns, and municipalities created planning boards and passed zoning ordinances, all in the hope of gaining some control over the growth they knew was coming. These administrative changes, this addition of new governmental bodies, could hardly match the changes to the landscape, of course. After voters approved a $15 million bond issue in 1924, Moses, appointed by Smith to serve as president of the Long Island State Park Commission, began to assemble land for his park system. He planned to provide not just large woodland parks, such as Bethpage State Park, but also long beach parks, including those at Jones Beach and Fire Island. And they would be connected by beautiful parkways, with the Northern and Southern State Parkways leading out of the city, and several other parkways connecting motorists to their destinations.

Moses became the state's master builder, but others, too, would play a role in shaping the growth of the metropolis. Many of the roads and parks Moses would later champion were first proposed in the Regional Plan, among them the extension of Lexington Avenue through Gramercy Park, connecting it to Irving Place. This road, never built, would have bisected the park, effectively destroying its idyllic value and compromising one of the city's most successful neighborhoods, a proposed act of vandalism so grievous as to expose how much planners were willing to sacrifice simply to improve automobile traffic flow. Indeed, moving cars around the city became the primary goal of urban and regional planners in the twentieth century, much to the detriment of the state's environmental quality, both in cities and around them.

FRANKLIN DELANO ROOSEVELT

Smith's administration promoted conservation, but it was not nearly as important to the movement as the Roosevelt administration that followed. Like Theodore, Franklin Roosevelt expressed great confidence in government and saw a need for the regulation of individual and corporate behavior. He was born in 1882 on the Hyde Park property that would be his lifelong home. The family's estate inspired Franklin's deep connection to nature. Like his cousin, he became an amateur ornithologist at a young age, collecting specimens of all the bird species that frequented the area, and, through his childhood romps in the woods and countless rides with his father, Roosevelt acquired an intimate knowledge not just of the property but of the region's ecology. He knew the plants, the wildlife, the soil, the climate, and, after special study, he learned the history as well. In fact, as a young man Roosevelt well understood the connection between human history and environmental change; he knew that understanding a place required knowledge of both the landscape and the social, political, and economic events that had shaped it. The Hyde Park property had been farmed for over two hundred years, and now, Roosevelt understood, it could be regenerated through a long interval as forest. Just as forests could rejuvenate the human spirit, so too could they rejuvenate the land, restoring spent soils. This became Roosevelt's goal for his property and for upstate New York as a whole.

Roosevelt traveled far from his Hyde Park home, both in office and out, but he remained forever influenced by that place. The forests were so important to him that he thought of them even as president. Planting and harvesting trees remained central to his identity. He preached the practice of forestry for economic reasons rather than the preservation of forests for romantic reasons. He corresponded with foresters at Cornell and Syracuse, and he encouraged fellow landowners in New York to plant seedlings on their marginal lands and to learn more about the benefits of forestry, the value of trees. In 1923, while still recovering from the onset of polio, Roosevelt wrote to William Overfield, a Hyde Park farmer, offering members of the local Grange the opportunity to order trees from the State Conservation Commission without paying for delivery. Roosevelt himself had ordered a good number of trees for planting on his property—an annual occurrence at his estate. "I am firmly convinced that it pays to plant these trees," he wrote, "and almost every farm has some section of rocky or otherwise unsuitable land for crops which could be planted to trees which in time would have real commercial value." Over the course of his life, Roosevelt oversaw the planting of more than a half-million trees on the Hype Park property, and, just as important, he oversaw harvests as well, beginning in 1912. He was certain that scientific forestry could be made to pay for upstate landowners.

Roosevelt was keenly aware of the manifold problems signified by "idle land," acres that farmers could no longer make pay. Idle land symbolized the plight of farmers, the exhaustion of the state's soil, and the continued draw of large cities that threatened to change forever the character of his state. Forestry, Roosevelt argued, could help heal rural economies and rural lands. "We can help Nature to give us more and at the same time we can lessen the dangers to our civilization which have come with the growth of the cities," he noted in a 1921 speech.

"Would you, as a matter of preference, choose to have your boy grow up in a tenement on the East Side in New York?" Roosevelt, who had grown up in the country but with intimate familiarity with the city, feared the consequences of an ever-urbanizing society, and the reparation of rural America remained at the core of his political agenda, both at the state level and during his presidency. As both governor of New York and president of the United States, Roosevelt saw the nation's many depression-era problems through a lens shaped by his experience in upstate New York. Saving the country required saving the countryside.

Roosevelt began his public service career in 1911, after winning a seat in the New York State Senate. Because of his interest in the environment, he gladly became the chair of the Forest, Fish, and Game Committee. From this position he introduced what became known as the Roosevelt-Jones Bill, which proposed, among other things, that the state be empowered to regulate privately owned forest lands in the Forest Preserve counties. This proved a controversial proposal, and it was easily defeated by timber interests. Still, in his years in the state senate, which ended when President Woodrow Wilson appointed him assistant secretary of the navy in 1913, Roosevelt was a consistent voice for stronger government regulation of natural resources. After his long, partial recuperation from polio, Roosevelt reentered politics, running for the governor's office in 1928. While campaigning, he passed through upstate counties with their abandoned farmhouses and idle farmlands, and he became all the more aware of the state's rural poverty. Roosevelt won the election, partly because he had so effectively articulated a desire to improve rural life. He understood the interconnectedness of rural problems, which, he argued, required regional planning to solve.

Even before entering office, Roosevelt, along with Henry Morgenthau Jr., a wealthy Dutchess County farmer and the publisher of *American Agriculturist*, arranged an informal conference on the idle lands problem, inviting various experts to attend, including Franklin Moon, dean of the College of Forestry at Syracuse. Here Roosevelt confirmed his belief in the need to take unproductive lands out of agriculture by initiating an expanded reforestation program. Upon entering office, Roosevelt appointed Morgenthau to head the bipartisan Agricultural Advisory Commission, which made recommendations to the new administration, such as tax reform to equalize the burden of road building across the state. Morgenthau remained a trusted adviser to Roosevelt, and in 1930 he became the commissioner of conservation, the post from which he directed the reforestation program Roosevelt had envisioned in his campaign.

In a speech before the Cornell College of Agriculture in 1930, Roosevelt summed up the complexity of rural New York's needs: "All sorts of factors are involved: better roads, better markets, better schools, better health facilities, better churches, lower rates for electricity, lower rates for telephones." Although government could not solve all of these problems, the state could fund the scientific study of land, especially soil quality, agricultural yields, and forest cover. According to Roosevelt, this comprehensive study could direct state funds appropriately, encouraging reforestation here, better agricultural practices there. The study of soil quality might even aid in determining where the state should build roads and where electrification should be brought to the countryside—in sum, where farm communities should persist.

The state did fund a Cornell Department of Agriculture study of Tompkins County, which Roosevelt hoped would serve as a model for a statewide examination. He argued that the study of soil quality could lead to the efficient planning of farm-to-market roads, rural electrification, and the "scientific allocation of school facilities." A year later Roosevelt noted, "About 18,000,000 of the 30,000,000 acres in the State are now farm lands and the preliminary survey has shown that a very high percentage of the land now in cultivation has no right to remain as farm land." By one commonly repeated estimate, 4 million acres in private hands lay idle, adding nothing to the wealth of individuals or the state. Interestingly, however, even though farmers were abandoning up to 250,000 acres every year, Roosevelt wanted the state to create a land policy that would prepare New York for the movement of people out of cities and back to the country. The statewide study would identify the best places for this return.

During the Great Depression, cities seemed especially overcrowded, with the unemployed lining up for aid and some even building shantytowns on marginal urban lands. Roosevelt concluded that "the distribution of population during recent years had got out of balance, and that there is a definite overpopulation of the larger communities in the sense that there are too many people in them to maintain a decent living for all." Roosevelt hoped that revitalized and more efficient agriculture could serve as a catalyst for a rural revival, but he also hoped that government might encourage the location of industry in smaller towns and cities, with the goal of dispersing urban populations.

According to Roosevelt, the return to prosperity in New York would require finding productive uses for idle lands. During Roosevelt's administration

Figure 21. First as governor and then as president, Franklin Roosevelt was a champion of conservation. President Franklin Roosevelt, Governor Lehman, and Peter Lehman at the Fifty Years of Conservation in New York celebration held in Lake Placid in 1935. New York State Archives, Albany.

the state encouraged reforestation in a variety of ways. Most important, the state grew millions of trees in its own nurseries to plant on state lands, including the Forest Preserve. In 1931 state nurseries grew and distributed more than 40 million trees; altogether New York planted 40 percent of all trees planted in the United States. Reforestation was most effective when coupled with state acquisition of abandoned lands. By the fall of 1931 the state had acquired nearly 35,000 acres at an average price of just $3.67 per acre, meaning that these lands were now less valuable than they had been at their initial purchase more than a hundred years earlier. The state purchased property in more than a dozen counties, clustered in three areas where idle lands were especially abundant: in the western Southern Tier, especially Allegany County; in central New York, especially Cortland and Chenango counties; and in Schoharie County, west of Albany. The state planted nearly 30 million trees on these acquired lands in just two years. The state also provided inexpensive seedlings to counties, which together planted 5 million trees in county forests in 1930 alone. In addition, individual property owners purchased trees from state nurseries, as Brookfield's Alretha M. Honer did in 1932. She bought forty thousand evergreen saplings, including red pine, Norway spruce, and balsam. The Conservation

Department's preference for evergreens in reforestation altered forest composition over some parts of the state by introducing large stands of pine and spruce where previously mixed deciduous forests had prevailed. Many of these forests still stand, giving ample evidence of the transformative nature of depression-era conservation.

Much of Roosevelt's conservation policy derived from the long-term trend of farmland abandonment combined with the more recent agricultural depression, which persisted through the 1920s. The Great Depression, which began at the end of the decade, gave Roosevelt's administration the opportunity to take his ideas further. Unemployment could be attacked through conservation programs, especially tree planting, and so conservation took on new meaning. Repairing the land could help repair of the state's economy, in both the short term and the long term. Farmers in Chenango County, for example, overwhelmingly praised the reforestation project in their region, with over 90 percent of those who had sold parcels to the state claming that their lives were better since the sale. Many of those selling property to the state used the program to unload unprofitable parcels—those that were unconnected to the home farm or on back lots, at higher elevations. Fewer than a third of the parcels the state purchased in Chenango and Madison counties included the residence of the seller. Still, in some instances the reforestation program marked a great transition. In 1934 one Chenango farmer sold his 262-acre farm, the home where he had been born in 1886 and had lived his entire life. By the time he left his property, he was the only one remaining in what had been a neighborhood of farms. Henceforth, of course, it would be a forest, mostly of pine and spruce. This marked a significant environmental shift, resulting from the combination of a pro-forestry policy and a poor agricultural economy. The environment itself played a role, of course, since the state pursued parcels at higher elevations, where soils were thin and farms were iffy propositions even in good times.

Roosevelt argued for a more expansive reforestation program in 1931, supporting a constitutional amendment to allow the state to purchase lands outside the Blue Lines that enclosed the Adirondack and Catskill parks but inside the Forest Preserve counties for the purpose of reforestation. The amendment, which was identified as the Hewitt Act, named for the legislator who introduced it, would also approve the spending of $20 million over the course of eleven years for what became known as the "Enlarged Reforestation Program." In lobbying for the amendment, Roosevelt said in a radio address: "Annually, hundreds of thousands of acres in this State are being abandoned for farm use.

We propose to put these abandoned acres back, as far as we can, into their natural and profitable use, the use for which nature intended them, of growing trees for us." The passage of the Hewitt Amendment allowed the state to acquire more than 400,000 acres before the beginning of World War II. As Roosevelt declared: "Heretofore our conservation policy has been merely to preserve as much as possible of the existing forests. Our new policy goes a step further. It will not only preserve the existing forests but create new ones." Significantly, these new forests would be owned by the state. By the fall of 1934, the Conservation Department controlled more than 2.5 million acres of land, mostly in the forest preserves, but also in specified reforestation areas, game refuges, game farms, fish hatcheries, tree nurseries, and historic sites. This diverse list of types of state properties represented the state's expanding role in resource management, a role that would continue to grow throughout the remainder of the century.

THE GREAT DEPRESSION

After the stock market crash of 1929, the Great Depression spread from the countryside into the cities. As unemployment rose and paychecks shrank, a growing number of New Yorkers found themselves in need of assistance. By the winter of 1931–32 more than a quarter of New York City residents needed help; half the residents of Harlem could not pay for food and rent. The following summer Binghamton and Johnson City initiated programs of subsistence gardens to relieve hunger. Churches, charities, and local governments could not provide enough help. Roosevelt's active governance in New York State, which included hiring ten thousand men to work in forestry in 1932, helped him gain the Democratic presidential nomination and ensured his victory that November.

As president, Roosevelt addressed the depression with a number of policy initiatives, including those informed by his conservationism. In his acceptance speech at the Democratic Convention in Chicago, Roosevelt cited his New York experience to claim that emergency reforestation efforts could employ a million men, providing immediate relief for the economy and long-term benefits for the environment. As part of his first hundred days, Roosevelt put before Congress his idea for an emergency conservation corps that would consist of unemployed men. These men would engage in conservation work, particularly planting trees, largely replicating the program Roosevelt had begun in New York. Created by

Figure 22. During the Great Depression the Civilian Conservation Corps undertook tree-planting projects across the state, especially in counties where agriculture was struggling. CCC crew planting on hillside, Allegany County (1936). New York State Archives, Albany.

Roosevelt's signing of "An Act for the Relief of Unemployment through the Performance of Useful Public Works and for Other Purposes," the Civilian Conservation Corps initially recruited 250,000 men across the nation.

Roosevelt kept a keen eye on the activities of the CCC, even tracking the locations of camps and the work in which they were engaged. The CCC became one of the most popular components of the New Deal, and when Congress renewed the program in 1935, it increased the participation limit to over 350,000. In his 1936 report summarizing the CCC's first two years, director Robert Fechner described the corps as giving "jobs to hundreds of thousands of discouraged and undernourished young men, idle through no fault of their own, to build up these young men physically and spiritually and to start the nation on a sound conservation program which would conserve and expand our timber resources, increase recreational opportunities and reduce the annual toll taken by fire, disease, pests, soil erosion and floods." As Roosevelt proclaimed, these were considerable accomplishments in husbanding the nation's human and natural resources.

The Civilian Conservation Corps lasted until the United States entered World War II. During its nine years of existence, the CCC engaged in a wide variety of work, taking young men out of cities and into the national parks and forests of the West. But the program was also very active in New York, where plans for the first two camps were initiated less than two months after Roosevelt took office. These camps, which would house about two hundred men each, operated under the direction of the State College of Forestry in the Adirondacks, one near Newcomb which eventually took the name Roosevelt Wildlife Experiment Station, and the other on Cranberry Lake. Other camps opened under the guidance and with the cooperation of the Conservation Department, including a camp at Fish Creek Pond, one of the earliest, where young men labored to expand the campgrounds and other recreational facilities in the Saranac region of the Adirondacks. Eventually the CCC established dozens of camps in the state, from Salamanca in the west to Paul Smiths and Fishers Landing in the north, to Cornwall along the Hudson and Yaphank on Long Island. In the summer of 1935 New York's Conservation Department oversaw sixty-seven camps, though many of them would be short-lived.

Enrollees signed up for six-month stints in the CCC, and even though many signed up again and again, for some just a half-year in the woods could be transformative. Company 1297, for example, occupied a camp at the Huntington Wildlife Station, a thirteen thousand–acre parcel donated to the State College of Forestry in 1932. The camp, near Newcomb, was almost thirty miles from the nearest train station at North Creek. The main camp was quite isolated, and some workers went even further into the wilderness, to side camps. In the summer of 1936, twelve men lived for five weeks in two log cabins on the shore of Catlin Lake. They engaged in surveying, maintaining trails, and making repairs to their own camp. When not working, they enjoyed the wildlife, including a small beaver they briefly held captive for study, and the lake itself, which provided opportunities for swimming and boating. That fall the main camp gained the services of Noah La Casse, an Adirondack guide who had gained some renown for having accompanied Theodore Roosevelt on Mount Marcy back in 1901 as McKinley lay on his deathbed. Theodore Roosevelt's route out of the mountains, which passed by the camp, had already taken the name Roosevelt-Marcy Trail. La Casse regaled the young men with tales full of adventure and wisdom gained from a life in the woods. All together, this

Figure 23. The CCC completed a variety of projects in the area formerly known as Kaaterskill Park, including building a dam at North Lake to improve recreational opportunities. North Lake, Catskills, CCC work (1934). New York State Archives, Albany.

was precisely the type of wilderness experience both Theodore and Franklin Roosevelt would have wanted for young American men, especially men born and raised in the city.

If the CCC was able to transform the enrollees themselves, it surely transformed New York's environment. Although nearly all the work took place on public lands, by the mid-1930s, decades of state land purchases—in the forest preserves, for the park system, and for historic preservation and wildlife refuges—meant that CCC camps could engage in a variety of work in many locations. The CCC developed campgrounds, such as those at Devil's Tombstone in the Catskills and Lake George Battlefield and Hearthstone Point in the Adirondacks. It provided nearly all the labor for the state's ongoing reforestation program through the mid-1930s. During 1935 CCC laborers planted over 37 million trees in New York, reforesting more than 32,000 acres. Enrollees constructed hiking trails and ski trails through state lands; they cut truck trails through reforestation areas as a fire protection measure. CCC workers also built a small dam to raise the water level of North Lake in the historic Kaaterskill Park; the larger lake would allow more swimming and boating opportunities at the campground there. They replaced a dam at Cedar Lake, near Indian Lake, in an effort to improve fishing.

Much of the labor took place on Forest Preserve lands, but the CCC also established camps at state parks, including Gilbert Lake State Park in Laurens, where crews built dams to create recreational lakes and other facilities. The CCC built the extensive stone pathway through Watkins Glen after a flood severely damaged the largely wooden structures that had allowed tourists to explore the beautiful gorge for nearly one hundred years. CCC labor also allowed the state to become more aggressive in wildlife conservation. Workers enlarged and improved the Saranac Fish Hatchery. From a CCC camp at Pharsalia Game Refuge, land the state had purchased in 1926, workers made improvements to nearby Sherburne Game Farm, constructed a dam across the South Otselic River, and built ponds in the refuge itself. They constructed dikes, water control facilities, and a pheasant brooding facility at Howland's Island Game Refuge, created through purchase of a farm in 1932. In the Catskills the CCC improved trout habitat by reworking streams, adding dams and deflectors to create pools, and improving stream banks with log cribbing to reduce erosion and planting trees to provide shade. The CCC's work was not always ecologically sound, however, and increasingly the organization earned criticism for intrusive projects, especially road building.

The CCC was by far the best-known federal workforce in natural areas during the depression, but other organizations were active as well. The Civil Works Administration, which operated during the winter of 1933–34, and the Works Progress Administration, created in 1935, hired men for a variety of projects, including expanding and maintaining recreational facilities. For example, a WPA camp at Stony Brook State Park constructed roads and trails, planted trees, and improved stream banks. The WPA undertook similar work in Taughannock Falls State Park on Cayuga Lake. The depression also witnessed the first significant federal land purchases in New York for conservation purposes. Beginning in 1938 the Department of Agriculture oversaw the purchase of more than one hundred farms in the Finger Lakes region. Initially managed by the Soil Conservation Service as a mixed reforestation project and demonstration farm, the property was named Hector Land Use Area. In the 1950s the U.S. Forest Service took over management of the land, and finally, in 1985, it became the Finger Lakes National Forest.

The CCC and other federal programs could not fix all of the countryside's problems, of course. Weakness in agriculture persisted, especially in dairy, which produced half of the state's farm income. When farmers suspected that some distributors were buying milk at untenably low prices, they organized a movement to boost prices. In 1932 several farmers from dairy counties, including Jefferson and Lewis, visited New York City to conduct store checks, searching for underpriced milk. Farmers worked through the Dairymen's League Cooperative Association in an effort to rein in distributors who underpaid farmers for milk, and they even threatened strikes against offending distributors. By early 1933 the situation had grown worse for some farmers, including those in Monroe County, where a strike led to the dumping of thousands of gallons of milk and a revolt against the apparently ineffective Dairymen's League. Not until a milk control bill passed through the state legislature did the conflict subside. The health of the dairy industry was a chronic problem for New York, however, and milk prices remained a near constant concern. Throughout the remainder of the twentieth century, viable dairies continued to grow in size while family farms continued to go under, trends that had serious consequences for rural economies and rural landscapes.

CITIES IN THE DEPRESSION

If the Great Depression left the countryside transformed, changes were equally obvious in the state's cities. The economic crisis and the ever-increasing use of automobiles sapped the vitality of American downtowns. Just as significant, both state and federal policies encouraged demographic dispersal, an intentional attempt to diminish the importance of dense central cities to the American economy. Roosevelt, who had grave concerns about the fate of rural communities, had no such concerns about cities. Although federal aid poured into the cities, in the form of direct assistance and government jobs, Roosevelt's administration developed no policies designed to save urban communities. Indeed, federal housing and transportation policies emphasized the reduction of congestion in the urban core and the demolition of problematic urban neighborhoods.

Across New York State, commercial districts suffered as discretionary spending plummeted. Many store owners could no longer make the rent. Office space, too, became vacant, as employers cut back or went out of business. Some property owners found themselves with empty, aging buildings in and around faltering downtowns. Rather than renovate these buildings to make them more attractive in the very soft market, many owners demolished them. The empty lots that replaced these buildings could at least serve as parking lots, which were in demand as more commuters drove to work. Parking lots could provide enough income for owners to pay the property taxes. These "taxpayers," as they were called, were meant to serve as placeholders until the urban office or retail market improved, at which time new buildings might attract new tenants. Unfortunately, many urban real estate markets only partly rebounded after the depression, and parking lots accumulated in urban landscapes as older buildings continued to come down—a trend that transformed the upstate cities of Buffalo, Syracuse, and Utica in particular.

While poor market conditions led to demolitions around downtowns, federal policy encouraged more aggressive destruction in surrounding neighborhoods. The poorest city residents lived in older, ill-kept housing with poor ventilation, shoddy electrical systems, and inadequate water supplies and bathroom facilities, among other problems. These urban slums had been the concern of housing reformers for decades, but the depression gave the nation an opportunity to pursue bold solutions. Several New Deal programs provided funding and labor for urban renewal projects, including the Lakeview Project in Buffalo, where Public Works Administration money and WPA labor helped clear a neighborhood to make way for public housing. Like the Lakeview Project, just north of Buffalo's central business district, most urban renewal demolition occurred in the neighborhoods nearest downtowns, in minority communities. The public housing that replaced demolished tenements was clearly of better quality but generally of lesser quantity. Slum clearance had multiple consequences for cities, including the reinforcement of residential segregation by race and class, and the dispersal of impoverished minority residents into new "second ghettos."

Although demolition transformed urban landscapes, the most important shifts in housing and retail took place far from downtown. The Home Owners Loan Corporation (HOLC), created in 1933, attempted to enliven the moribund housing market by lowering mortgage rates. HOLC helped transform typical mortgages, allowing more New Yorkers to buy their own homes, but an anti-urban bias, combined with racism, made the purchase of homes outside the city more likely, at least for whites. In policies that persisted well into the postwar era, the federal government backed mortgages for new single-family homes in suburbs while placing red lines around mixed-race urban communities, consigning them to even further deterioration.

Urban environments also changed in more positive ways. The depression gave New York City the opportunity to expand its park system and greatly improve recreational facilities in existing parks. Up to seventy thousand CWA and WPA workers made improvements to public lands throughout the city, mostly under the guidance of Robert Moses, head of the newly consolidated Park Department. Moses hired hundreds of engineers, planners, and landscape architects to help him redesign the modern city. Workers planted trees, reseeded lawns, added playground equipment, benches, bathhouses, boathouses, tennis courts, ball fields, and other recreational infrastructure. Brooklyn's Prospect Park gained a new menagerie; Riverside Park gained a boat basin. Every existing park saw some improvement—a skating rink here, a golf course there. The city built 288 new tennis courts in all, along with 673 baseball fields. In 1936 the Astoria Park pool and play area opened on the Queens waterfront, with stunning views of the new Triborough Bridge. It was just one of eleven large pools built in the 1930s, pools that together could accommodate nearly fifty thousand swimmers simultaneously. Only one, however, Colonial Park pool in Harlem, admitted African Americans. The city also built 255 new neighborhood playgrounds in the 1930s, though most appeared in white neighborhoods and only one in Harlem. In this way and others, the new recreational landscape of the city reflected and even reinforced the city's racism.

Still, these park and playground improvements represented a significant investment in the urban landscape and a new understanding of how urban residents should best use their leisure time. No longer just quiet places for contemplation and relaxation, as Frederick Law Olmsted had conceived of them, urban parks would be active places, places of motion. At the same time, Moses and his engineers knew that New Yorkers, both in and out of the city, would increasingly hop in their cars to seek recreation, and so park developments inevitably accommodated automobiles. A host of parkways, especially in Queens and on Long Island, connected people and parks with pleasing drives. In an effort to ease travel and reduce congestion, Moses emphasized limited-access highways, designed with gracefully sweeping interchanges that engulfed the urban and suburban landscape. In the 1920s and 1930s he approved and pushed into existence 416 miles of parkways extending out from New York City—the Mosholu, Sprain Brook, Cross County, and Hutchinson parkways to the north;

to the east the Grand Central, Belt, Cross Island, and Interborough, and the Northern and Southern State parkways.

At the ends of these pleasure drives one needed places to put all those cars, and so the modern park included large parking lots. The lot at the newly constructed Orchard Beach in the Bronx consumed forty acres. Jacob Riis Park included a lot that could hold nine thousand cars. Jones Beach State Park, at the ends of the new Meadowbrook and Wantagh State parkways, was little more than a string of bathhouses fronted by acres of parking connected by yet another parkway. This was just the beginning, of course, for after World War II the nation would turn ever more completely toward the automobile and the vast infrastructure necessary to make it work. New York would be a leader in that movement, too.

THE LONG TRANSFORMATION

Through forty years of policy implementation and experimentation, conservation transformed New York's landscape. Greatly expanded public lands supplied the state with new park systems, historic landmarks, wildlife refuges, and an enlarged state forest. Greatly expanded government authority gave future state and local officials the ability to regulate and plan land use, to regulate energy production, and to add further to the public domain. The long conservation movement left New York's environment more thoroughly protected than ever before, and it had just as great an effect on the entire country. Through this long conservation era, New York served as the nation's most important incubator of ideas and careers.

Conservation was a national movement, to be sure, but New York sent to the national stage politicians, Theodore and Franklin Roosevelt among them, who kept conservation on the federal agenda. The state produced influential theorists and activists, too, from George Bird Grinnell, the Brooklyn native who edited *Forest and Stream* magazine for more than thirty years, to Rexford Tugwell, the Sinclairville native and Columbia University economist who helped formulate New Deal agricultural policy. Bob Marshall became the nation's leading wilderness advocate, and Robert Moses the nation's premier park builder. Altogether these New Yorkers revealed the power of individuals to shape environmental politics and the landscape itself.

Aspects of New York's environment clearly improved because of the conservation era's activist government. New parks gave urban residents much-improved recreational opportunities both in the city and beyond. Reforestation and other policies gave rural lands an opportunity to recover. On the landscape, however, lay ominous signs for the postwar era, as new parkways and parking lots foreshadowed sprawling development and new toxic threats. As the nation turned its attention to defeating Imperial Japan and Nazi Germany, new enemies of a healthy environment loomed on the home front.

6

Tracing Man's Progress in Making the Planet Uninhabitable

Environmental Interest Groups and Postwar Threats

I n July 1946 Governor Thomas Dewey turned the first shovel of dirt in a kickoff ceremony for the construction of the New York State Thruway. Standing near the midpoint of the 486-mile route, Dewey compared the Thruway to the Erie Canal, predicting that the new six-lane limited-access road would spark growth in commerce, industry, and agriculture. The Thruway would nearly connect the George Washington Bridge with Albany and then Utica, Syracuse, Buffalo, and the Pennsylvania border along Lake Erie. "Transportation has always been the cornerstone of the social and economic progress of any people," Dewey announced before extolling his state's leadership role in pressing new transportation innovations. Designed by the state Public Works Department, the Thruway reminded many observers of Norman Bel Geddes's vision of the future unveiled just seven years earlier at General Motors' "Highways and Horizons" pavilion at the New York World's Fair. It was a sleek, modern roadway with no traffic lights and few interchanges. Dewey and others hoped that it would sustain the economic growth sparked by World War II, believing that better transportation, especially for trucks, would have a real economic impact. The Thruway held much symbolic value as well, for it so clearly represented the modern era; it was big, fast, efficient, and thoroughly planned by experts.

Earlier that summer Dr. Evarts B. Greene had delivered an insightful speech at the Hudson River Valley Conference, arranged to bring together various parties interested in the region's protection. Greene, a prominent historian, discussed the long effort to preserve the historic landmarks of the Hudson Valley, beginning in 1849 with the state's acquisition of Hasbrouck House, which had served as Washington's headquarters in Newburgh. Greene recognized the diversity of organizations involved in conservation, and his inclusiveness foreshadowed the complexity of the environmental movement. As if to ensure that his audience understood the potential of historic preservation to support larger environmental goals, he noted, "An important part of the conservation movement has been the service of the historical societies, and notably the New York Historical Society and the New York State Historical Association." Greene also understood that preserving the area's historical resources required the protection of the Hudson Highlands themselves. Referring to these Revolutionary War sites, Greene said, "I should like to point out that here we have not only specific structures of the time—houses, public buildings or military remains— but a kind of documentation of the military scene—the physical situation in which the events of the war took place." Greene knew that the landscape itself could serve as a historical document, and he hoped to secure the preservation of the Highlands, with their panoramic views of wooded mountains. "Across the River here is a stretch of some twenty-five miles of notable landscapes, rich in historical associations—not only of the Revolution, but of the earlier and later periods of the river from the days of Henry Hudson, through the busy years of eighteenth-century river traffic, to Fulton and the era of steam navigation." This special role in American history, Greene concluded, required that the entire region should receive special protection.

NEW MOVEMENTS

Greene's speech was remarkably prescient. Not only did he understand how the two preservation movements could work toward the same goal—the preservation of both historical and natural landscapes—but also he understood how important the Hudson River Valley had been and would continue to be in these efforts. Ten years earlier, activists had formed the Hudson River Society (an umbrella group that included garden clubs, historical societies, and hiking clubs) dedicated to the preservation of the valley's scenic and historic value. Its leading founder was William Church Osborn, and among its leadership were Laurance Rockefeller and Carl Carmer. The organization, which soon became the Hudson River Conservation Society (HRCS), developed a diverse agenda, from protecting historic buildings to lobbying for better sewage treatment. The HRCS also had a diverse mission statement, which by 1961 read: "To protect and maintain the beauties of the Hudson Valley; to preserve its scenic and historic landmarks; to eliminate the pollution of its waters and air; to develop its recreational values; to cooperate with industry and where necessary to seek its regulation in order to help achieve these aims." The group expressed a pragmatic environmentalism, comprehensive in scope but realistic in goals. By the late 1950s the power company Consolidated Edison had become a member of the HRCS, reflecting the conservative nature of the organization. Indeed the society's conservatism ensured that it would not play a leading role in the postwar environmental battles in the Hudson Valley.

Still, in the way that it brought together diverse groups and individuals, the HRCS did reflect the growing complexity of environmental issues and interest group politics. After World War II the Hudson Valley would see movements for regional planning, for improved water pollution control, for the protection of environmental aesthetics, and for balancing the need for economic growth with other human needs. It also witnessed critical battles against continued highway construction and obtrusive industrial and power plants. These battles inspired the creation of several new public interest groups. All of them would be more assertive than the HRCS.

New York's environment faced multiple threats in the postwar decades, even beyond the Hudson Valley, most of them related to suburban development and an intensifying industrialization that was increasingly reliant on dangerous chemicals. Air and water pollution, serious problems even before World War II, continued to worsen. Untreated sewage fouled the state's waterways, and phosphates from detergents caused algal blooms, especially in Lake Erie. Manhattan's air became thick with auto exhaust and incinerator ash, and air pollution increasingly lingered over Syracuse and Buffalo. New toxic threats developed, including those from nuclear weapons testing and the powerful pesticides increasingly used to control insects in forests and farm fields. Around the state, but especially in the counties near New York City, unregulated growth threatened to permanently alter historically significant, aesthetically attractive, and ecologically important landscapes. As early as the 1950s it became apparent that some urban neighborhoods would not recover their vitality, and many of the state's historic downtowns began a long economic slide. Garbage accumulated in empty lots, and empty lots accumulated in formerly vibrant neighborhoods, indicative of a demographic shift that would remake the state's physical and social landscape. These cumulative environmental threats sparked a multifaceted response, as movements for historic preservation, regional planning, and environmental protection evolved into a powerful environmentalist political force.

Beginning in May 1959 E. B. White, writing in the *New Yorker*, brought his numerous concerns about the environment together in a periodic column, published as "These Precious Days." He began, "Because the slaughter of innocents continues, here and abroad, and the contamination of air, sea and soil proceeds apace, The New Yorker will undertake to assemble bulletins tracing Man's progress in making the planet uninhabitable." The compendium of shocking news that followed over the next year focused on nuclear fallout from hydrogen bomb tests, the unregulated spraying of DDT, the terrible soot problem in New York, and water pollution around the globe. White, like many others in the nation, feared for the very survival of humanity in an increasingly poisoned world.

Although White made no political demands in his column, many New Yorkers did demand more from their government, arguing that the gathering environmental threats required a vigorous regulatory response. New Yorkers therefore built a new political movement, one that went beyond the conservationism of the prewar era. This new movement at first retained that old moniker, but it eventually became known as the *ecology movement*, in light of the growing role of science in environmental politics. By the 1970s, of course, the movement had become known as *environmentalism*. This evolving terminology reflected the evolving nature of the movement, which increasingly linked numerous problems in an agenda larger than the protection of an individual parcel or species. Conservation still had its place, certainly, but to an ever greater extent, environmentalists were simultaneously concerned with human and ecological health. Since so many environmental problems were interconnected, and tied to demographic and economic growth, environmentalists searched for more holistic solutions. In late 1969 Ada Louise Huxtable, architecture critic of the *New York Times*, described a "crisis of the environment" composed of threats to both the country's natural assets and its communities, as bulldozers tore through the countryside and urban neighborhoods alike. Picking up the theme laid down by White and others during the 1950s, Huxtable argued that, given the environmental crisis, "the question is survival."

Environmental activism took many forms, reflecting the diversity of the movement and its concerns. In an era of increasing distrust of both big corporations and big government, concerned citizens often relied on themselves and the organizations they created to protect the environment. Public interest groups began to take center stage in environmental politics, keeping issues in the press, demanding effective government action, and suing when other avenues failed. Interest groups were not new to environmental politics, of course, but they were increasingly important in the postwar era. Some of these groups predated the war, such as the Sierra Club, the Wilderness Society, and the Hudson River Conservation Society, but others were new, including the Committee for Smoke Control, Scenic Hudson, Natural Resources Defense Council, Environmental Defense Fund, and the New York Landmarks Conservancy. Sometimes acting in concert, sometimes alone, these interest groups and hundreds of others revealed the power of collective action even in the face of growing corporate power and political inertia—and, unfortunately, in the face of ever more complex and intractable environmental threats.

THREATS FROM INDUSTRIAL GROWTH

World War II brought a boom in industrial production around the state. New York received $21.5 billion in wartime federal contracts, more than any other state. General Electric, Kodak, and other New York companies thrived as they contributed to the war effort. The war brought recovery from the depression and investments in new industrial plants that promised continued prosperity after the fighting ended. The aircraft industry boomed on Long Island, with Grumman in Bethpage employing 85,000 at its peak, and in Cheektowaga and Tonawanda, where Curtiss-Wright employed additional thousands. In a trend that lasted through the postwar era, companies built new plants on suburban land, where open space and inexpensive real estate allowed the construction of massive facilities. These factories meant good jobs and economic growth, but they brought dangers as well to nearby residents and the environment. For example, the aircraft industry used large amounts of aluminum, the shaping of which required cadmium, a dangerous chemical that seeped into Long Island's groundwater. The growing chemical industry brought even more apparent threats, including those from AlliedSignal, which began manufacturing chlorine and other chemicals at its facility on Onondaga Lake in 1946. Discharges of mercury from the plant, formerly known as Solvay Process Company, entered the lake, adding to the already heavy pollution load.

Threats from the chemical industry were especially grave in the Niagara region, which witnessed dramatic growth during World War II and the years thereafter. Among the growing companies was Hooker Chemical, one of the leading employers in the city of Niagara Falls. Hooker manufactured diverse chemicals, most of them chlorine based, including lindane, an extremely potent pesticide. From 1940 through 1953 the company's sales expanded more than fivefold. Indeed production grew so quickly, the plant could no longer dispose of waste products on its own property. Nor could Hooker simply discharge all its wastes into the city's waterways and sewers, long the primary means of disposal in the chemical industry. Instead Hooker made an arrangement to create a dump offsite, in the eastern section of the city. In 1941 the company began trucking wastes to the old Love Canal, which had for decades sat unused, save by local children who swam and fished in the water-filled ditch.

Hooker fenced off the property, pumped out most of the water, and more or less systematically filled the canal with 25,000 tons of chemical wastes over a twelve-year period. By 1953, suburban growth around the sixteen-acre site made the continued operation of a toxic waste dump untenable, so Hooker closed the site, covered the dump with topsoil, and sold it to the Niagara Falls Board of Education, which was then in search of properties on which it could build schools for the city's growing population. Hooker never hid the fact that Love Canal was a chemical dump, and school officials surely knew how Hooker had used the canal. All the same, a working-class neighborhood of small ranch and bungalow homes took shape around the grassy rectangular property, at the center of which the Board of Education built the Ninety-ninth Street School and its playground.

The growth of the Niagara region reminds us again of the interconnections among environmental issues in the postwar era. The neighborhood around Love Canal, which became known as LaSalle, was in many ways typical of idyllic postwar expansion. Its prosperity was based on good industrial jobs; Hooker employed over two thousand people in the Niagara Falls area, which was also home to eight other major chemical manufacturers. LaSalle residents purchased single-family homes and led lives dedicated to raising their children and educating what they hoped would be the most fortunate generation of Americans yet. Here suburban development and toxic industrial by-products would come together, with tragic consequences.

THREATS FROM SUBURBAN DEVELOPMENT

Even as large industrial employers opened new facilities on the outskirts of cities, more and more New Yorkers sought homes in the suburbs, sometimes to

Figure 24. The postwar decades witnessed intense suburban development, especially on Long Island, where parkways allowed longer commutes to work and reshaped the landscape with expansive interchanges designed to keep cars moving. Northern State Parkway–Wantagh Road, N.Y. (1949). UCLA Department of Geography, Benjamin and Gladys Thomas Air Photo Archives, Fairchild Collection.

be closer to jobs, but more often to avoid the problems of urban life: cramped living, bad air, and, increasingly, poor schools and violent crime. Suburbanization predated World War II, of course, but the postwar years saw a dramatic surge in development beyond municipal boundaries. The slow pace of home-building through the Great Depression and the war meant that nearly an entire generation of buyers awaited homes in the 1940s, and developers could not keep pace with demand. In 1947 Abraham Levitt and his sons initiated a series of innovations that would help speed the delivery of houses to customers, reduce their cost, and set an example for the entire industry. Working on two thousand acres of former potato farms on Long Island, the Levitts at first planned a community of two thousand rental homes, each built on a concrete slab and

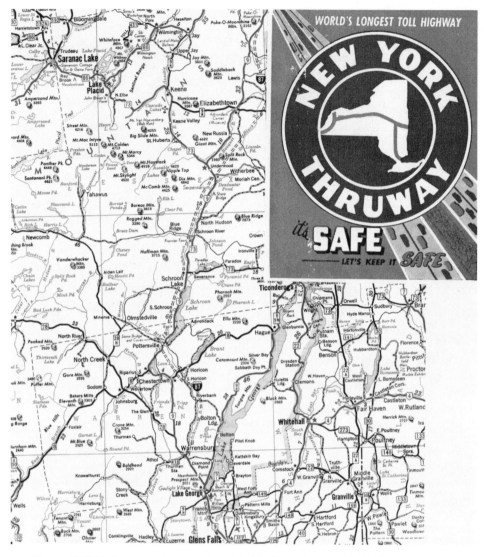

Figure 25. With the proposed construction of the Northway, shown on this 1960 map as a dashed line, a modern highway appeared poised to remake the Adirondacks in the same way the New York Thruway had reshaped other parts of the state, as symbolized in this window sticker. Author's collection.

containing the latest appliances. The units rented so quickly, however, that the builders added four thousand more and offered them for sale. Levittown, as it became known, was so successful that by the end of 1951 it contained over seventeen thousand homes.

In many respects Levittown was a remarkable achievement, one to be copied, even if on a smaller scale, throughout the United States. It offered inexpensive, comfortable housing with small private yards, accessible to schools and play-grounds; it offered relief from the high prices and congestion of the city. The development's success, however, was predicated on automobile commuting. Although residents could drive up to Hicksville to catch the Long Island Rail-road, they were much more likely to hop on the Wantagh Parkway, the Southern State, or the Northern State. Even more troubling, Levittown's success was founded on racial exclusivity. In the 1950s Levittown grew to 82,000 residents, all of them white. Not all New York suburbs imposed such strict segregation, but African Americans did find it much more difficult to escape from troubled urban neighborhoods, ensuring that the postwar era would be one of growing inequality in environmental experiences based on race.

As suburbanization drew more middle-class New Yorkers out of cities, white-collar jobs began to follow. In 1954 General Foods became an early and impor-tant example of this trend when it moved a thousand employees from three buildings on Park Avenue to a three-story building in a park-like setting in suburban White Plains. A company announcement touted the "hushed change from the turbulence and tempo of New York" that the move would bring, add-ing that large windows would let in ample sunlight, neither filtered by the city's smog nor obscured by neighboring skyscrapers. In a sign of things to come, soon after the move a commercial real estate advertisement in the *New York Times* offered "6.6 Acres, Opposite General Foods." Growth begat growth in the suburbs, threatening to alter the state's countryside permanently, marring it with highways, office parks, parking lots, smokestacks, and sprawling housing developments. Farmland was disappearing, and not just on Long Island and in Westchester County. Suburban parklands grew crowded. The construction in the late 1960s of the Northway extension of the Thruway, into the Adirondack Forest Preserve, threatened suburbanization even in the North Woods. More and more New Yorkers grew wary of all this development, this growth in the countryside concentrated along new expressways.

AIR POLLUTION

In commenting on the growing suburbanization trend in 1947, the *New York Times* editorialized, "It is reasonable to assume that smoke and soot are partly responsible for some of the migration from New York to the suburbs, which, in itself, is an economic loss to the city in taxes and business." Four years later, freelance writer Tom Huddleston noted that New Yorkers continued to "move out of town to escape the smoky miasma." New York City's air quality declined rapidly in the 1940s. The city had turned toward dirtier coal during the depression, and after the war, New York's air pollution was worse than ever. One study estimated that on average nearly three thousand pounds of soot fell on every Manhattan block each month. "Soot is the topsoil of New York," quipped E. B. White in 1954. In addition to health problems, soot caused millions of dollars in damage. But the postwar pollution problem was more complex than the smoke problem of an earlier generation. Automobile exhaust increased, and emissions from incinerators grew problematic as residents burned more and more plastic. Invisible but dangerous gases mingled with ash in the clouds above the city. Responding to public pressure, the city created a new Bureau of Smoke Control in 1949, which initiated inspections and forced corrections at polluting smokestacks. Still, the pollution persisted, as did the complaints.

Several organizations began a campaign to control the pollution, aided by the *New York Times*, which ran dozens of articles and editorials on the problem. After the passage of the 1949 ordinance, the *Times* published a letter from "An Irate Housewife from Gramercy Park," which asked if something might be done about incinerators in the city. The writer, who had attended an anti-smoke meeting organized by the Outdoor Cleanliness Association, complained not just about the impossibility of keeping her apartment clean because of the soot, but also about the possibility that the smoke might cause cancer. In the summer of 1950, as the city debated an ordinance that would restrict the use of dirty coal, many women expressed outrage at the city's poor air quality. At one public hearing before the Board of Smoke Control, attended by about four hundred people, two women from Yorkville won the day even after experts from the coal industry testified on the importance of allowing customers flexibility in fuel choice. One of the women, Mrs. Daniel Dolan, pulled a shirt and a sheet from a bag, complaining that her clean laundry had been soiled as it hung on the line. She blamed the smoke from a nearby bakery, but she might also have blamed neighborhood incinerators and an Interborough Rapid Transit power-house. When the women finished, there was a burst of applause from the audience. With wide public support, the new ordinance passed.

Enforcement remained lax, however, causing Elizabeth Robinson, a leader in the New York Federation of Women's Clubs, to organize a new interest group, the Committee for Smoke Control, in early 1951. The committee drew its energy from women activists for cleaner air; although several members of

Figure 26. Consolidated Edison was a conspicuous contributor to New York City's air pollution problem, a fact that complicated the search for new sources of electric power. Midtown Manhattan (1949). UCLA Department of Geography, Benjamin and Gladys Thomas Air Photo Archives, Fairchild Collection.

its advisory board were men, its eleven-person executive board was all female. With the ongoing support of the *Times*, which ran a stream of air pollution articles and editorials, Robinson and her committee kept the smoke issue before the public. Robinson, a housewife from Forest Hills, Queens, helped define the smoke problem. "Women are thinking of the health of their children," she said, "and where that is at stake, a woman will fight as primitively as any tiger in a jungle." In its first year the committee published a twenty-two-page pamphlet, "The Next Breath You Take," invoking the "carbon-blackened lungs" of New Yorkers and connecting increased pollution with an alarming increase in lung cancer. The pamphlet exhorted action: "As long as *you* tolerate conditions in New York, cleanliness is next to—impossible!"

The agitation for better air quality led to more government action. In 1952 the Department of Air Pollution Control replaced the Bureau of Smoke Control. Though largely an administrative move that had no real effect on air quality, the name change revealed a growing awareness that more than just smoke hung over the city. Air pollution was an increasingly complex problem, as tailpipe and incinerator exhausts bathed the city in an unknown variety of chemicals. The city attempted to regulate the thousands of apartment building incinerators by restricting hours of operation and requiring simple filters. If there was any progress, however, residents didn't notice it. After the American Cancer Society announced that air pollution was probably contributing to rising rates of urban lung cancer, and after London experienced a death-dealing smog episode in late 1952, the *Times* editorialized that "we have, in New York, something to worry about." The warnings and agitation continued, but so did the pollution—in New York City, Buffalo, Syracuse, and municipalities around the nation.

NUCLEAR THREATS

Even as the Committee for Smoke Control worked to improve air quality in the city, New Yorkers gained a new atmospheric threat. A decade of testing nuclear weapons in the arms race between the Soviet Union and the United States had polluted the entire globe with strontium 90, a radioactive isotope created during hydrogen bomb explosions. Scientists first raised the alarm about strontium 90 in 1956, claiming that the isotope could be found in the nation's milk supply. Americans were justifiably horrified, particularly mothers with children who consumed lots of milk and, of course, dairy farmers, who couldn't afford another threat to their industry. Among those who took action was Florence Loozis, of New Hyde Park, who wrote to the *Times* to express concern about giving milk to her children, asking, "Am I giving them a cancer-producing substance which will accumulate in their bones and bring on this dread disease in twenty years?" Loozis also concluded that the nonchalance of the Atomic Energy Commission left "the average citizen in a state of fear and perplexity and shakes his confidence in Government." By the time Loozis wrote her letter, scientists were regularly checking the strontium levels in milk, which fluctuated with the seasons and the test explosions of bombs in the American West, the Pacific Ocean, and Siberia. After more than a year of such reporting, another "Worried Mother" wrote the *Times* about her anxiety, noting that "experts" could not even agree on safe levels of strontium. Together these two letter writers captured not only the special fear felt by mothers feeding milk to their children but also a growing distrust of both the government and technology. This distrust became a hallmark of modern environmentalism.

By the early 1960s an organized movement to end atmospheric testing had developed around the strontium threat. In New York the Scientists' Committee for Radiation Information, founded at the Rockefeller Institute, gave free presentations on atomic radiation, educating the public at a variety of forums. Another organization, Women Strike for Peace, founded in Washington, D.C., staged demonstrations at the United Nations in New York City, with monthly marches growing to 3,500 participants. Together the education of the public and the public demonstrations, two additional hallmarks of the modern environmental movement, helped force the superpowers into the Limited Test Ban Treaty in 1963, which ended Soviet and U.S. atmospheric tests.

Fear of radioactive fallout subsided after the passage of the treaty, but the consequences of nuclear technology remained a concern, especially in connection to nuclear power plants, several of which were planned for New York. Postwar industrial growth strained the state's electrical power supply. Demand was further intensified by demographic growth and a consumer culture that featured numerous energy-intensive products, such as television sets, refrigerators, washers and dryers, and, most important, air conditioners. Power companies scrambled to plan and build sufficient generating facilities, but public activism concerning air pollution sent them in search of better power sources, not sooty coal-burning plants. Although power companies couldn't develop hydroelectric facilities on a large scale, the state could. The New York Power Authority, created by Franklin Roosevelt in 1931, opened two massive hydroelectric plants in the postwar era, one at the St. Lawrence Seaway project in Massena in 1958, and another three years later at Niagara Falls. One of the world's largest hydroelectric facilities, the Niagara Power Project would have made the quixotic visionary King Gillette proud. The structure used water redirected from the Niagara River to power turbines at the appropriately titled Moses Generating Station, named for that other visionary Robert Moses, who had a hand in both of the hydroelectric installations. Although the Niagara facility diminished the flow over the falls, complaints about aesthetics were drowned out by praise for the pollution-free power. Hydropower couldn't bring social equality in the way Gillette had hoped, but it could at least help keep Niagara's air cleaner during the postwar economic expansion.

Since the state's private power companies couldn't increase supply through hydroelectric development, they turned to a variety of other facilities, including nuclear plants. In 1963 Niagara Mohawk announced plans to build a nuclear plant on the upper Hudson, across the river from the Saratoga National Historic Park, which celebrated the turning point in the American Revolution by offering visitors a chance to stand overlooking the beautiful and strategic Hudson River. Historians and other concerned citizens, including many who worried about the consequences for the river itself, successfully battled against the plan, which Niagara Mohawk dropped in 1968.

At the same time, another battle raged on Cayuga Lake, where New York State Electric and Gas Corporation (NYSEG) hoped to build a nuclear plant. Just twelve miles from Ithaca, the proposed plant attracted extraordinary attention from scientists at Cornell University. Ecologists argued that the nuclear plant would pollute Cayuga by heating the water, thereby changing the lake's nutrient levels and sparking the growth of aquatic plants, a process called eutrophication. Concerned citizens, including Cornell faculty, created the Committee to Save Cayuga Lake, which quickly gained hundreds of members and the support of other organizations, including sporting groups. NYSEG, based in Ithaca, couldn't overcome this organized opposition, which worked to educate the public about the threat of eutrophication with publications, lectures, and open hearings. NYSEG postponed its plans indefinitely in April 1969 and never renewed efforts to build a nuclear plant on Cayuga. Cornell responded to the debate by creating a new Science, Technology, and Society program, which provided faculty and students a structure within which similar issues could be studied and debated in the future.

STORM KING

Cayuga Lake was spared a nuclear plant, but New York State was not. Consolidated Edison had opened Indian Point in 1962, a nuclear plant along the Hudson River. Con Ed eventually built three reactors at Indian Point, but ongoing protests about fish kills in the Hudson caused by the plant's intake and discharge of river water for cooling purposes, combined with fears of nuclear disaster, convinced the company that nuclear power alone could not meet growing demand. The same year that Indian Point began operations, Con Ed announced plans for the world's largest pumped storage facility across the river at Cornwall. There, at a massive rock face that plunged into the Hudson, Con

Ed would pump the river's brackish water up and through the mountain—Storm King—to a reservoir. When demand spiked—during summer days, for example—the water would be released to generate power. Since electricity would be required to pump the water up the mountain, the new plant would create no net power, but the facility would make additional plants unnecessary by allowing Con Ed to cover peak demand through existing generating capacity. With its many coal-fired plants, including a particularly obtrusive steam plant along the East River in midtown Manhattan, Con Ed was New York City's largest polluter, and the Storm King project was part of its effort to increase electricity production without increasing emissions in the city.

Most Cornwall residents supported the Con Ed plan because the plant would bring jobs and tax revenue, and because the company promised to build a new riverfront park atop rock spoils from tunnels dug through the mountain. The Storm King proposal sparked immediate protest, however, from conservation organizations concerned about Hudson River scenery and historic landscapes. The project would scar Storm King itself and, at least in its initial incarnation, require the building of huge transmission towers that would mar even more of the Highlands' beauty. To battle the proposed plant, activists gathered at the home of Carl Carmer, who had written the volume on the Hudson River in the "Rivers of America" series in 1939. That 1963 gathering included Leo Rothschild, from the New York–New Jersey Trail Conference; Walter Boardman, executive director of the Nature Conservancy; and Harry Neese of the Sierra Club. The group decided to call their collaboration Scenic Hudson Preservation Conference.

Scenic Hudson hoped to block Con Ed's plan by persuading the Federal Power Commission not to issue a permit, largely on the basis of inevitable aesthetic damage. The FPC held public hearings, including two days of testimony at the Bear Mountain Inn and five days in Washington, D.C. At the latter hearings in 1964, Carmer offered his defense of the Hudson, emphasizing the historic importance of the river, and especially the scenery, which had long inspired great art and, he noted, continued to do so. Supporters of the power plant argued that it represented the march of progress, but Carmer questioned a definition of progress that included marring such a place. Instead, Carmer argued, "progress is made when the people preserve their inheritance of scenic, historic and recreational values." Carmer poetically captured a growing environmentalist sentiment, one that linked historic and natural preservation in an effort to control growth and limit the damaging effects of development, especially around expanding cities. "There is ominous talk along the Hudson today," he warned, "talk from self-appointed oracles who declare the march of cities inevitable. In only a few years, we are told, the City of New York may stride like a wild irresistible monster in mile by mile steps up the Great River of the Mountains. Soon the clamor of machines may be echoing from the Palisades—soon the noiseless deeps below the peaceful highlands may be sucked into the maw of the city." Clearly Carmer knew that more than just Con Ed's plans threatened to transform the Hudson Valley.

Despite Carmer's vivid testimony, the FPC seemed inclined to support the new plant. Each hearing, however, brought new publicity, increasing awareness of the impact this facility would have on a beloved landscape. In turn, opposition grew. More activists, even beyond New York, came to believe, as Carmer did, "that all of America stands at a crossroads and that the Hudson, being what it is, should be the spear-point of the national drive against all agencies that would separate our people from their love of the American landscape as it has always been." When the FPC did grant the permit, Scenic Hudson sued, claiming that the commission had ignored or excluded relevant environmental and historical evidence.

In its ruling in *Scenic Hudson v. Federal Power Commission,* the United States Court of Appeals, Second Circuit, agreed that federal law required the FPC to hear complete testimony, noting, among other things, that the commission had failed to make a study of alternatives to Storm King. The court also agreed that the Hudson Highlands had "unique beauty" and "major historical significance," and indeed that this stretch of the Hudson offered "one of the finest pieces of river scenery in the world." In addition to sending the issue back before the FPC, the court established the right of Scenic Hudson to sue in the matter, noting that the group easily qualified as an "aggrieved party." Significantly, the court justified the public's interest in protecting the river by quoting Theodore Roosevelt, who as president vetoed a bill that would have granted water power sites to private interests. Roosevelt had supported the development of water power, but he was wary of monopoly. In another passage quoted by the court, Roosevelt emphasized that government agencies had an obligation to "coordinate the points of view of all users of waters." Henceforth, according to *Scenic Hudson,* the environmentalist point of view had legal standing, an outcome that allowed the flowering of environmental law and by itself ensured the lasting significance of the Storm King battle.

Following court orders, the FPC reopened hearings in 1966 and took new testimony, not just on the historic and scenic value of the region but also concerning fish stocks in the river. Incredibly, in supporting the Storm King plant again two years later, an FPC examiner claimed that there was no evidentiary support of the argument that "these installations would scar and change scenic values associated with the mountain." After a delay caused by New York City's concern that the Storm King plant would compromise the nearby Catskill Aqueduct, in 1970 the FPC finally granted a license for the plant, sparking another lawsuit from Scenic Hudson. This time, however, the court found that the FPC had adequately considered alternatives and heard extensive testimony concerning natural resources and natural beauty. Therefore the license stood. Fortunately for opponents, however, the battle had lasted so long, the publicity had been so great, and opposition had grown so strong that Con Ed had lost state and municipal support. The company finally abandoned its Storm King plan in 1980.

Opposition to Storm King spanned the development of the environmental movement, and the diversity of people lined up against Con Ed revealed the growing diversity of environmentalism. Wealthy conservationists, including Laurance Rockefeller, spoke out against the plan, as did radical activists such as folk singer Pete Seeger. In 1969 Seeger launched a Hudson River sloop, *Clearwater,* which has since plied the Hudson offering education about the river's ecology, history, and continuing environmental threats. Another prominent opponent was Robert Boyle, a journalist who published early environmentalist pieces in *Sports Illustrated.* An avid angler, Boyle helped create the Hudson River Fishermen's Association in 1966, hoping to alert the FPC to potential fisheries damage that would be caused by the water intake system at Storm King. In 1983, after the Storm King threat had finally passed, the Fishermen's Association created the Riverkeeper program, and eventually the groups became one, under the latter title. The Hudson Riverkeeper watched over the Hudson, alert for pollution and other threats to the river's ecology. The organization served as a model for dozens of others around the country, including those in Puget Sound, Casco Bay, and San Diego. All of these Keepers adopted regional approaches to their environmental problems, basing their action on ecological knowledge, another hallmark of the evolving environmental movement.

The Riverkeepers represent a significant, lasting institutional result of the Storm King battle, but perhaps not the most significant. Two of the lawyers in the battle against Con Ed, Stephen Duggan and Whitney North Seymour Jr., continued their work on environmental issues after their Storm King appeals were exhausted. In early 1970 they hired John Adams, a New York City–based lawyer, as the foundation of a new legal organization called National Resources Defense Council (NRDC). Under Adams's leadership the NRDC became a leading force in environmental law, especially active in securing the Clean Water Act in 1971, which allowed citizens to sue polluters to force abatement. This was precisely the type of suit the NRDC hoped to encourage. The NRDC went on to address dozens of important issues, from phasing out leaded gasoline to protecting the ozone layer from chlorofluorocarbons. Together Scenic Hudson, the Riverkeepers, and the NRDC reveal the critical importance of public interest groups in environmental protection in the 1960s and beyond. This marked a shift in environmental politics. Although expertise—especially in science and law—continued to hold special sway in the policy arena, the second half of the twentieth century witnessed a growing role for average citizens. Citizen activism, especially as organized through interest groups like those that saved Storm King, lay at the heart of the environmental movement.

LONG ISLAND AND DDT

NRDC wasn't the only environmental organization to develop around legal challenges and ecology in New York. Citizen concern over the widespread aerial spraying of DDT by government agencies sparked legal action as early as 1957, when New York prepared to participate in a three-state effort to control the spread of the gypsy moth, an invasive species that had been slowly moving west from its accidental release in Massachusetts. Gypsy moth caterpillars can infest hundreds of acres of forest, denude them of leaves, and threaten tree health. Before the spraying could begin, however, several residents of suburban Long Island first complained about and then sued over the plan, which involved spraying thousands of acres in residential communities that probably had no gypsy moths. One of the plaintiffs was a dairy farmer, who worried about milk tainted with DDT; another was an organic farmer, who wondered why the government should have the power to dose her land with chemicals she would never use herself. A federal judge denied a temporary injunction, however, and the spraying began in a twenty-five-mile zone that reached from the Adirondacks to Long Island. Despite this setback, the court case persisted. Plaintiffs could now demonstrate damages from DDT, one of several persistent chlorinated hydrocarbons used as pesticides in the postwar era. Sometimes used in shockingly large quantities over great expanses of crops and forests, these pesticides were eventually linked to human health problems and, more immediately, to ecological disruption, especially declining bird populations.

Meanwhile, state and federal agriculture officials had faith in the ability of DDT to eradicate gypsy moths, assuming that aerial spraying across a wide swath of land would remove the pests. The utility of DDT had been demonstrated during World War II, when the military used it to control the spread of lice-borne disease, apparently with no adverse effects on humans. In addition, the war supplied scientists with the language they would use in "the battle" against gypsy moths. The moths had made a "bulge" across the Hudson, and had to be "pushed back," according to an oft-used metaphor. Eradication of the "evil enemy" was necessary for "victory." In this battle, scientists expected a certain amount of collateral damage, including fish kills—which officials tried to keep to a minimum—and the destruction of other insect life, including honeybees. One of the plaintiffs against the state's spraying was Robert Murphy, a former curator at the Museum of Natural History, who claimed that biological control would be more effective than chemicals. Proponents of spraying countered that control was inferior to eradication, and only massive pesticide use could bring about the latter. The government needed total victory.

Human health became an issue in the case, heard in the U.S. District Court in 1958, but as the judge noted, only one living physician in the country had "engaged in experimental work as to the effect that DDT has on human beings." Rather than finding that so little evidence could not prove the chemical's safety, the judge instead noted that the defendants could not claim that the DDT had made them ill. (The potential long-term consequences of spraying did not trouble the judge.) Despite the anecdotal testimony of physicians from around the country, the judge determined that DDT was indeed safe for humans when used in the quantities sprayed on Long Island.

Murphy and his fellow petitioners lost the court case, but not before appealing it all the way to the Supreme Court, where Justice William O. Douglas issued a dissent that questioned the claim that the spraying had caused no damages to the defendants. The dairy farmer's cows continued to deliver DDT-tainted milk five months after the spraying, and both federal and state law prohibited the sale of milk that contained any trace of DDT. Another claimant had spent considerable money turning her land into an organic farm, only to have the government fly over her property and spray it with the pesticide. Two other claimants complained about dead fish and birds. All of this caused Douglas to wonder how previous judges could have found that there were no damages. He concluded, "The need for adequate findings on the effect of DDT is of vital concern not only to wildlife conservationists and owners of domestic animals but to all who drink milk or eat food from sprayed gardens." After this case Douglas went on to become the most famous environmentalist to sit on the Supreme Court.

In writing his dissent in the Long Island case, Douglas cited an essay that had appeared a year before in the *Washington Post* written by Rachel Carson, in which she described the dangers of DDT, especially to birds. That piece, combined with the evidence from Long Island, clearly raised concerns for Douglas about DDT. Still, the Long Island plaintiffs were unable to stop the widespread use of chlorinated hydrocarbons, even in Nassau County. The situation changed dramatically with the publication of Carson's fuller exploration of the dangers of DDT under the title *Silent Spring*. With the encouragement of E. B. White, Carson's work appeared first in serial form in the *New Yorker* in June 1962. Carson, a trained biologist, had gathered together anecdotal evidence about powerful, persistent pesticides, such as DDT, dieldrin, and heptachlor. Her elegant and urgent writing both tapped into and fostered anxiety about modern technology and distrust of experts. *Silent Spring* inspired growing numbers of people to question whether heavy pesticide use was in the public interest.

In addition, scientists increasingly began to wonder whether the benefits of pesticide use outweighed the costs, or even if the costs and benefits could ever be fully accounted. Three of the scientists raising questions were George M. Woodwell of the Brookhaven National Laboratory, and Charles Wurster and Robert Smolker of the State University at Stony Brook, who joined with other concerned citizens to create the Brookhaven Town Natural Resources Committee in 1965. This group might have remained unknown to history, except that it joined forces with a Long Island lawyer named Victor Yannaconne. In 1966 Yannaconne's wife, Carol, became concerned about the effect of DDT on Yaphank Lake, which had experienced fish kills after the Suffolk County Mosquito Control Commission (MCC) dumped in thousands of gallons of DDT solution to kill larvae. Using the scientists as his expert witnesses and his wife as the plaintiff, Yannacone sued the MCC, a case that took the name *Yannacone v. Dennison*. Yannacone argued that the MCC, employed to kill mosquitoes, was actually killing much, much more. In his testimony before the court, Wurster compared using DDT to kill mosquitoes to using atomic bombs to fight crime. After hearing the evidence, the judge determined that "it is reasonably apparent that DDT is capable of and actually has to some extent caused extraordinary damage to the resources of this county," particularly by reducing wildlife. In fact the MCC admitted this point, but argued that the benefits of reducing the mosquito population outweighed the costs imposed by DDT. In the end, the judge decided that collateral deaths were acceptable in the war against mosquitoes.

Technically the Yannacones lost this battle, though the MCC soon decided to stop using DDT because of the negative publicity. More important, the organization Victor Yannaconne helped create with scientists on Long Island, which took the name Environmental Defense Fund in 1967, eventually won the war against DDT when the Environmental Protection Agency banned it, along with several other chlorinated hydrocarbons, in 1972. The long effort to end the use of persistent pesticides had another lasting consequence as well: the establishment of the Environmental Defense Fund as another prominent national environmental interest group. The Environmental Defense Fund, now called Environmental Defense, took up a series of important issues in the 1970s, including acid rain, which revealed the advantage of bringing science and law together to force better government regulation of the environment.

PLANNING AND THE QUIET REVOLUTION

Interest group activism transformed politics in the postwar decades, but government itself underwent changes, continuing the trend toward greater regulatory authority. New planning bodies sprouted around the state, many of them with considerable powers to shape future land use. In 1971, writing for a new federal office, the Council on Environmental Quality, Fred Bosselman and David Callies described this growing trend as, in the words of the title of their report, *The Quiet Revolution in Land Use Control*. In part this was a governmental response to rapid growth, especially along urban fringes. But perhaps in greater part it was a response to the increasingly important role of the automobile in shaping this growth—the low-density, high-acreage demands for transportation infrastructure and requisite parking. By the 1950s planners had accumulated effective tools such as zoning, had acquired access to new technologies such as limited-access highways, and had gained new authority in the state. Urban and suburban problems were accumulating, and planners were among those who claimed to have solutions. There were two different sides to postwar planning. In the countryside there was an effort to control growth with old tools—especially zoning—to diminish sprawl and encourage the preservation of scenic views, open space, and agriculture. In the city, planning devolved largely into a set of traffic and parking solutions.

In 1959 Governor Nelson Rockefeller praised the foresight of the state, and the activism of Robert Moses, in creating state parks for its growing urban population, but more was needed. "In our own lifetime," he remarked, "we have seen lands and waters around our cities engulfed by construction and preempted for outdoor recreation at an astonishing rate. Many areas which should have been reserved for public parks and recreation are already gone forever." He claimed that only a bold stroke could save remaining resources. Rockefeller's bold stroke was a $75 million bond for the state's purchase of new recreation lands. "Simply stated, our people need more outdoor living space—and wise, far-sighted provisions must be made for it," he declared while commemorating the creation of the state parks system at Jones Beach. To develop support for the bond act, Rockefeller initiated a recreation survey. Not surprisingly, that survey noted the rapidly increasing use of state facilities and recommended passage of the bond proposition, which occurred in 1960. Of the $75 million, $35 million was set aside for state purchases, while $40 million was allocated to cities, counties, and towns for local parks. Among the many parcels purchased with the funds were Prince's Bay and Pleasant Plains parks on Staten Island and the Catskill Mountain House property in the Catskills, where the old hotel sat in ruins, perched above the Hudson. Since this bond issue was such a great success—and the money was spent so quickly—in March 1962 Rockefeller supported another bond issue, of $25 million, which the state's voters passed that November.

Expanding state and local park systems could not solve all the problems caused by sprawling growth, of course, and New Yorkers hoped that planning and zoning could offer protection. Regional planning was particularly important in the Hudson Valley. In 1966 New York State created the Hudson River Valley Commission, which had several goals, including the rather ambitious objective of encouraging "all beneficial uses of the lands and waters of the Hudson Riverway including, but not limited to, commercial, industrial, and other economic development consistent with the preservation and rehabilitation of the natural, scenic, historical, and recreational resources of the Hudson Riverway." In other words, the commission would encourage any development that wouldn't alter the Hudson Valley. By May 1967 the commission was at work, attempting to develop a comprehensive plan for the Hudson River Valley. In addition, the commission was empowered to review any project within one mile of the shore of the river or within two miles of the shore and visible from the Hudson. Any project that would destroy historic or recreational resources or change the appearance or use of the water in the Hudson River or the surrounding land would be subject to review and public hearings, a hallmark of 1960s politics. The commission's geographical scope—limited by visibility—confirms that its primary concerns were aesthetic rather than ecological.

Not strictly an environmental body, the commission was designed to be a conservative force in the valley. The interdisciplinary staff of the commission revealed the complexity of its task and the complexity of modern environmentalism's goals. On staff were urban and regional planners, architects, landscape architects, engineers, geographers, economists, an ecologist, an organic chemist, a sociologist, and specialists in public administration and municipal finance. Altogether the commission and its review process provided yet another means through which residents could express their own ideas about what their communities should be, how they should change, and how they should not. Unfortunately, the commission was broken upon the shoals of the Storm King controversy when it was caught between Governor Rockefeller's support for the power plant and the environmental community's overwhelming opposition. The commission became a target of environmentalists, ensuring that it would be short-lived and relatively ineffective.

The battle against sprawl spread throughout New York, as the construction of residential subdivisions and expansive retail centers fanned fears that agriculture would slowly but surely disappear from the state. As shopping plazas popped up on former farm fields and new residential streets curved through former pastures, some New Yorkers began to lament the changes to the landscape. Rural residents worried about the encroaching city; suburban residents complained about the loss of the open space that farms provided—one of the amenities that had drawn them to the suburbs in the first place. Some farmers feared that they simply couldn't continue farming in areas where property values were rising in the face of suburban demand.

In the hope of protecting the farm economy—and agricultural landscapes—the state established the Commission on the Preservation of Agricultural Land in 1966. Over the next several years the state devised policies to aid farmers, especially through tax relief. The most important step came in 1971, with the development of the agricultural district concept, designed to give a variety of help to farmers who wanted to continue farming. These districts, created at the local level and initiated by interested farmers, functioned as special tax zones, in which large landowners could be taxed at a much lower rate if they kept their lands in agricultural uses. Although farmers created these districts around the state, they are particularly common in the counties just north of New York City, where property values and tax assessments are high and development pressures are intense.

Sprawling development threatened more than just the state's farmland. Even more powerful preservation movements gathered to protect the Adirondacks and Catskills, where new subdivisions of second homes threatened to alter both the culture and the environment in the mountains. In 1968 Governor Rockefeller initiated a Temporary Study Commission on the Future of the Adirondacks, followed by a similar commission for the Catskills. One of the recommendations of the Temporary Commission was the creation of a permanent body to address issues in the Adirondacks. The legislature created this body, the Adirondack Park Agency (APA), in 1971, which immediately undertook a major planning initiative. At the time the state owned just 40 percent of the land in the Adirondacks, so planning required accounting of both private and public lands. The first planning document was the State Land Master Plan, completed in 1972, in which the APA recommended the creation of new classifications for all state lands determined by use and characteristics.

The most important of these classifications was wilderness, which was defined as land that contained neither roads nor buildings and, if the wilderness designation passed, would never contain them. For twenty years the state had been debating how to deal with the growing intrusion of motorized vehicles in the Adirondacks—from jeeps and other four-wheel-drive vehicles to motorboats. In 1959 the Legislative Committee on Natural Resources began a study of all Forest Preserve lands with the goal of determining which might be "reserved solely for wilderness recreation," and "through which people who are harassed by modern tensions can obtain the quiet and solitude they so badly need." This effort to set aside wilderness was part of a nationwide reaction to the intrusion of the automobile and other motorized vehicles in otherwise protected lands. As committee chairman R. Watson Pomeroy summarized in 1961 as he worked to pass a state law authorizing the creation of wilderness areas in the Forest Preserves, "If the unique natural qualities which these areas now possess are to be preserved unspoiled for the enjoyment of future generations, they must be protected against the depredations caused by modern motorized transportation devices."

The state's efforts to create wilderness protection sparked considerable opposition, especially from Adirondack locals who feared that stiffer preservation would further limit economic development. Among those who protested the wilderness proposal was Gerald Hull, president of the Oval Wood Dish Corporation in Tupper Lake. Hull complained that the wilderness provision would prevent all but a small minority of New Yorkers from making good use of the Forest Preserve. He found an ally in Robert Moses, who had long expressed opposition to wilderness preservation. Since the 1940s Moses had worked repeatedly, and unsuccessfully, to amend the state constitution to allow recreational development on Forest Preserve lands. As Moses had declared in 1947, "The average city family cannot live in any comfort in a leanto or hut, and a few days of rain and cold on the bare ground make them sick and miserable." Moses wanted the Forest Preserve opened to a larger number of New Yorkers, not kept remote and useless for all but "a handful of fanatics." Fourteen years later Moses had not changed his mind, calling the Pomeroy bill "the silliest piece of legislation I can remember" and complaining, "This is not a step toward zoning the Adirondacks, but an attempt to lock it up still tighter for imitation Indians and mountaineer Scouts." Local opposition to wilderness designations prevented the passage of the Pomeroy bill, but in 1964 Congress passed the Wilderness Act, fulfilling the dream of wilderness activist Bob Marshall. The subsequent establishment of wilderness areas in federally owned land was a great victory for wilderness advocates. But since the federal government owned no lands suitable for designation in New York, the state would have to create its own wilderness act to ensure similar protections of state lands.

Despite strong upstate opposition, wilderness protection remained on the state's agenda, supported by Paul Schaefer, a Schenectady resident who had developed a great love for the Adirondacks. Schaefer had also developed a strong friendship with Howard Zahniser, a leading figure in the Wilderness Society. Since 1946 Zahniser had summered in an Adirondack cabin with his family, and although he pursued a national agenda for wilderness, he and Schaefer became effective advocates for preservation in the Adirondacks. In the summer of 1972, eight years after Zahniser had been the principal author of the federal Wilderness Act, the creation of wilderness areas became a central feature of the State Land Master Plan for the Adirondacks. Although the plan established guidelines for all state lands in the Forest Preserve, its major accomplishment was the protection of over 1 million acres of the Adirondacks as wilderness, through which no roads would be built. These lands contained 748 bodies of

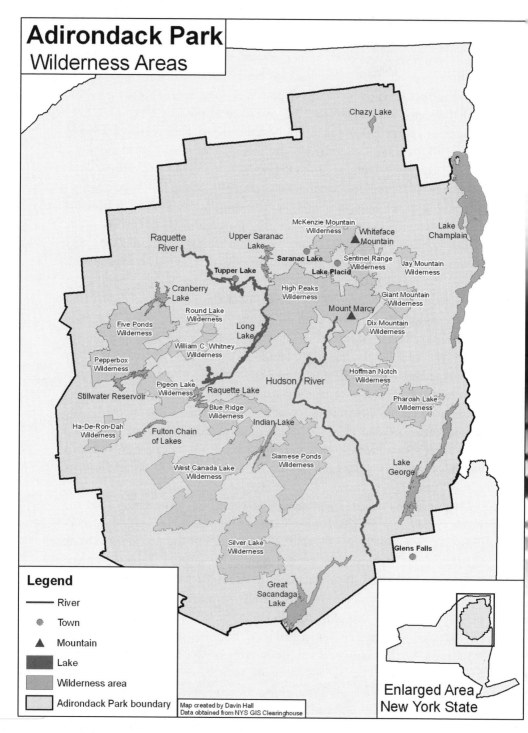

Adirondack Park
Wilderness Areas

Chazy Lake

McKenzie Mountain
Wilderness
Whiteface
Mountain

Raquette
River

Upper Saranac
Lake

Lake
Champlain

Saranac Lake

Sentinel Range
Wilderness

Jay Mountain
Wilderness

Tupper Lake

Lake Placid

Cranberry
Lake

High Peaks
Wilderness

Giant Mountain
Wilderness

Round Lake
Wilderness

Mount Marcy

Five Ponds
Wilderness

Long
Lake

Dix Mountain
Wilderness

William C. Whitney
Wilderness

Pepperbox
Wilderness

Pigeon Lake
Wilderness

Raquette Lake

Hudson River

Hoffman Notch
Wilderness

Stillwater Reservoir

Blue Ridge
Wilderness

Indian Lake

Pharoah Lake
Wilderness

Ha-De-Ron-Dah
Wilderness

Fulton Chain
of Lakes

West Canada Lake
Wilderness

Siamese Ponds
Wilderness

Lake
George

Silver Lake
Wilderness

Glens Falls

Great
Sacandaga
Lake

Legend

— River

● Town

▲ Mountain

■ Lake

Wilderness area

Adirondack Park boundary

Map created by Davin Hall
Data obtained from NYS GIS Clearinghouse

Enlarged Area
New York State

Beginning in 1972 the State Land Master Plan set aside wilderness areas in the Adirondacks.
Today eighteen wilderness areas cover more than a million acres in the Adirondack Park.

water, on which no motorboats could be used. Fittingly, many of these bodies of water were in the Five Ponds Wilderness south of Cranberry Lake, the former stomping grounds of Bob Marshall. The largest wilderness area included the High Peaks south of Lake Placid, covering nearly 200,000 acres. In addition to protecting these Adirondack lands, the state eventually set aside four wilderness areas in the Catskills, totaling nearly 120,000 acres, much of it around Slide and Panther mountains. More than three hundred years after European colonization began and more than a hundred since Natty Bumppo lamented the passing of New York's wilderness, the state set aside sizable tracts for permanent protection.

URBAN PLANNING, HIGHWAYS, AND HISTORIC PRESERVATION

While the protection of wilderness and open space ruled rural planning in the postwar decades, decentralization remained the watchword in city planning. Since planners still considered congestion at the urban core the fundamental flaw of cities, they attempted to pull cities apart. The construction of new highways could allow commutes over long distances and, as a bonus, enable cities to destroy problematic neighborhoods as acres of limited-access highways replaced acres of degraded housing. In 1951 Robert Moses, still at work shaping New York City and beyond, wrote an essay in aid of the city's effort to develop a civil defense plan, which appeared in the *New York Times Magazine*. Moses also published the essay as a pamphlet, containing the epigraph "Traffic Relief: A vital necessity, bombs or no bombs, to safeguard our lives and to make the city function." In other words, saving the city would require better management of automobiles, whether the Soviets attacked or not.

Moses had already laced the region with highways, but he had many more to build. Among his proposals was a Midtown Expressway that would cut across Manhattan mostly above grade just south of Penn Station and the Lincoln Tunnel. He claimed that this was the only way to deal with congestion, save perhaps "demolition of half the buildings and drastic limits on future construction." Moses also hoped to transform the dense neighborhood of Williamsburg, Brooklyn, and his pamphlet included a dramatic image of the yet-to-be-built Brooklyn-Queens Expressway running through a massive renewal project, looking very much like Le Corbusier's towers in a garden, the quintessential modern vision of efficient urban life.

Moses built many expressways and parkways, but not all of the highways he supported came into existence. A powerful anti-highway movement developed in New York, beginning with a long battle in the 1950s to protect Washington Square Park from a sunken roadway that would ease north-south traffic but divide the park. Moses envisioned this roadway as part of a broader remaking of the neighborhood south of the park. He hoped to remove the existing housing and replace it with new, taller buildings, along the lines of Stuyvesant Village, where a series of apartment towers had been set among landscaped lawns. This road through Washington Square was also intended to connect with the proposed Lower Manhattan Expressway, which had been in the works since 1940. Moses underestimated the opposition that would build in Manhattan as he dreamed up better traffic flows around and through the island—opposition that caught fire in Greenwich Village under the leadership of average residents, like Shirley Hayes, a mother of four who hoped to protect Washington Square, and who eventually helped improve it dramatically. Hayes led the Washington Square Committee, a group that also garnered support from Jane Jacobs, who began to develop planning ideas nearly diametric to those of Moses and other modernists who envisioned an auto-centric city filled with characterless towers set in small patches of grass and larger patches of parking.

In 1961, with the fate of many of Moses's highway projects still undetermined, Jacobs published an influential critique of postwar planning orthodoxy, to great effect. *The Death and Life of Great American Cities* revealed how destructive decentralizing planning had been to large cities, including New York City. Ideal urban neighborhoods, Jacobs thought, looked much like her own Greenwich Village—bustling with diverse populations, laced with active sidewalks and narrow streets. Green space was limited, but the street life was vibrant. Jacobs lovingly described the "ballet" of sidewalk movement on Hudson Street, where residents, workers, and visitors kept the rich urban neighborhood alive and, most important in this era, safe. According to Jacobs, planners had it all wrong when they attempted to segregate uses and demolished older, dense blocks and replaced them with towers surrounded by grass. She argued that "the rebuilt portions of cities and the endless new developments spreading beyond the cities are reducing city and countryside alike to monotonous, unnourishing gruel," all of it derived from "the same intellectual dish of mush."

What Jacobs expressed was just part of a growing anti-highway sentiment. As planning for an expressway linking the Holland Tunnel and the Williamsburg Bridge gained momentum in the 1960s, it also gained opposition from the

Joint Committee to Stop the Lower Manhattan Expressway. Public opposition developed as well against the proposed elevated Mid-Manhattan Expressway, which Moses hoped would connect the Lincoln and Queens-Midtown tunnels. With growing opposition and soaring price tags, political support for these projects waned, especially after Moses lost influence during Nelson Rockefeller's administration. By the 1970s both projects were officially dead. Of course, New York did get its share of new highways, some of them partially funded by the federal government through the Interstate Highway Act, passed in 1956. Among the most important—and the most disruptive—was the Cross Bronx Expressway, constructed between 1948 and 1963. The building of the Cross Bronx may have seemed necessary to some people—especially planners. To thousands of Bronx residents, however, including many in the East Tremont neighborhood, it undoubtedly seemed like the purposeful demolition of their homes and neighborhoods. Although it clearly wasn't the only cause of problems in the borough, the Bronx declined precipitously during and after the construction of the expressway.

Other urban highways did not displace as many residents as the Cross Bronx, but many were remarkably disruptive of the urban environment—adding noise, air pollution, and physical barriers to what were in some cases already deteriorating areas. In Buffalo, for example, engineers ran the Niagara section of the New York State Thruway, designated I-190, between downtown and Lake Erie. The highway continued north along the Niagara River for several miles, diminishing the value of the river as a recreational asset to Buffalo's northern neighborhoods. In Syracuse, I-690 passes along the shore of Onondaga Lake and through the heart of the city, where the elevated roadway is a physical barrier and an eyesore. Perhaps the most obtrusive urban highway, however, is Albany's I-787, constructed in stages from 1965 to 1985. It gave drivers excellent access to downtown from Interstates 87 and 90, but it also separated the entire city from the Hudson River, and it filled valuable urban acres with tangles of interchanges. Today Albany is a stunning example of urban planners' priorities in the second half of the twentieth century. Automobiles had to be accommodated. Even small cities struggled with increasing traffic, and no solution seemed ideal. In Poughkeepsie, for example, the introduction of one-way traffic and the widening of several downtown streets may have improved traffic flow, but it also made being in the center of town very uncomfortable for pedestrians.

Planners often coupled highway construction with urban renewal projects that brought even more demolition to New York's cities. Albany again provides the most striking example. In the early 1960s the state began clearing ninety-eight acres of central Albany to make way for the Empire State Plaza. By the time it was completed fourteen years and $2 billion later, the plaza had long since become a symbol of government inefficiency and hubris. It had also become emblematic of modern architecture's propensity to forget about human needs and desires in an urban setting. In the huge open mall even the trees were planted in concrete boxes and pruned into squares, creating a sterile atmosphere that was neither urban nor natural. The mall was punctuated by oddly shaped buildings, every surface seemingly covered in marble or poured concrete. In appraising the plaza in the *New York Times*, Paul Goldberger noted that it appeared to be of "the planet Krypton" rather than New York State. If the mall seemed out of place (and out of time), it had also obliterated a broad swath of the city, not just by so completely removing what had come before, but by creating a space that didn't work the way cities traditionally had. The new highways were connected directly to an enormous parking garage under the mall, meaning, as Goldberger noted, "that every mall occupant can live out the suburban dream of never having to set foot on a city street." Certainly the plaza had its supporters and its successes, such as a new performance space affectionately called "the Egg," but mostly what the state had built was a monument to the anti-urban thinking that dominated modernist architecture and to the adage that power corrupts.

By the time the Empire State Plaza was finally completed, protests against large-scale urban renewal projects had slowed the damage around the state. For decades planners had included demolition among their most powerful weapons against urban blight, and since the 1930s they had removed entire blocks and replaced them with public housing or redevelopment projects such as Lincoln Center, built in stages in the 1960s. At first, aside from those who got displaced, few people protested against urban renewal demolitions, knowing that these were mostly failed buildings in failed neighborhoods. But the pace of demolition picked up in the postwar era, and more than just troubled housing faced the wrecking ball. In 1964 Pennsylvania Station, one of the city's great landmark buildings, was demolished to make way for a new Madison Square Garden.

The combined loss of spectacular individual buildings like Penn Station and the ongoing loss of entire neighborhoods through urban renewal and highway construction sparked a broad movement to save landmarks and the urban fabric. As Jane Jacobs noted in her critique of planning orthodoxy, "Cities need old buildings so badly it is probably impossible for vigorous streets and districts to grow without them." A year after the loss of Penn Station, New York City created the Landmarks Preservation Commission, granting it considerable power to protect even privately owned buildings from demolition. The commission could also create historic districts, where the entire urban fabric could be protected. Many historic preservation societies predated the postwar era, including the Landmark Society of Western New York, created in 1937 to preserve one of Rochester's great Greek Revival mansions, but the preservation movement became much more influential in the 1960s. Rochester, for example, established its first historic district, along East Avenue, in 1969, after years of hard work by the Landmark Society. Although the movement for historic preservation developed quite apart from the wilderness movement, they were intimately related; they were both largely a reaction to the destruction wrought by the remaking of landscapes to suit the automobile, even at the expense of fundamental human needs.

The evolving historic preservation movement was concerned with more than just saving old homes and spectacular edifices like Grand Central Terminal, which for a time also appeared destined for demolition. Historic preservationists also worked to retain the urban fabric, to protect streetscapes and neighborhood character. They worked to preserve historic sites as well, including the Saratoga Battlefield. In 1965, responding to calls to prevent the piecemeal removal of one of the state's great structures, New York began the process of creating the Old Erie Canal Historic Park, which preserved about a tenth of the canal, creating opportunities for hiking, biking, and other recreation, as well as public history sites, such as the Canastota Canal Town Museum.

EARTH DAY

The strength of the environmental movement became clear on April 22, 1970, the first Earth Day. Planned over the preceding months by the Washington-based Environmental Action Coalition, the nationwide teach-in included locally organized events from lectures to cleanups to protests. In Syracuse roughly five hundred people participated in a "Sludge Trudge," marching through downtown and demonstrating their concern for the environment. At the event Mayor Lee Alexander offered his analysis of how cars were ruining the city with air pollution, parking problems, and traffic. Elsewhere in the city, Students for a Livable Environment, a Syracuse University organization, led boat tours around Onondaga Lake, pointing out sources of pollution. In Manhattan, over the course of the day, perhaps 100,000 people passed through Union Square. Con Ed gave money in support of the events and handed out brooms and rakes to fourth graders organized for a cleanup, in the hope of diverting negative attention from the power company, then still engaged in the Storm King battle. That didn't dissuade a theater troupe from acting out a play on Fourteenth Street in which a bear awakens from hibernation to find a Con Ed nuclear plant outside his cave. Other activists linked improving the environment to ending the war in Vietnam; still others continued the call for civil rights for African Americans. Even as activists pushed their own agendas, the theme of the day's events was not lost. In a brief speech Mayor John Lindsay posed the question of the day: "Do we want to live or die?" Although critics continued to attack environmentalists for putting wild creatures or pristine nature ahead of the needs of people, this criticism missed the point altogether. As E. B. White had written eleven years earlier, the environmental crisis facing New Yorkers had to do with the earth's very habitability. Saving the planet was really about saving humanity.

Protests and speeches notwithstanding, the value of Earth Day emerged mostly through the demonstration of the power of collective action to make change. The environmental movement, still gathering momentum on that day, would rely on the work of interest groups, many of which had been created in New York, such as Riverkeepers, the Environmental Defense Fund, and the National Resources Defense Council. Other interest groups would come and go, like the Washington Square Committee that worked to protect the only significant open space in Greenwich Village, and the Committee to Save Cayuga Lake, which helped block the construction of a nuclear power plant. On Earth Day people gathered in all types of groups to do what they could, at least on that day. Four hundred members of Clearwater Crew cleaned up the boating lake in Central Park. All over the state, students from high schools cleaned up neighborhoods and parks. The Dalton School's Yorkville Environmental Protection Association led a "sweep-in" around Gracie Mansion, in which a hundred people participated. Students from Highlands Junior High School attended to the railroad station in White Plains. In Rockland County, students cleaned up the stream that runs through the village of Pearl River. Picking up trash and painting buildings were easy steps toward reversing the problems of litter and urban neglect. But much more complex problems loomed in the decades ahead, some of them lingering threats and some of them new.

7

We Live in This Filth

The Urban Crisis, Environmental Justice, and Threats from Beyond

In the spring of 1971 Mayor John Lindsay toured some of New York's most degraded neighborhoods with mayors from other cities. After seeing Brownsville in Brooklyn, Boston's Kevin White declared that the area "may be the first tangible sign of the collapse of civilization," a phrase that echoed the concerns of urban Progressive reformers seventy years earlier. Poverty concentrated in Brownsville as the middle-class fled, leaving behind a neighborhood of deteriorating housing, growing numbers of vacant buildings, and rubble-strewn lots. So many of the area's buildings were in such an obvious state of decay that Lindsay referred to the neighborhood as "Bombsville." Abandoned cars littered the neighborhood, along with broken appliances and discarded furniture. Residents complained of rats feasting on uncollected garbage along curbsides and in the basements of vacant buildings. One study found that 45 percent of children in the neighborhood suffered from lead poisoning. In 1970 one resident, standing before the local Black Panther Party headquarters, taunted a *New York Times* reporter: "We live in this filth. You don't and the politicians don't." Brownsville had become the poster child of the urban crisis.

The urban crisis and the environmental crisis had much in common, in both causes and effects. Although the postwar economy was booming, not all places fared well. Most new jobs appeared on the edges of cities, sometimes far from the neighborhoods that had the highest unemployment. Older factories shed workers or closed altogether. Cities that had taken growth for granted found

themselves shrinking for the first time in their history, with demographic con-
traction generally reflecting economic woes that would only deepen over time.
Decline was especially evident in upstate cities. Buffalo, Rochester, Syracuse,
Albany, Elmira, Binghamton, and Newburgh all reached their peak population
with the 1950 census. These seven cities combined lost almost half a million
residents over the next forty years, nearly 35 percent of their population. Other
cities fared even worse. Schenectady and Utica had both seen their population
peak in 1930, while Cohoes's had peaked in 1910.

This decline in urban population had many causes and, as New Yorkers would
gradually discover, many environmental consequences both in and outside of
cities. Declining industry left empty facilities and growing problems, many
associated with unutilized, deindustrialized parcels called *brownfields,* where
pollution played a significant role in preventing new investment. Even beyond
brownfields, industrial wastes, many of them toxic, proved increasingly troublesome, and they became a critical issue in evolving environmental politics. The
burdens of waste fell unevenly across the state's population, with minorities and
the poor experiencing more negative consequences, a fact that largely explains
the growing diversity within environmental activism in the 1960s and 1970s.
Once largely the province of the middle class, environmental politics now involved all types of New Yorkers.

THE UNLIVABLE CITY

The urban crisis deepened in the 1960s, fueled at least in part by the disorder associated with racial violence—the riots of the Long Hot Summers—and
increasing street crime, both of which further encouraged white flight from
large cities. No doubt many urban residents fled for environmental reasons, too,
as they had over the previous century. Air pollution had become an intractable
problem in much of urban America, in part because of unregulated automobile exhaust. In 1966 Syracuse began its air pollution control program, at first
tackling large polluters, including industry, which it hoped to move from dirty
coal to cleaner natural gas. That same year Mayor Lindsay appointed a new task
force on air pollution in New York City. It quickly issued a series of warnings
concerning both the chronic health consequences of bad air and the possibility that a temperature inversion, during which pollutants accumulated in the
region's still air, could cause a major disaster like the one that killed hundreds
in London in 1952.

In the following months the interconnectedness of so many of the city's problems came into focus. The city's air had deteriorated because the region had turned so fully toward automobile transportation; it couldn't end the use of terribly polluting incinerators for fear of garbage accumulating in densely populated neighborhoods; and it was demanding that Con Edison provide increasing amounts of electricity but from cleaner plants, while protests continued against the plan to build a nonpolluting hydroelectric plant at Storm King. The problems of air quality, transportation, sanitation, energy, and the preservation of natural scenery all flowed together in the accumulating smog over the Thanksgiving weekend of 1966. As the city warned people with lung and heart troubles to stay inside, it closed all eleven municipal incinerators, among the most polluting smokestacks in New York. As the smog thickened, the city asked residents to avoid unnecessary driving, a task made easier by the holiday weekend. Officials asked that apartment buildings stop incinerating trash, too. The excess garbage would be taken to the massive Fresh Kills landfill on Staten Island with the aid of forty scows working overtime. After the weather shifted and the smog cleared, a study found that 10 percent of city residents had experienced some ill effect from the pollution, be it stinging eyes, coughing, or difficulty breathing. A study of mortality over the course of the episode determined that the city had suffered 168 excess deaths attributable to the pollution.

One didn't have to be an ecologist to understand that the problems that plagued New York were all linked together. The age of abundance had given way to an age of unpopular choices. Lindsay, who served as mayor through some of New York's darkest moments, described a number of those choices in his 1969 book *The City*, noting, "You begin to recognize what may be the prime fact of municipal life—the essential interdependency of problems and solutions." As mayor, Lindsay struggled with several environmental problems, including air pollution, but he recognized the difficulty of taking on one problem at a time. "Every time you shut down an incinerator, you increase the amount of garbage on city streets," he wrote. But Lindsay understood that more than the environmental problems themselves were interconnected. So too were the urban and environmental crises. Environmental problems helped spur middle-class flight from the city, weakening municipal financial and human resources. At the same time, those who remained in the neighborhoods saw environmental problems, especially uncollected trash, as emblems of larger governmental neglect and social inequality. Solving the urban crisis would require solving environmental problems, making the city attractive again to the middle class and acceptable to all its residents.

Air pollution might best typify the filthy urban environments of the 1960s, but other issues also gained increasing attention. Lead poisoning in particular became emblematic of both the urban and environmental crises. Although the problems caused by lead paint had been discussed for decades, not until 1959 did New York outlaw those toxic products for indoor use. For more than a decade, however, that ban had a negligible impact, since many housepainters continued to use lead paint, even into the 1970s, and since old lead paint remained on walls throughout the city. In 1967 New York City alone had 642 reported cases of lead poisoning, mostly involving young children who had eaten paint chips and peeling plaster in their poorly maintained apartments. These were just the acute poisonings. One survey of children in the South Bronx led to an estimate that citywide, between nine thousand and eighteen thousand children under the age of seven had suffered lead poisoning. A year later the estimate of poisoning cases rose to as high as thirty thousand per year, with large percentages of children in the poorest neighborhoods suffering from symptoms such as nausea, vomiting, and lethargy. After a door-to-door survey in Brownsville, Brooklyn College announced that up to 45 percent of that neighborhood's families might have lead poisoning. Since lead poisoning in children can cause learning disabilities, some observers noted that the schools couldn't possibly solve all of the problems caused by inner-city environments.

The lead problem gained an important voice for change when Jack Newfield described the city's "Silent Epidemic in the Slums" in a September 1969 issue of the *Village Voice*. Frustrated by the lack of media attention to lead poisoning, Newfield told the story of Brenda Scurry, a young African American mother of three. Scurry lived in a decaying neighborhood in the South Bronx strewn with garbage and punctuated by burned-out houses. Her twenty-three-month-old daughter, Janet, died from lead poisoning after eating paint in her apartment. Tragically, hospital workers had failed to diagnose and treat the poisoning simply because they were not alert to the problem. After Newfield's exposé, followed by his opinion piece in the *New York Times*, lead poisoning increasingly became a recognized disease of the urban environment. Cities around the state took steps to remove or cover up the paint, long and expensive processes that are still under way.

In the summer of 1970, just months after the first Earth Day had succeeded in raising New Yorkers' awareness of myriad environmental problems, the urban and environmental crises came to a head. In Brownsville, frustration with horrible environmental conditions boiled over. In a protest against lax sanitation, two residents piled uncollected garbage in the street and set it afire. When

police attempted to arrest the men, who were clearly making a political statement rather than simply engaging in mischief, other residents began scattering
garbage and threatening police. By day's end the violence had spread to arson
and looting, leaving Sutter Avenue looking like a war zone. Sanitation crews
arrived in force over the next several days to clear away the riot's mess and the
offending piles of refuse. Two weeks later, however, the neighborhood remained
strewn with abandoned cars, filthy vacant lots, and of course some of the worst
housing in the city. Clearly more regular garbage pickups could not solve all of
Brownsville's problems.

The violence in Brownsville served as a model for other neglected urban
neighborhoods. In August residents of East Harlem set refuse and abandoned
cars afire as a protest. On 110th Street discarded furniture and bedding were
stacked to make a bonfire. Ten days later, garbage fires burned on Lenox Avenue
in Harlem in an organized protest against inadequate trash pickup. Four hundred people participated. That same night a smaller crowd in Crown Heights,
Brooklyn, hurled garbage into the streets. Over the next year the city responded
with more garbage trucks and more sanitation workers, even sending three hundred men out into the streets with push brooms, recalling turn-of-the-century
efforts led by George Waring. Sanitation workers also helped organize and
equip self-help cleanup efforts, which altogether collected more than ten thousand tons of trash in Brooklyn alone in 1970.

In all of these instances uncollected garbage was a very real problem, but for
residents it also represented a host of environmental problems related to un-
satisfactory city services and inadequate housing. In 1967 Harlem activist Jesse
Gray had led a demonstration in Washington as the House of Representatives
debated a bill to control rats in America's cities. "Rats cause riots," the dem-
onstrators chanted, succinctly connecting environmental and social disorder.
Three years later other New York City residents burned trash as a broad form
of protest. Organized by the Young Lords, a Puerto Rican nationalist group,
the arson in Spanish Harlem was designed to protest a lack of heat and hot
water in buildings around 110th Street. In this and many other ways the urban
and environmental crises overlapped. Even crime became an environmental
issue, as urban scholars looked to the cityscape to explain skyrocketing violence.
Architect Oscar Newman studied New York City's extensive public housing,
which contained 528,000 people, and determined that better design could prevent crime. Some public housing had diminished surveillance from the street
and even from apartments, allowing for greater mischief in public areas such as
hallways, stairwells, and playgrounds. Perhaps modern design, like that found

in public housing, had played a role in creating a less livable city, as Jane Jacobs had claimed a decade earlier, but only partly because it made it harder for police to conduct their patrols. Just like more regular garbage pickup, by itself improved police surveillance couldn't possibly solve the urban crisis.

Upstate cities suffered many of the same problems that faced New York City, but none could match the crisis that revealed itself in neighborhoods like Brownsville, Harlem, and the South Bronx, where troubles only deepened in the poor economy of the 1970s. In the spring of 1977 Bill Moyers brought his *CBS Reports* team into the South Bronx to investigate a piece they would call "The Fire Next Door." Ostensibly Moyers came to report on the wave of arson that was changing the face of the neighborhood. Fire, long a human tool for transforming environments, was now clearing out urban deadwood—abandoned and decaying buildings. In the previous ten years, thirty thousand buildings had been set on fire, as the South Bronx emptied out and residents turned to arson for entertainment and, sometimes, for profit. Moyers used the same tactic Newfield had employed eight years earlier. To make the crisis more real to his audience, Moyers told the story of one woman, an Irish immigrant who had lived in the same apartment for thirty-eight years but now felt compelled to leave because of the deteriorating conditions, especially crime. Despite Moyers's touching reporting, most New Yorkers retained a distant view of the unfolding urban crisis.

As the summer of 1977 heated up, disaster struck New York. Lightning north of the city caused a cascading power failure that eventually affected 9 million people. When darkness fell, looting ripped through commercial districts in several parts of the city, an outcome that had commentators around the nation lamenting the collapse of urban civilization. That fall, as the New York Yankees pursued a World Series championship in their South Bronx stadium, Howard Cosell directed television viewers' attention to the troubled neighborhood. "Ladies and gentlemen, the Bronx is burning," Cosell announced, as cameras were trained on an abandoned elementary school ablaze nearby. The Bronx had replaced "Bombsville" as the poster child of the urban crisis.

LOVE CANAL AND SUPERFUND

In most cities the crisis was not so obvious or dramatic, and in some places it involved no flames or riots or accumulating garbage or troubled youth in poorly designed public housing. Instead it involved the slowly accumulating knowledge that industrial cities contained hidden dangers. Such was the case in Niagara Falls, where in the spring of 1972 eleven-year-old Debra Gallo and her playmates found lumps of a hard chalklike substance near a swing set. They used it to draw on the sidewalk, and as the lumps crumbled into powder, Debra rubbed her eyes. They began to burn so badly she had to be taken to an emergency room. Several of the other children also burned their eyes and faces. The Niagara Falls Fire Department investigated, as did the safety supervisor from Hooker Chemical, the city's largest employer and the former owner of the land where the girls had been playing. The chalky substance, it turned out, was benzene hexachloride, also known as lindane, a powerful insecticide and a suspected carcinogen. The girls all recovered from their burns, but the neighborhood was just beginning a long, tragic relationship with Hooker and its buried wastes.

In the same year Debra Gallo learned not to play with white lumps she found around the playground, Lois Gibbs moved with her husband and a baby boy to a small house on 101st Street. Six years later her son began to attend the Ninety-ninth Street School, near which the girls had found the lindane. After a few months of school, he developed epilepsy. That same year, 1978, Michael Brown, a reporter for the *Niagara Falls Gazette*, began to investigate complaints about chemicals in the area around the school property, complaints that had been growing in frequency since 1976, when heavy rain and snowfall raised the water table and apparently initiated extensive underground leakage of toxic chemicals. Unbeknownst to Gibbs and many other residents of the LaSalle neighborhood, the Niagara Falls Board of Education had acquired the property on which the school sat from Hooker Chemical in 1953. The contract gave the Board of Education sixteen acres of land in the rapidly growing eastern part of the city, not far from the river, for just one dollar, but with the stipulation that Hooker would bear no responsibility for damages caused by chemical wastes buried at the site—the former Love Canal.

Brown's *Gazette* articles addressed the neighborhood's growing health concerns, especially among the families whose homes backed onto the old canal, and where, without publicity, the Department of Environmental Conservation had begun studying the chemical composition of surface and sewer water. All of this greatly concerned Gibbs, who rapidly evolved from a stay-at-home mom into an environmental activist, first by going door-to-door in the neighborhood talking to people about health problems, and later by leading her neighbors in a multiyear battle for a satisfactory governmental response. Early in the summer

Figure 27. In the postwar decades a suburban neighborhood developed on either side of the former Love Canal, with the 99th Street School built directly atop the former chemical dump. This 1978 aerial photograph reveals the close proximity of the homes to the former canal. Courtesy Buffalo State College *Courier-Express* Collection.

of 1978 she had spoken to enough of her neighbors to conclude that practically the entire community seemed to be sick. Of course Gibbs wasn't the only concerned resident. Karen Schroeder had grown up in the neighborhood and now lived on Ninety-ninth Street with her husband and four children, one of whom had been born with a host of birth defects. Schroeder had complained to the *Gazette* and politicians, sparking investigations. Heavy rains had left her yard sodden with dangerous chemicals that had spilled out from the poorly capped dump. Tests conducted by the Department of Environmental Conservation (DEC) and the Federal Environmental Protection Agency (EPA) had found eighty-two different chemicals in backyards and basements, including benzene hexachloride, chloroform, toluene, and, perhaps most frightening of all, trichlorophenol, which contained the highly toxic chemical dioxin. Residents complained of headaches, respiratory problems, and even burns and rashes from contact with water in their yards, while studies found that Love Canal residents had experienced an excessive incidence of miscarriages and birth defects. Residents themselves began to connect cancers, liver and kidney problems, and any number of diseases to the chemicals.

On August 2, 1978, New York State health commissioner Robert P. Whalen closed the Ninety-ninth Street School and recommended that pregnant women and infants leave their homes around Love Canal immediately. "There is a great and imminent peril to the health of the general public," he announced. Suddenly, growing concern among residents escalated into panic. If infants shouldn't live near Love Canal, why should any child, or any adult for that matter? But how could they leave, anyway? How would they pay their mortgages and moving expenses plus rent for new places at the same time? The next day Whalen arrived at a meeting in the school auditorium to field these and other questions, none of which he could answer satisfactorily. Local politicians didn't attend the meeting, but Michael Brown did. He later summarized the mood of the room: "Young mothers sat in the auditorium, children on their laps, and openly wept. Others looked blankly toward the podium dazed." Their world had fallen apart; their families, their homes, their finances were all in jeopardy. The quiet working-class subdivision had suddenly become international news. Henceforth the name Love Canal would be forever linked with toxic waste, which in turn would become the most pressing environmental issue in the nation.

Two days after Whalen's visit, residents gathered to form the Love Canal Homeowners Association, electing Gibbs president. Schroeder became secretary. Overnight the association had 550 members and the stated goal of a

Figure 28. Lois Gibbs became an environmental activist as she battled to protect her family's health, helping to spark a nationwide concern about toxic wastes. This May 1980 photograph captures Gibbs engaged in the hard work of organizing. Courtesy Buffalo State College *Courier-Express* Collection.

compensated evacuation for everyone who wanted to leave. As the crisis intensified, Governor Hugh Carey visited Love Canal, and in a heated public meeting declared that the state would purchase the houses in the first two rings of streets around the canal. Two hundred thirty-five families would be relocated. Appraisals, purchases, and relocations proceeded quickly, and by the end of the month, ninety-eight families had evacuated. But not everyone was satisfied, including Gibbs, whose own home was beyond the first two rings. New research suggested that swales had carried chemicals well away from the canal. Gibbs and dozens of other residents stepped up their protests, carrying picket signs and keeping media attention on the unfolding disaster. As the state began remediation efforts, attempting to put in drains that would keep leaking chemicals out of the neighborhood, the disturbed soil sent odors into the air, spiking concern yet again for those families that hadn't relocated.

It wasn't until May 1980, however, that a new EPA study brought the matter to a head. That study revealed that eleven of thirty-six tested residents around

Love Canal had shown evidence of chromosomal damage, presumably from the chemical wastes. Gibbs and the Homeowners Association were furious and frightened. Two days later they took two EPA officials "hostage" in a Love Canal home, holding them until media coverage became sufficient to force a federal solution. That came just two days later, when President Jimmy Carter declared a state of emergency—the second in two years at Love Canal—and pledged federal support for the relocation of the entire neighborhood, more than nine hundred families altogether.

Although considerable controversy surrounded the health data, with some people claiming that adverse effects from the chemicals were either slight or nonexistent, the mental health consequences of the Love Canal crisis were real. Residents lost their sense of security in their own homes, the value of which plummeted as buyers refused to gamble with their health by moving into the area. The specter of cancer or birth defects in the next generation would follow them even after they moved out of the neighborhood. They had been exposed, they knew; what that would mean over the long term, they did not. One mother who had lived in the third ring around Love Canal summarized: "I don't care what they tell me about the health effects of Love Canal. I'm convinced that it did affect my son and will affect him and will affect me for the rest of my life. Physically, emotionally, mentally, financially. The total impact of the thing is something you will never recover from."

By this point Love Canal residents had had years of experience with foot-dragging government officials, especially from the city of Niagara Falls; they had spent years listening to Hooker Chemical officials explain away their decision to sell a chemical dump for use as a school and playground. Some residents, especially Lois Gibbs, had become their own experts, studying the chemicals in question, digging up information on health effects, and, perhaps most important, learning how to become effective advocates for themselves and their neighborhood. The Love Canal Homeowners Association became one of the most important environmental organizations in the nation, not least because it revealed the ability of average people, especially women, to make a difference in environmental politics.

In large part because of the Love Canal activism, fear of toxic exposure spread well beyond Niagara Falls, as did suspicion of government and industry. A growing number of Americans no longer trusted the corporate establishment. Government officials scrambled to get a handle on the situation. The DEC released a list of firms that had handled hazardous chemicals around the state and initiated an investigation into eighty-five "high-priority" cases. Citizens began to realize how widespread the hazardous waste problem really was, as one survey found 215 dumps in Erie and Niagara counties alone. In Niagara Falls, even at some distance from Love Canal, soil samples contained high levels of benzene, groundwater samples contained pesticides such as heptachlor and aldrin, and the air contained tetrachloroethylene. Heavy metals were everywhere in the city. Indeed the region contained so many chemical production sites and so many waste dumps—Niagara County had thirty-eight known industrial landfills—that health officials began to wonder about safety throughout Niagara Falls.

It didn't stop there. People all over the country began to suspect that nearby dumps might contain toxic chemicals. The fifty-five-gallon industrial drum became the very symbol of toxicity, and fear spread wherever those barrels were found. Although New York State contained up to five hundred waste disposal sites, Oswego County gained special attention, as the state located thirty thousand barrels of waste on abandoned sites. Tests of public wells turned up contaminated water on Long Island, where 100,000 residents suddenly found themselves questioning the safety of their tap water, and in the summer of 1980 more than 100,000 gallons of PCB-contaminated oil sat at College Point in New York City, awaiting disposal, a prospect that grew dimmer as the nation suddenly took intense interest in hazardous wastes. No one wanted PCBs in their backyard. Citizens had become alerted to the hazardous waste issue, and to their own power to control their communities. When faced with the prospect of a new PCB dump in their community, citizens of Warren County, North Carolina, gathered in protest in 1979. They demanded that their community not become "another Love Canal." In just this way, Love Canal had become both a negative and a positive example for people around the country.

If the federal reaction to Love Canal had been halting, now Congress acted quickly. On the last day of 1980 Carter signed the Comprehensive Environmental Response, Compensation, and Liability Act (CERCLA), better known as Superfund. The act empowered the EPA to identify and study hazardous waste sites in order to develop remediation plans. To fund this work, it created a new tax on oil and chemical companies. In addition, the EPA could sue responsible parties for reimbursement of cleanup costs, when they could be identified and pursued, a step the EPA took against Hooker Chemical in a case that dragged on until 1995, when Occidental Chemical Corporation, the parent company, agreed to pay $129 million to cover cleanup and relocation costs.

Eventually the EPA investigated nearly two thousand sites in New York State, adding over one hundred of them to the National Priorities List. More than thirty of these were in the two suburban Long Island counties alone. Some sites, such as the C & J Disposal Leasing Company, outside Hamilton, were relatively small. This site held up to one hundred waste drums, apparently containing hazardous organic compounds such as phthalates and phenols. The EPA oversaw the site's cleanup, which involved the complete removal of the wastes and the soil around them, a task accomplished within four years of the initial investigation. Other sites, however, such as Onondaga Lake, polluted by several industries outside Syracuse, and the upper Hudson River, contaminated by General Electric's PCB discharges, comprise expansive polluted areas and will require lengthy remediation. Although Superfund came under intense criticism from both industry and environmentalists, some New York Superfund sites, including Love Canal and the C & J site, have been delisted, owing to successful remediation. This process was greatly aided by a state bond issue, passed in 1986, which allotted over $1 billion to clean hazardous waste sites, augmenting federal dollars and speeding recovery.

NIMBYISM AND ENVIRONMENTAL JUSTICE

By the mid-1980s a new term had entered the national vocabulary: "NIMBY," an acronym of "not in my backyard." Although the term eventually described citizen-led efforts to block all types of developments, including homeless shelters, jails, cell phone towers, and big-box retail stores, NIMBYism had its roots in the anti-toxics movement of the early 1980s. Heightened awareness of the dangers of toxic waste made the disposal of such materials extremely difficult, and proposed landfills almost always garnered serious local opposition. Residents even battled against sanitary landfills designed simply to accept household waste, leaving many municipalities struggling to expand capacity for ever-growing volumes of consumer trash. Eventually movements to stop the construction of roads, electric power lines, and, in New York City, garbage transfer stations all took on NIMBY characteristics. Many participants in NIMBY movements had learned directly from Love Canal. Neither businesses nor government could be trusted to protect public health and safety. Residents had to do it themselves. They had to become health experts, to learn the details of proposed construction, to determine the risks that would come with it. After the 1969 passage of the National Environmental Policy Act (NEPA), all projects

receiving federal dollars required environmental impact statements and a process through which the public could voice concerns. The State Environmental
Quality Review Act (SEQRA), passed five years later, required environmental impact statements for any project receiving state funding or state sanction
through permits. Together NEPA and SEQRA revolutionized development
in New York, greatly increasing the public's role in determining what changes
would be made in communities.

Because NIMBY movements became so common—and frustrating to those
who supported economic development—the term took on a connotation of
obstructionism pure and simple. But use of the term often ignored complex
realities. Many communities protested against new environmental hazards not
because they had pristine environments to protect, but because they already
bore heavy environmental burdens. In the late 1980s, for example, Nassau
County proposed building a sludge treatment plant in Bay Park, which already
contained several troublesome facilities, including a sewage treatment plant.
Sludge would be dewatered at the new plant, part of the process by which the
county would meet a new federal law preventing the ocean dumping of sewage
sludge. In 1992 the New York Department of Environmental Protection allowed construction of the Bay Park plant and another dewatering plant at Cedar
Creek, but not before two citizens' groups presented their concerns. Homeowners Opposed to Polluting the Environment (HOPE), created by Bay Park
residents, and Stop Cedar Creek and Recover Our Environment (SCARE), created by residents near the second proposed plant, both hired lawyers and made
presentations before the DEC. Although they lost their battles to prevent the
plants from being built, the process required an openness that earlier generations of activists would have envied, and community activism would at least be
rewarded with the new plants' adherence to environmental laws.

By the time HOPE and SCARE had lost their battles against sewage sludge
plants, movements to ensure environmental justice had taken shape around
the state. Using the lessons of Love Canal and often the processes required by
NEPA and SEQRA, some minority communities gathered together to protest
both ongoing and new environmental threats. In New York City many of these
movements involved the handling of trash, especially after a 1996 law required
that the city close the poorly built Fresh Kills landfill in 2001. The largest un-
lined landfill in the world, Fresh Kills loomed over Staten Island, leaching fouling waste into the Kill Van Kull. The closure of Fresh Kills required the city
to rework its system of garbage disposal. The last municipal incinerator had

closed in 1990, ocean dumping had been outlawed, and the city had no space for a new landfill, meaning that officials had to devise a way to get 3.5 million tons of trash out of the boroughs every year. Evolving plans included building new transfer stations where trash could be loaded onto barges or trains, a process that would require hundreds of trucks to converge on handling facilities proposed for Hunts Point in the South Bronx and Red Hook and Williamsburg in Brooklyn. One Williamsburg high school student protested to the City Council, "Communities of color are treated as if they weren't human." Activists pointed out that building more waste-handling facilities in already polluted neighborhoods simply made environmental burdens more unequal.

Even as minority neighborhoods worked to keep out new trash-handling facilities, activists for environmental justice took on the problem of air pollution, which also disproportionately affected poor and minority neighborhoods. For example, in Brooklyn's Williamsburg neighborhood, residents worked through El Puente, a community center and school, to study asthma. The neighborhood, which includes the industrial zone along Newtown Creek, contained dozens of polluting and potentially dangerous facilities, and when community researchers found elevated occurrences of asthma, they linked the disease to these environmental burdens. El Puente's research helped spark a growing awareness of asthma as an urban disease and an environmental justice concern. At the same time, the South Bronx Clean Air Coalition worked to force the closure of the last incinerator in the city of New York, a medical waste incinerator run by Browning-Ferris Industries, one of the nation's largest waste-handling companies. Altogether the environmental justice movement earned significant victories, improving the conditions in minority neighborhoods and, especially, raising awareness of the disproportionate environmental burdens poorer New Yorkers continue to bear.

The closure of Fresh Kills did more than fuel the environmental justice movement in New York. It also punctuated the landfill scare that had developed in the 1980s as municipal dumps began to reach capacity and NIMBY movements made opening new landfills difficult. In 1987 the wanderings of a garbage barge, the *Mobro*, made national news, as reporters tracked the unsuccessful voyage of New York trash in search of a willing dump along the Atlantic seaboard. Eventually the barge came home, and the trash was burned in Brooklyn and the ash buried on Long Island. The *Mobro*'s journey helped elevate garbage to crisis status, and New Yorkers sought new solutions to this very old problem. In 1982 New York had passed a bottle bill, which charged a nickel deposit on most aluminum cans and glass bottles. The new rules met with great support around the state, and even if New York's waste stream was only marginally reduced, roadside trash did diminish noticeably. The popularity of recycling increased in the 1980s, as environmental interest groups lobbied for curbside pickup of glass, plastic, paper, and metal, and the passage of a 1988 law required municipalities to develop recycling programs by 1992. Five years after that deadline, industrial and municipal recycling efforts were diverting more than 40 percent of the state's waste stream from landfills.

ACID RAIN

All over the state, local groups took on local problems, but not all environmental threats were homegrown. In the mid-1970s New Yorkers began to learn more about the dangers of acid precipitation. Earlier in the decade reports out of Scandinavia indicated that highly acidic rain and snow were damaging northern European forests. Scientists blamed the tall smokestacks of western Europe, which released sulfur dioxide high into the air, where it mixed with water vapor, creating sulfuric acid. By 1974 Cornell University researchers had discovered the same phenomenon in the United States, as coal-burning plants in the industrial heartland sent tons of sulfur aloft, some of which fell back to earth in New York. Many researchers focused on the Adirondacks, where soil types made forests and surface waters especially susceptible to damage from acidification. Early studies suggested that native brook trout and spotted salamanders in particular might be threatened by the changing pH of Adirondack waters. These early academic studies inspired the DEC to undertake its own, more comprehensive study, focusing on the effects of acidification on fish and the potential of adding lime to lakes to reduce acidity. The state also studied how the culprits—sulfur and nitrogen oxides—were transported in the air. The DEC concluded that 80 percent of the sulfur deposited in the Adirondacks came from outside the state. Because so much of the acid that fell on New York came from the industrial Midwest, especially the tall-stacked coal-fired plants of the Ohio Valley, state officials agreed that federal involvement would be necessary to solve the problem.

In 1980 a congressional subcommittee held acid rain hearings, in which Congressmen Robert McEwen and Donald Mitchell, who represented districts in the Adirondacks, summarized what scientists had thus far discovered. At the center of their concern were Adirondack lakes, hundreds of which no longer contained fish. A continuation of this trend could mean the loss of millions of tourist dollars to the region. They also feared the effects of increasing quantities of heavy metals, leached from soils and bedrock and entering the region's waters. Commissioner Robert Flacke of the DEC testified on the need for the federal government to establish new regulations that would reduce sulfur and nitrogen emissions. Adirondack Park Agency commissioner Anne LaBastille prepared a report for the subcommittee, which concluded, "Cleansing devices should be installed in car and steel factories, fossil fuel and smelting plants, and vehicle emission systems at the earliest date, and costs should *not* be the limiting factor." LaBastille and others who had studied acid rain knew that the technology to solve the problem already existed. The question was one of political will.

Acid rain became the most important environmental story in New York in the 1980s, as acidification threatened the state's most precious natural landscapes. New concerns about diminished agricultural yields and the corrosion of public art and stone buildings also added heat to the political debate. More frightening, the national political climate did not augur well for a quick solution. In the last year of the Carter administration, the EPA announced that scientific study had proved the need for federal action to stem the consequences of acid precipitation. In 1981, however, the Reagan administration swept into office on the promise of decreasing federal regulation as a means of stimulating the flagging American economy. Now led by Reagan's appointees, the EPA determined that it needed to study the issue before tightening regulations. Environmentalists and other concerned citizens saw this call for more research as merely a stalling tactic. New York politicians, including Senator Daniel Patrick Moynihan, continued to press for federal action, as did Canadian politicians, who hoped to negotiate a treaty that would reduce pollution entering Canada from the United States. More than any previous environmental debate, the acid rain discourse focused on a cost-benefit analysis, with conservative politicians and industry spokesmen arguing that the nation could not afford expensive solutions to all environmental problems, often explicitly blaming the environmental regulations of the 1970s for reducing America's competitiveness in the global economy. Many politicians argued that the nation should not invest billions in a solution that would not provide an adequate return. Under this market-oriented philosophy, only problems with quantifiable economic implications deserved solutions. So supporters of regulation did the math: acid rain cost the nation millions of dollars a year, particularly through damage to timber and crops, and would continue to do so for the foreseeable future.

With the Reagan administration dragging its heels, New York State passed its own Acid Deposition Control Act in 1984. The first acid rain legislation in the nation, it reduced pollutant contributions from inside the state and set an example for the federal government. Within five years, sulfur emissions from New York State utilities were down 23 percent from 1980 levels. Of course, since New York could not regulate the sulfur emitted beyond its borders, the acid rain problem was far from solved. In the face of continued delay at the federal level, New York sued the EPA to force the federal government to regulate sulfur emissions, which could be reduced significantly by the installation of smokestack scrubbers. Despite legal victories, however, real progress did not come until Reagan left office. In 1989 the first Bush administration proposed legislation to reduce sulfur and nitrogen emissions. In 1990 Congress obliged by passing the Clean Air Act Amendments, which regulated power plant emissions through an innovation called "cap and trade." Reflecting the political culture of the era, this approach used a modified market solution, moving away from the command and control philosophy of the 1970s. The law set up a market for emissions permits, which could be sold among polluters, with the most efficient plants reaping benefits from their cleanliness. Highly polluting plants, meanwhile, had to pay extra to continue their polluting ways. This law proved remarkably effective, with sulfur emissions dropping even faster than projected. Unfortunately, the law allowed cleaner New York plants, which had already reduced emissions to meet the state requirements, to sell their permits to dirtier plants in the Midwest, a process that blunted the law's effect on the acid precipitation over New York State.

Sulfur emissions declined significantly during the 1990s, continuing a trend that had begun before the 1990 legislation. Sulfur dioxide emissions dropped by two-thirds in the twenty-five years after 1980, while nitrogen dioxide emissions remained essentially unchanged. Public attention decreased along with the sulfur emissions levels, perhaps because many assumed that the new laws had solved the problem, but the Adirondacks in particular continued to experience the negative effects of acidification. In 1999 a coalition of interest groups took out a full-page ad in the *New York Times* announcing "Your Best Chance to Stop Acid Rain Once and Forever." Lobbying for further reductions in sulfur and nitrogen emissions, the coalition included older organizations, such as the Association for the Protection of the Adirondacks and the National Audubon Society, as well as newer ones, such as the Environmental Defense Fund. Even the National Trust for Historic Preservation joined the fight, revealing how broad the threat from acidification was, and how broad the environmental movement had become.

GLOBAL WARMING

Acid rain wasn't the first transnational environmental threat. Nations had already come together to ban atmospheric testing of nuclear weapons in the 1960s, and again in the 1970s the world's developed nations agreed to stop the production and use of chlorofluorocarbons in an effort to protect the ozone layer. But in one way the 1980s acid rain battle set an example for another international threat. The Reagan administration's failure to act on acid rain foreshadowed the federal government's inaction on global warming. As early as 1979 the National Academy of Sciences had issued a warning about the consequences of increasing quantities of carbon dioxide in the atmosphere. Scientists had long debated the role that increased pollution might play in changing the global climate, especially by trapping heat that would otherwise dissipate into space. That debate persisted, along with uncertainty regarding precisely how warming of the earth would affect everything from rainfall and cloud cover to ocean currents and sea levels, but by the early 1980s a preponderance of the evidence suggested that the greenhouse effect would raise global temperatures over the next century, especially if industrial nations took no steps to curb the burning of fossil fuels, the major source of atmospheric carbon dioxide.

The public discourse on global warming took on a new urgency in 1988, when an extremely hot summer was accompanied by drought and fierce forest fires in the American West. Combined with accumulating research concerning the consequences of warming, the historically hot weather of the late 1980s convinced many people that carbon dioxide production had to be curbed—both in the United States and around the world. American politicians, however, emphasized the cost of action, especially related to developing cleaner energy technology. The environmental community for its part emphasized the consequences of inaction, often articulated in doomsday scenarios that inspired unintended reactions, including a sense of hopelessness among believers and ridicule from the unconverted. The result was a complete lack of policy progress.

All the while, New Yorkers heard more and more about the probability that rising sea levels would jeopardize homes and compromise water supplies on Long Island. Scientists also linked global warming to receding waters in the Great Lakes, noting that warmer temperatures sped evaporation. In Oswego,

Hamburg, and other snow-belt areas, the talk was of even greater lake-effect snowfalls that would come when the Great Lakes failed to freeze over. In 1989 Hurricane Hugo devastated South Carolina, sparking concern in New York about the predicted growth in the frequency and intensity of tropical storms and the potential for disaster should a great storm strike New York Harbor. Other scientist warned of crop failures and species shifts that would accompany increasingly erratic but generally warmer weather. When the spruce trees atop Whiteface Mountain began dying, leaving stark stands of dead trees around the Veterans Memorial Highway, tourists and scientists alike wondered about the logic of waiting to act until all the science was understood.

In 1989 Adirondack environmentalist Bill McKibben described one of the consequences of global warming: the very idea of a nature separate from human influence had been lost. As he put it in *The End of Nature,* "we have changed the atmosphere—changed it enough so that the climate will change dramatically." Even in the deep woods of the Adirondacks, out the back door of McKibben's Johnsburgh home, one could no longer escape into untouched nature. Despite mounting scientific evidence and the activism of people like McKibben, Washington continued to stall regulation. Especially during the second Bush administration in the first decade of the new millennium, global warming became a partisan issue as conservatives questioned the science and the motives of environmentalists. Some political commentators even speculated that Al Gore and his fellow activists had drummed up the issue as a way of forcing increased governmental regulation—regulation that did not come.

INVASIVE SPECIES

By the 1990s another threat gained national attention: invasive species. Nonnative species have arrived in New York throughout history, sometimes in great numbers, as during the colonial period, when Europeans brought with them wheat, pigs, cattle, rats, and numerous other species. This earlier invasion was remarkably transformative of the state's environment, of course, but the new species kept coming, including Ailanthus, the tree of heaven, an ornamental favored by Frederick Law Olmsted, who admired the "pseudo tropical" beauty of the Chinese tree, which he planted in Central Park. The tree of heaven didn't stay in the park, of course, and by the 1910s it had become nearly ubiquitous in the troubled inner-city neighborhoods of New York. As the star in Betty

Smith's 1943 novel *A Tree Grows in Brooklyn,* Ailanthus became a symbol of survival in the difficult environments of impoverished urban America. "No matter where its seed fell," Smith wrote, "it made a tree which struggled to reach the sky. It grew in boarded-up lots and out of neglected rubbish heaps and it was the only tree that grew out of cement. It grew lushly, but only in the tenement districts." As the urban environment continued to deteriorate, however, the tree of heaven spread, becoming a symbol of neglect and blight as much as survival.

The purposeful importation of ornamentals continued, but more and more invasive species were unintended and unwanted arrivals, often diseases. In the early twentieth century the chestnut blight crept through the state, beginning on Long Island, where it had arrived with trees imported from Asia. After appearing in the Bronx in 1904, the disease spread quickly, until by the 1930s the chestnut had been all but eradicated from New York State. At about that time Dutch elm disease began to threaten another of the state's great trees. A favorite ornamental and street shade tree, the elm has held on longer than the chestnut, in part because of the decades-long struggle to protect healthy trees, both by quickly removing diseased trees and, after World War II, using pesticides to control the beetles that help spread the disease.

The public was deeply concerned and saddened by the disappearance of chestnuts and elms, a transformation made all the more difficult by having to watch individual favorite trees die. But a more general alarm about invasive species awaited the 1990s, when heightened awareness about the importance of biodiversity, combined with the arrival of several aggressive new species, convinced some observers that regional ecosystems were gravely threatened, especially as the globally integrated economy accelerated the transportation of goods and species across international boundaries. A strong philosophy of wildlife preservation and increasing ecological knowledge also contributed to a growing sense of crisis, as environmentalists feared that lands protected from human actions might now be jeopardized by other species.

Among those garnering the greatest concern was the zebra mussel, an Asian species that came to the Great Lakes in the bilge of a trade ship. Its arrival portended more invasions resulting from increasing global trade and improved water pollution laws, which kept bilge water clean enough for organisms to survive long voyages. After its initial appearance in 1988, the zebra mussel spread quickly, out-competing local mussels and threatening fish populations by consuming great quantities of food. The zebra mussel prefers moving water, and so it often makes its home in intake pipes, where it can grow so thickly as to block the flow. By 1990 it had already clogged intake pipes at the Dunkirk power plant on Lake Erie and the Niagara Power Project on the Niagara River, where management hoped to try chlorine to control mussel growth. After moving throughout Lakes Erie and Ontario, the mussel began appearing in many of the state's smaller lakes. In 1998 Charles O'Neill, director of the National Zebra Mussel and Aquatic Nuisance Species Clearinghouse, noted: "Between the exotic plants, animals and bacteria coming over, I don't think a week goes by that we don't hear of another potentially harmful critter. It never ends." Among the most prolific aquatic plants was Eurasian water milfoil, a fast-growing weed that began choking out native plants and threatening lake and pond ecosystems. Milfoil spread by motorboats, mostly, used in one body of water and moved to another with plant fragments still attached. Management of milfoil included mechanical removal, which provided only minimal relief, and the use of herbicides.

Forests, too, saw their share of invasions. In the early 1900s gypsy moths spread from Massachusetts, where they had been accidentally released in the late 1800s, and by the 1920s New York State had begun a long "war" against the pest. In the 1930s the Civilian Conservation Corps sponsored many camps dedicated in part to seeking out and destroying gypsy moth eggs and larvae. In the 1950s DDT became the favored response to infestations. By the 1980s, when the moth again appeared in large numbers, many had realized that the pesticide solution may have been worse than the problem; biological controls, such as the distribution of bacteria and parasitic wasps, became more popular. In addition, scientific study had revealed that the moth need not cause excessive concern, since healthy trees could survive periodic infestations. But as worries about the gypsy moth eased, other invasive species gained more attention. The 1990s brought increasing concern about spreading ornamentals, such as the Japanese barberry and honeysuckle, which had established themselves along trails in several major parks. And in wetlands, purple loosestrife, a beautiful ornamental, had begun to overrun marshes and wet meadows, creating dense, expansive stands and diminishing diversity. More recently, giant hogweed has begun to appear in the fields of western New York and is raising special concern because of its toxic sap. Taken together, the invasive species threaten to reduce the ecological value of nature preserves throughout the state, while also threatening timber and crops. Environmentalists and the state have recognized that preservation must be active rather than passive, since the protection of intact ecosystems requires considerable regulation and management.

GENERAL ELECTRIC, STERLING FOREST, AND THE PRESERVATION OF OPEN SPACE

In the story of invasive species we see the confluence of several important trends, including increased outdoor recreation, improved ecological knowledge among the public, and the seriousness with which New Yorkers take the project of preservation. Yet despite the threats posed by nonnative species, the direst environmental problems in recent years have still derived from human action—especially global warming, for which no solution appears imminent. Other lingering environmental issues have met with some resolution, however. For instance, in 2006 the Environmental Protection Agency reached an agreement with General Electric regarding that company's pollution of the Hudson River. General Electric has been a major employer in New York and also a major polluter. Beginning in 1947, GE's capacitor manufacturing plants in Fort Edward and Hudson Falls began discharging PCBs into the Hudson. Eventually the plants released up to 1.3 million pounds of the toxic chemical into the river. GE stopped active discharges of the chemical in the 1970s, but it continued to seep into the water from heavily polluted sediment on the river bottom, especially above the Fort Edward Dam. When the dam was removed in 1973, sediments began to move downstream in larger quantities. The next year studies revealed high PCB levels in Hudson River fish, and by 1976 the state had outlawed fishing on the river between Fort Edward and Albany. Other restrictions limited fishing farther downriver, including a ban on commercial striped bass fishing, once a lucrative business.

The EPA and the state knew the source of the PCBs, but the question was what to do about them. In 1984 the Hudson River became a Superfund site, and General Electric and the EPA began intensive studies of the river's sediments and contaminated sites along the banks. The 2006 agreement finally determined that General Electric would dredge the most polluted stretches of the river. The sediments would be processed at a massive new facility, built by GE, in Fort Edward. Although General Electric would pay for the dredging, and the removal of tons of PCBs from the river is certainly a happy prospect, many people complained that the dredging process itself would introduce higher levels of PCBs into the water. And some had cause to wonder what would become of the tons of polluted sediment once removed from the Hudson? One possible solution was the CWM Chemical Services waste facility just north of Model City in Niagara County. Model City, where William Love began building his ideal unpolluted industrial community, continues the long tradition of chemical waste storage around Niagara Falls. In a terrible irony, Love left behind the canal that would eventually become the most famous waste dump in American history, Love Canal, and, ten miles away, the small crossroads community of Model City, home to the last toxic waste dump in the Northeast.

Other environmental victories have come in response to the continued pressure of suburban sprawl. Since the late 1970s, development has spread away from long-suburbanized counties, particularly Nassau and Westchester, and into more distant counties, such as Rockland, Orange, Dutchess, and Suffolk. Sprawling subdivisions of homes and suburban-style retail with expansive parking lots and ever wider streets led to significant losses of farmland, especially noticeable in Orange County along State Route 17. Closer to the city, where older suburbs became more densely developed, residents expressed concerns about growing traffic problems, for example, along the I-287 corridor through Westchester, where offices and retail continued to cluster near the General Foods headquarters. Upstate metropolitan areas grew much more slowly, if at all, but the growth that did occur appeared around the edges, in Manlius, for example, south of Syracuse, and Colonie, between Schenectady and Albany. Environmentalists complained about poor land use decisions and the creation of energy-intensive communities, but in a region with little economic growth, victories for those who hoped to prevent development were rare.

Concern about sprawl flared with the announcement of plans to develop as many as fourteen thousand homes in forested lands in southern Orange County, in a beautiful expanse of the Hudson Highlands known as Sterling Forest. Owned by an insurance company, the eighteen thousand acres had formerly supported mining and had been in the Harriman family. Hilly topography and marshy lands had delayed development, but the Thruway passed near the eastern edge of the forest, making it very accessible to New York's northern suburbs. The city was just forty miles away. In a case in which the State Environmental Quality Review Act helped opponents both delay development and rally support, the proposal met a series of obstacles, most of them erected by citizen activists. A significant victory for environmentalists came in 1997, when the Trust for Public Land and the Open Space Institute finalized plans to purchase most of Sterling Forest. The groups also led a successful lobbying effort at the state and federal levels to secure funding for the purchase and to ensure that the forest and wetlands would become Sterling Forest State Park, New York's largest park acquisition in fifty years. In 2006 the state purchased the final 575-acre parcel of Sterling Forest, ending the possibility of any non-park development. Sprawl in the Highlands had been defeated, at least in the forest. Altogether Sterling Forest Park offered habitat protection, recreational opportunities, and also historic preservation, since these lands had been home to the mines and the forge that had created the chain links that spanned the Hudson during the Revolution.

The creation of Sterling Forest Park was just one of many major environmental successes during the three-term administration of Governor George Pataki. Other accomplishments followed the 1996 passage of the $1.75 billion Clean Water/Clean Air Bond Act, which overcame opposition from those who feared more roadblocks to economic development and increased borrowing for a state already deep in debt. Just six years earlier, upstate opponents to a 1990 environmental bond act had blocked Governor Mario Cuomo's plans to make large state land purchases for the purpose of recreation and preservation; but Pataki loaded his proposal with a grab bag of programs that would send funding all over the state. There would be money to close Fresh Kills, to clean up brownfields, upgrade water supply systems, purchase natural gas–fueled buses for New York City, clean up Onondaga Lake, improve sewage treatment on Long Island and in Westchester County to protect Long Island Sound, and of course money for land acquisition, including funding for Sterling Forest. In lobbying for the bond act, Pataki linked environmental protection to economic success, and supporters noted the jobs that would be created, especially through water supply and sewage treatment construction projects. Governor Pataki went on to become a remarkably strong supporter of environmental protection, and by the end of his third term in 2006, his administration had protected over a million acres of land through purchase and easements.

Purchases for preservation purposes continued after Pataki left office, and some of them have been dramatic. In two important cases the Nature Conservancy, rather than the state, played the critical role. In 2007 the Nature Conservancy, with the help of the Open Space Institute, purchased 161,000 acres of land in the Adirondacks from Finch Paper, a company with deep roots in Glens Falls and a still active paper mill. The purchase allowed the Nature Conservancy to preserve the forests around seventy lakes and on ninety mountains in the central Adirondacks, primarily east of Long Lake. Significantly, the agreement with Finch ensured that even as the Nature Conservancy managed the land for ecological diversity and recreation, it would also remain at least in part a working forest producing wood for the mill. Thus this 2007 purchase revealed how wrongheaded anti-environmentalists could be. Preservation, recreation, and conservation could all coexist with industry. As supporters of purchase boasted, this agreement proved that economic and environmental objectives are not always in conflict. Just a year later the Nature Conservancy made a much smaller purchase, but one with symbolic importance: Follensby Pond, home of the Philosophers' Camp of Ralph Waldo Emerson, Louis Agassiz, and others, would now become part of the Forest Preserve, protected as wild forever.

Observers looking for an environmental success story in the last few decades need not tramp to the Adirondack wilderness, however. They need only walk through one of the most popular spaces in New York State: Central Park. Having fallen on hard times along with the city around it in the 1960s and 1970s, Central Park had become graffiti-covered and litter-strewn, its lawns bare from overuse, its structures crumbling from neglect. Worst of all, it had gained a national reputation as a high-crime zone as much as a recreational park. In 1980 concerned citizens created the Central Park Conservancy, part of New Yorkers' push back against urban decay. In a public-private partnership, the conservancy improved the care of plants, preserved structures, and removed graffiti. Repairing and finding a new use for the Belvedere Castle was one of the first projects. Without a sense of irony, the Central Park Conservancy 1982 annual report noted that the castle "had fallen into near ruin," forgetting that the castle had been built to function as a ruin, adding a touch of antiquity to the landscape. By the 1980s, old abandoned buildings had taken on new meaning in the city. No longer did they suggest a rich past, the way Calvert Vaux had intended in the 1850s. Now they simply represented a troubled present and an uncertain future. Too many ruins scarred the city's neighborhoods. The conservancy's Management and Restoration Plan, initiated in 1981, has been a great success, and once again Central Park might easily be judged the most important park in the world. It attracts local and regional residents and tourists by the millions from near and far. The park exemplifies the diversity of New York's culture. Visitors sunbathe, walk dogs, toss Frisbees, take in plays, gather around street performers, strap on roller blades, and dance; they play bocce, soccer, and softball. Some visitors even engage in the quiet contemplation Olmsted hoped his design would inspire. They stroll through the landscape, admire the rustic architecture, and linger at the zoo.

Perhaps just as important, Central Park's revival matches that of the city as a whole. Wealth has congregated around the park, in the remarkably successful Upper East Side and Upper West Side neighborhoods. By the 1990s even Harlem had begun a reversal of fortunes, as wealthier New Yorkers sought more reasonably priced real estate north of the park. Harlem's gentrification caused consternation and some conflict, as longtime residents found themselves living in a neighborhood they increasingly didn't recognize, or worse, feared they could no longer afford, but Harlem's recovery from decades of concentrated poverty and physical deterioration reveals much about Manhattan's economic and environmental health. The revival of Central Park and the neighborhoods around it represents hard work, dedication, and the coming to fruition of one central idea: this place is too important to allow it to deteriorate.

AGRICULTURAL DECLINE AND THE RETURN OF THE FOREST

Over the last several decades the public sector has led a remarkably successful effort to preserve New York's cultural and natural heritage. In the private sector, however, broad economic decline—especially in agriculture—has brought equally dramatic environmental change. From the suburbanizing counties of Putnam and Rockland, north to St. Lawrence and Clinton counties, and across dozens of upstate counties, including Delaware, Madison, and Cattaraugus, the number of farms and the number of acres in farmland have dropped considerably. Recent declines continue long-term trends. In the late 1800s, near the peak of agriculture's influence over the landscape, New York State had more than 240,000 farms. By 1959 it had fewer than 83,000, and by 2007 it had just over 36,000. Much of the recent decline is due to the continuing difficulty of making dairy farms profitable. The state's population of milk cows has dropped by 500,000 head since the late 1950s. Some sectors have seen some growth, including vineyards in western New York. Indeed grape production remains strong along Lake Erie, where Concord grapes supply juice, and along the western Finger Lakes, which have long provided the thriving wine industry with many varieties of grapes. In addition, over the last couple of decades the organic farm movement has brought a significant increase in mixed agriculture, as small farms have dedicated their environmentally sensitive production to local and regional consumption. Still, the stable agricultural sectors, such as viniculture, and the few growing sectors, such as organic production, have not stemmed the overall decline of farming in the state.

Figure 29. In this 1917 photograph Rudolph family members stand beside a barn on their Red Hill farm in the town of Denning, Ulster County. Courtesy Rudolph Farm Collection.

The shrinking agricultural sector has brought wrenching economic change for many small upstate communities, but it has also brought significant environmental change, as literally millions of acres of former farmland have slowly reverted to forest—both through the intervention of reforestation programs and as a consequence of ecological succession. Throughout much of the state, land use has evolved from pasture to meadow and, eventually, to forest. In the late 1800s, New York had nearly 23 million acres dedicated to agriculture. Today it has just over 7 million acres of farmland, fewer than 5 million of which are in crops every year. In some places the decline has been stunning. Madison

Figure 30. This 2009 photograph shows the corner of the same barn, with the reforestation of the old farm evident in the background. Like many other counties in upstate New York, Ulster has experienced considerable reforestation largely because of the economic failure of agriculture over the last century. Copyright Michal Heron Photography, reprinted with permission.

County had over 4,600 farms in 1875. It had just 744 in 2007, and the county's total area in cropland had diminished by almost 200,000 acres. In Essex County, along Lake Champlain, the decline has been even more complete, with both numbers of farms and numbers of acres in crops declining by 90 percent since the 1870s. Around Essex County, and around the state, fewer fields have mostly meant more forests. This is not a return of the same forests that were cleared by settlers more than a century ago, of course. There are no chestnuts among the saplings; the elms die young. The evolving fields contain honeysuckle and other invasive species. Still, wild meadow and young forests have increased habitat for many species, including some that represent a remarkable ecological recovery. Turkeys are abundant, as are beavers. There may be as many as thirty thousand coyotes in the state; bears may number as many as eight thousand, concentrated mostly in the heavily forested areas of the Adirondacks, the Catskills, and the Allegheny region. Even in formerly well populated and extensively farmed regions, one can sense that the frontier is slowly sweeping back, taking the least profitable farms and filling them with trees. In parts of New York State, it almost feels as if the wilderness is howling again.

Epilogue

Finding Places in History

On the way to Niagara Falls one summer, my family and I took a little detour. We drove into the community called Black Creek Village. We passed dozens of small, well-kept homes in a neighborhood that looked like so many other working-class subdivisions on the outskirts of American cities. This was no ordinary community, however, as the eight-foot fence surrounding seventy acres at its heart made clear. We drove around the fence and the long, grassy mound that it enclosed. We found no signs, no explanation or interpretation of what we were circumnavigating. Of course, I already knew. This was Love Canal. As we passed down streets where the state had acquired and demolished dozens of homes, down streets that were unsurprisingly empty and ill-kept, I told my children the story of the toxic dump and the health problems faced by the people who had lived there. My daughters were deeply empathetic, as children tend to be, and they asked if everyone is okay now and if they are still alive. I didn't know. Perhaps unsatisfied because I could tell them more about the past than about the present, my girls became impatient. My youngest asked, "Why do we have to go to places like this?"

I knew my girls wanted to see the falls, not a former toxic dump, so we drove on, through the chronically depressed city of Niagara Falls. And I'm still thinking of a good answer to the question my daughter posed. Perhaps the best I can do is claim that like books, places tell stories. Landscapes are valuable documents that can help us understand environmental history; they can reveal something about how people have lived on the land, how they shaped and reshaped the places where they lived, worked, and played. And we should visit the places like Love Canal, where important events have happened, and while we are there, we should tell the stories that mark these spots. Of course, to gain a more complete understanding of environmental history, we need to visit a wide variety of places, to see what stories they can tell us, what lessons they might impart.

Tourists tend not to stop at Love Canal, or even drive around its fence. The nearby LaSalle Expressway, taken by most American visitors to the falls, passes just a few yards from the southern end of the filled canal, but no historic markers encourage drivers to pause. Undoubtedly this absence is partly in deference to neighbors who would rather not have the constant reminder of that episode in the history of this place, and to the entire city of Niagara Falls, which is trying to be something other than a postindustrial city. Still, even without a museum or a historic marker, the landscape can tell us a great deal about this complex story. The grassy mound behind the chain-link fence and the streets that mark a neighborhood removed are sure signs of disaster. But the landscape reveals conflicting views as well. A few scattered houses on 101st and 102nd streets mark the places where holdouts saved their homes but lost their neighborhood. These remaining houses remind us that some residents didn't believe that Hooker's chemicals were doing harm, and instead blamed activists for disturbing their peace and breaking their community apart.

A few years ago the EPA declared Love Canal clean, its toxic wastes now sealed, the site properly drained and monitored. The state has sold more than two hundred homes north of the dump. Questions linger, of course, because toxic chemicals are so mysterious to most of us. Is it safe to go back, safe to rebuild here? Can the former Love Canal stop being the former Love Canal and truly become Black Creek Village? Over time, this neighborhood may blend more completely into the landscape of the Niagara Frontier, a landscape largely built during the postwar boom and largely undone by a lost wager on a chemical industry that brought jobs and trouble. Someday Love Canal may be simply one of many abandoned industrial sites in the region, deemed safe, but not for redevelopment. The Niagara Frontier is lousy with chain-link fences that surround places that used to be something else. Each of these fences is an object lesson in the dangers of the modern chemical industry and of weak industrial regulation and oversight. For decades to come, even without a formal public history installation, Love Canal's chain-link fence and grass-covered mound will tell that cautionary tale.

You need not visit a former toxic dump to find a cautionary landscape. Take a completely different kind of place, such as Long Island's Levittown. Drive around it—I recommend a summer Saturday—on quiet, curvilinear streets, some of them ending in cul-de-sacs and most of them with children on bikes or on foot, doing what children do in safe and spacious neighborhoods. Pass the single-family homes that still represent economic security for all these families. You can watch the traffic on the larger streets that run past the shopping plazas on their way to the highways. Levittown is the quintessential post–World War II suburb, its name synonymous with sprawling communities of modest homes surrounded by little patches of grass. Sixty years after its construction, Levittown is still a model of suburban living and, perhaps, of how not to build a metropolis. Here we see a New York distended by long commutes and divided by race and class. The 2000 census listed 53,000 people in Levittown, only 387 of whom were African American. A town born segregated remains so.

As in most places, Levittown's landscape tells conflicting stories. Success is evident here in the comfortable houses, the parks and playgrounds. But in Levittown success occurs mostly at the individual or familial level—each single-family home a potentially happy story. The broader landscape, though, offers a more troubling narrative, one told at the societal level. This is a landscape built for cars and in support of racial segregation. Although these two evident facts may seem to have little in common at first glance, they both reflect a deep desire for security. Indeed the entire community still reflects the dominant postwar fears surrounding race mixing, rising crime, even nuclear war. The single-family homes, surrounded by lawn, surrounded by more homes, all of them occupied by people who shared common values and, more important, a common skin color, reflect a landscape of security. Levittown's success, in both the short and long term, reveals a broad desire among white New Yorkers to distance themselves from the city and to distance themselves from diversity. Levittown served those purposes in the 1950s, and it still does.

To fully appreciate sprawling suburbia as a cautionary landscape, you must travel well beyond the boundaries of any one community. In the endless subdivisions of Nassau County, you can find places—such as Mineola, Hicksville, Plainview—that may represent some type of success when viewed individually, in the way that the homes of Levittown can. But together they create a landscape of flight, built over a long era of prosperity, consumption, and shortsightedness. Driving through neighborhoods that pushed farther and farther into farm fields and forests, I am reminded of Carl Carmer's warning that New York's countryside "may be sucked into the maw of the city." Today, expensive gas and global warming haunt our auto-dependent suburbs, on Long Island and elsewhere, and in the heat of the summer, stuck in traffic on the Long Island Expressway, surely everyone can appreciate the broadest lesson that this landscape teaches: planning matters over the long term.

Carmer wasn't concerned about the disappearance of potato fields on the Hempstead Plains of Long Island. He feared that the city would reach up the beautiful Hudson Valley, where sprawl has indeed arrived in the last fifty years or so, but not to the extent it has on Long Island. Along the Hudson you'll find a different landscape, filled with state parks and historic sites. Tourists drive up both sides of the river in every season. Some of them head to Hyde Park and the former home of Franklin Roosevelt. If Levittown is a landscape of security, Hyde Park is a landscape of privilege. Wander the Springwood estate of Roosevelt the tree farmer and you can learn a great deal about the role of wealth and power in securing environmental protection in New York—even without poring over the rich archival material in his presidential library, which is also on the property. The estate itself is an object lesson in preservation.

You can hike through the forests around Springwood on well-maintained trails, one of which connects Springwood with the Vanderbilt mansion and Eleanor Roosevelt's cottage, Val-Kill. The preservationist organization first formed to combat Con Ed at Storm King, Scenic Hudson, has been instrumental in creating the trail through the purchase of land and the improvement of paths. But it is no coincidence, of course, that this lovely trail through fine woods connects three National Historic Sites. Scenic Hudson has long supported the preservation of historic landscape, one that includes forests, fields, and buildings. Historic preservation has been an especially powerful force in the Hudson Valley, as New Yorkers have struggled to preserve a rich heritage, especially through the protection and display of important homes: Roosevelt's Springwood, Frederic Church's Olana in Hudson, Thomas Cole's across the river in Catskill, and the list goes on. At Springwood, then, Roosevelt's home reminds us not just of his important role as an individual but of the preservation movement's concern for the cultural landscape.

At Springwood, overlooking the Hudson River, trying to locate John Burroughs's home, Riverby, across the water, you will also be reminded of the Hudson Valley's centrality to the evolution of environmentalism in New York State. You might also be reminded of Robert Boyle's words, written to describe the changing landscape up and down the Hudson Valley. "Though the scenes vary," he wrote, "they have a common theme—a sort of fairy-tale magic that lingers in the mind from childhood, the notion that this is the way the world ought to look." Boyle wrote these words over forty years ago, but they remain just as true today. They remind us of the power of culture, of Cole and Church and Burroughs and others, to create ideal landscapes, landscapes that have inspired historic preservation and natural resource conservation, landscapes that have inspired modern environmentalism. This is a landscape replete with meaning, one of the places where New Yorkers affirm their identity. They want to sit where Roosevelt sat, to overlook the Hudson and the valley that Cole and Church and others helped elevate to international importance.

Beyond the historic homes, the Hudson Valley contains many places that remind us of successful preservation efforts, from the Palisades to Storm King. But those seeking evidence of the success of environmental protection would probably head farther north, to the Adirondacks. This expansive park is full of preserved landscapes, such as those in the High Peaks, around the Saranac lakes, and what the Sierra Club calls the Great Oswegatchie Canoe Wilderness, half a million acres that run west of Long Lake, containing more than four hundred Adirondack lakes and ponds. The Sierra Club would like the state to make additional purchases here, bringing the entirety of the great expanse between Raquette Lake and Cranberry Lake into the state Forest Preserve.

In 2006 Bill McKibben took a celebratory canoe trip through a small part of this wild land, marking the Nature Conservancy's purchase of Round Lake and 26,000 acres from International Paper. McKibben praised the landscape, but he knew where he was. "Though very wild, the land we'd be traveling for the rest of the week isn't wilderness," he acknowledged. "People have used it, and in some cases used it hard, since the late 19th century." He and his companions paddled and portaged past former great camps, such as the Whitneys' summer estate on Little Tupper Lake, and past logging railroads and dams that raised water levels to facilitate floating out logs. Little Tupper is now part of the Forest Preserve, and it will remain wild forever, as will the larger Five Ponds Wilderness to the west, one of the original Adirondack wildernesses designated in the 1970s. Over much of this landscape only a careful eye like McKibben's would catch evidence of human use. "The Adirondacks are perhaps the world's greatest experiment in ecological recovery," McKibben wrote, "a place hard used a century ago and now slowly reverting, slowly proving that where humanity backs off, nature rebounds." McKibben's essay reminds us of the difficulty of learning from landscapes alone. Ecological recovery, in the form of a second-growth forest, can obscure the past, as clear cuts and logging roads slowly disappear.

Paddling through the Adirondacks one can almost forget the larger threats—of continued acid rain and global warming, the losses from which McKibben himself has written about so extensively. Protecting the entire wilderness through purchase can't solve these problems. The Great Oswegatchie Canoe Wilderness reminds us of New York State's leadership in preservation, and certainly of the activism of Bob Marshall, the Wilderness Society, and other champions of wild nature. It reminds us of the long effort to expand the public domain through land purchases, and not just in the Adirondacks. This wilderness might also represent the broader ecological recovery under way in the state. People even hear, though rarely see, moose in the North Woods. All of this is good news, of course, and reflective of good environmental policies: hunting regulations, the DDT ban, strategic land acquisition and easements. The recovery reflects the growing influence of ecology in public discourse and in policymaking. Some of the ecological recovery, however, reflects darker trends, related to the poor economy of the last several decades, the lack of demographic growth, and the failure of so many upstate farms.

You need not head to the wilderness to find either nature or landscapes that hold lessons in environmental history. In fact, do just the opposite: find the most intensely urban place in the state and look around. The Meatpacking District in Manhattan might do. Wedged between the West Village and Chelsea, the Meatpacking District is a collection of warehouses and markets that evince the ever-changing metropolis. Historically it was, just as its name suggests, a butchering and wholesaling district centered at the Gansevoort Meat Market. When I visited in the summer of 2008, this historic use was largely gone, and developers couldn't build there quickly enough. There were new condo towers, new restaurants and clubs. The tiny neighborhood had all the energy of a twenty-four-hour city, all the energy of capitalism's remarkable agility. Developers, entrepreneurs, investors long for and help create these hot neighborhoods, where early investments in forgotten corners of the city can be parlayed into huge profits.

But the Meatpacking District also reveals how citizens have used the power of government to reshape and regulate the urban environment. In response to development pressure, preservationists have successfully worked to create overlapping city, state, and national Gansevoort Market historic districts, garnering the modest protections and tax incentives those designations afford. More obvious to visitors is the High Line Park, opened in 2009 atop the elevated railroad line that ends at Gansevoort Street. This long-abandoned freight line, built in 1929, helps define this neighborhood as postindustrial space, and its redevelopment as a linear aerial park speaks to the city's ever-increasing emphasis on environmental amenities. Other changes in the area also reflect this trend, including the Ninth Avenue bike lane. More obvious, on the other side of the neighborhood the still-evolving Hudson River Park, stretching from Fifty-ninth Street to Chambers Street, already offers new public spaces. In Greenwich Village a series of piers provides a variety of recreational spaces, including lawns for sunbathing and relaxing—the kind of open space the Village hasn't had since the early 1800s.

Walking through the Meatpacking District today, you might think back to the Ladies Health Protective Association, organized in the 1880s in the attempt to make the urban landscape more livable, part of a broader effort to tame the worst qualities of industrialization. The crowded industrial city continues to morph into a crowded postindustrial metropolis, but as the rapid changes along Manhattan's west side reveal, the quest for a more livable city is never-ending.

Every place has a story, and in New York State that story is almost always more complicated than it first appears. North of Hamilton, for instance, a stretch of the abandoned Chenango Canal retains its water, and the village has set aside the towpath for recreation. The canal's nearly stagnant water is mostly uninteresting for walkers. The path's real attraction is on the other side, another body of water called Woodman's Pond, a modest lake with no camps or other buildings along its shore, no docks, no boats—a rarity in this part of New York. Its quiet waters make a fine resting place for reclusive waterfowl, like snow geese and wood ducks. This is a wonderful place for birding. Walking along this path feels like walking between two worlds, the wild Woodman's Pond, with its irregular, marshy shore, and the manmade canal, a measured line in a messy world. At the end of the walk, where Woodman's Pond reaches its southern bank, you can take another path along the lakeshore, following a small feeder canal that runs from Lake Moraine, the largest of the reservoirs built to supply water to the Chenango Canal. The path runs through the thick forest of willow, cedar, and ash that makes this part of Woodman's Pond so beautiful from a distance.

Here the story, and the geography, get complicated, for Woodman's Pond isn't exactly as it seems. The southern shore of the lake has been elevated by an earthen dam, the water level raised, its outlet built to pass under the feeder canal, where it can be funneled, if necessary, into the village water system. Woodman's Pond, it turns out, is as constructed as the canal, and both are maintained through the works of engineers and the force of law; the pond is posted: Keep Out, Public Water Supply. Clearly the towpath is a more porous boundary between manmade landscape and wilderness than I first imagined. (In some places the path is literally porous because muskrats and groundhogs have burrowed into the earth.) The kingfishers and great blue herons don't see a boundary at all, in fact, apparently as content to fish in the canal as in the lake. Over time, culture and nature have blended so thoroughly here that one might stand atop a dike and survey the stonework that funnels the water beneath the small feeder canal that carries water in another direction for different purposes, and still not appreciate how fully human hands have reworked this place. The lake is just that beautiful.

The last time I visited Woodman's Pond Wildlife Refuge, I stood upon that nineteenth-century stonework, at that very complicated place, and looked out across that lake and to the hillside beyond, where I saw something new: nearly a dozen windmills, the type that have been springing up across upstate over the last decade or so. In some places those massive white towers have sparked controversy, and people can reasonably debate their place in the landscape. But from this perspective, standing on a nineteenth-century dike, I thought they looked nearly as beautiful as the lake and, well, almost as natural.

Notes

Introduction

2–3 John H. Griscom, *The Sanitary Condition of the Laboring Population of New York* (New York: Harper & Brothers, 1845), 18–19.

3 William Cronon, "The Uses of Environmental History," *Environmental History Review* 17 (Fall 1993): 19.

11 Ebenezer Emmons, *Agriculture of New York* (Albany: C. Van Benthuysen & Co., 1846), 1.

13 Basil Hall, *Travels in North America* (Philadelphia: Cary, Lea & Cary, 1829), 57–58.

Chapter 1

14 Robert Juet, *Juet's Journal: The Voyage of the* Half Moon *from 4 April to 7 November 1609* (Newark: New Jersey Historical Society, 1959), 28.

21 Daniel Denton, *A Brief Description of New York: Formerly Called New Netherlands* (London, 1670), 3.

21 Kiliaen van Rensselaer quoted in Thomas E. Burke Jr., *Mohawk Frontier: The Dutch Community of Schenectady, New York, 1661–1710* (Ithaca: Cornell University Press, 1991), 49.

25 General Schuyler quoted in Lincoln Diamant, *Chaining the Hudson: The Fight for the River in the American Revolution* (New York: Carol Publishing Group, 1989), 9.

27 James Kent quoted in Alan Taylor, "'Wasty Ways': Stories of American Settlement," *Environmental History* (July 1998): 295.

27–28 William Cooper quoted in Alan Taylor, *William Cooper's Town: Power and Persuasion on the Frontier of the Early American Republic* (New York: Vintage Books, 1995), 97.

28 Otsego County settler quoted in Taylor, "'Wasty Ways,'" 296.

28 Dutch bounty cited in Thomas E. Burke Jr., *Mohawk Frontier: The Dutch Community of Schenectady, New York* (Ithaca: Cornell University Press, 1991), 51.

29 Alexis de Tocqueville, *Journey to America* (London: Faber and Faber, 1959), 129.

34 William Reed, *Life on the Border, Sixty Years Ago* (Fall River, Mass.: Robert Adams, 1882), 12, 19, 21.

38 William Edwards, *Memoirs of Col. William Edwards* (printed 1847), 71.

40 Peter Kalm quoted in Jill Lepore, *New York Burning: Liberty, Slavery, and Conspiracy in Eighteenth-Century Manhattan* (New York: Alfred A. Knopf, 2005), xii.

40 Visiting businessman quoted in Bayrd Still, *Mirror for Gotham: New York as Seen by Contemporaries from Dutch Days to the Present* (New York: New York University Press, 1956), 103.

41, 43 *New York Journal* quoted in Gerard T. Koeppel, *Water for Gotham: A History* (Princeton: Princeton University Press, 2000), 52.

43 Streets Commission charge cited in Edwin G. Burrows and Mike Wallace, *Gotham: A History of New York City to 1898* (New York: Oxford University Press, 1999), 420.

44–45 James Fenimore Cooper, *The Pioneers* (1823; repr., New York: Signet Classics, 1964), 233–35, 13–14.

45 William Cooper quoted in Taylor, *William Cooper's Town*, 33.

Chapter 2

46–47 Nathaniel Hawthorne, "The Canal Boat," *New-England Magazine* 9 (December 1835): 398–409.

50 Basil Hall, *Travels in North America* (Philadelphia: Cary, Lea & Cary, 1829), 57–58.

53 For a description of the dam, see Theodore Dwight, *The Northern Traveller: Containing the Routes to Niagara, Quebec, and the Springs, with Descriptions of the Principal Scenes, and Useful Hints to Strangers* (New York: Wilder & Campbell, 1825), 131.

53 Solomon Southwick, *Views of Ithaca and its Environs: By an Impartial Observer* (Ithaca: D. D. & A. Spencer, 1835), 5, 7.

55 Washington Irving quoted in Dorothy Hurlbut Sanderson, *The Delaware & Hudson Canalway: Carrying Coals to Rondout* (Ellenville: Rondout Valley Publishing Company, 1965), 9.

55 Cadwallader Colden quoted in Ronald E. Shaw, *Erie Water West: A History of the Erie Canal, 1792–1854* (Lexington: University of Kentucky Press, 1966), 136.

55–56 Hall, *Travels in North America*, 70–71.

56 John Fowler, *Journal of a Tour in the State of New York in the Year 1830; with Remarks on Agriculture in those parts most Eligible for Settlers* (London: Whittaker, Treacher, and Arnot, 1831), 85.

58 Abner Austin quoted in Martin Bruegel, "Work, Gender, and Authority on the Farm: The Hudson Valley Countryside, 1790s–1850s," *Agricultural History* 76 (2002): 3.

59–60 John Burroughs, *My Boyhood* (New York: Doubleday, Page & Company, 1924), 7, 17.

63 Forest Commission Report quoted in Karl Jacoby, *Crimes against Nature: Squatters, Poachers, Thieves, and the Hidden History of American Conservation* (Berkeley: University of California Press, 2001), 18.

64   L. M. Hammond, *History of Madison County: State of New York* (Syracuse: Truair, Smith & Co., Book and Job Printers, 1872), 183.

65   Burroughs, *My Boyhood*, 48.

66   Lockport description in Carol Sheriff, *The Artificial River: The Erie Canal and the Paradox of Progress, 1817–1862* (New York: Hill and Wang, 1996), 117.

67   Fowler, *Journal of a Tour in the State of New York*, 103–4.

67   Utica quotation in Mary Ryan, *Cradle of the Middle Class: The Family in Oneida County, New York, 1790–1865* (New York: Cambridge University Press, 1981), 8.

69   Kingston quotation in Stuart Blumin, *The Urban Threshold: Growth and Change in a Nineteenth-Century American Community* (Chicago: University of Chicago Press, 1976), 122.

74   Burroughs, *My Boyhood*, 28.

75   New York State Survey Board of Commissioners, *Report of the New York State Survey for the Year 1883* (Albany: Van Benthuysen Printing House, 1884), 42.

Chapter 3

76   Thomas Cole quoted in Louis L. Noble, *The Life and Works of Thomas Cole, N.A.* (New York: Sheldon & Company, 1960), 67.

79   Robert H. Boyle, *The Hudson River: A Natural and Unnatural History* (1969; repr., New York: W. W. Norton & Company, 1979), 17.

80   James Fenimore Cooper, *The Pioneers, or the Sources of the Susquehanna* (1823; repr., New York: Signet Classics, 1964), 279.

81   Thomas Cole, "Essay on American Scenery," *American Monthly Magazine* 1 (January 1836): 1–12.

81–82   William Cullen Bryant's "Forest Hymn" can be found many places on the Web, including Wikisource, at www.en.wikisource.org/wiki/A_Forest_Hymn.

82–83   Theodore Dwight, *The Northern Traveller: Containing the Routes to Niagara, Quebec, and the Springs, with Descriptions of the Principal Scenes, and Useful Hints to Strangers* (New York: Wilder & Campbell, 1825), 5, 22, 42.

83   Bayard Taylor, *At Home and Abroad* (New York: G. P. Putnam, 1860), 483.

84   Gideon Davison, *The Fashionable Tour: An Excursion to the Springs, Niagara, Quebec, and Boston* (Saratoga Springs: G. M. Davidson, 1825), 64.

84   Frances Wright, *Views of Society and Manners in America* (London: Longman, Hurst, Rees, Orme, and Brown, 1821), 238–44.

84–85   Nathaniel Hawthorne, "My Visit to Niagara," *New-England Magazine* (February 1835): 91–96.

85   Washington Irving, "The Catskill Mountains," in *Home Book of the Picturesque* (New York: George P. Putnam, 1852), 71–78.

86   John F. Sears, *Sacred Places: American Tourist Attractions in the Nineteenth Century* (New York: Oxford University Press, 1989), 22.

86   N. P. Willis quoted in Roland Van Zandt, *The Catskill Mountain House: America's Grandest Hotel* (Hensonville: Black Dome Press, 1991), 43.

86 John Fowler, *Journal of a Tour in the State of New York in the Year 1830; with Remarks on Agriculture in those parts most Eligible for Settlers* (London: Whittaker, Treacher, and Arnot, 1831), 172.

87 Nathaniel Hawthorne, "Old Ticonderoga: A Picture of the Past," in *The Snow-Image, and Other Twice-Told Tales* (Charlottesville: University of Virginia, 2003), electronic resource.

88 *The Erie Railway Tourist* (1874), 22.

90 N. P. Willis quoted in Van Zandt, *The Catskill Mountain House,* 44.

91 Andrew Jackson Downing quoted in Kenneth Jackson, *Crabgrass Frontier: The Suburbanization of the United States* (New York: Oxford University Press, 1985), 64.

91 Andrew Jackson Downing, *The Architecture of Country Houses* (New York: D. Appleton & Co., 1850), 344.

93 Frederick Law Olmsted, *Forty Years of Landscape Architecture: Central Park* (Cambridge: MIT Press, 1973), 357.

93 Olmsted, *Forty Years of Landscape Architecture: Central Park,* 356.

95 James T. Gardner, *Report of New York State Survey on the Preservation of the Scenery of Niagara Falls* (Albany: Charles Van Benthuysen & Sons, 1880), 7.

96 *New York Times,* July 15, 16, 1885.

97 Philip Terrie, *Contested Terrain: A New History of Nature and People in the Adirondacks* (Syracuse: Adirondack Museum/Syracuse University Press, 1997), 8.

97 Joel T. Headley, *The Adirondack; or, Life in the Woods* (New York: Baker and Scribner, 1853), 167, 62–63.

98–99 William H. H. Murray, *Adventures in the Wilderness, or, Camp-Life in the Adirondacks* (Boston: Fields, Osgood & Co., 1869), 8, 11.

100 Theodore Roosevelt quoted by Paul Cutright, *Theodore Roosevelt: The Making of a Conservationist* (Urbana: University of Illinois Press), 101–2.

100–101 George Perkins Marsh, *Man and Nature; or, Physical Geography as Modified by Human Action* (New York: Charles Scribner & Co., 1864), 235–36.

102 "Communication From the Comptroller Submitting Report of the Forestry Commission," Assembly Document no. 36 (January 23, 1885), 14–15.

102 Constitution of the Association for the Protection of the Adirondacks, June 20, 1902.

103 Bernhard Fernow quoted in Karl Jacoby, *Crimes against Nature: Squatters, Poachers, Thieves, and the Hidden History of American Conservation* (Berkeley: University of California Press, 2001), 17.

104–5 Association for the Protection of the Adirondacks, *A Plea for the Adirondack and Catskill Parks* (1903?), 25, 27, 28, 29.

Chapter 4

110 "Editor's Easy Chair," *Harper's New Monthly Magazine* 13 (July 1856): 272.

113 *Albany Express,* September 17, 1874, quoted in David O. Stowell, *Streets, Railroads, and the Great Strike of 1877* (Chicago: University of Chicago Press, 1999), 29.

114 *Buffalo Daily Courier,* August 19, 1873, quoted in Stowell, *Streets, Railroads, and the Great Strike of 1877,* 35.

116 John H. Griscom, *The Sanitary Condition of the Laboring Population of New York* (New York: Harper & Brothers, 1845), 4, 7.

117 Council on Hygiene quoted in Roy Lubove, *The Progressives and the Slums: Tenement House Reform in New York City, 1890–1917* (Pittsburgh: University of Pittsburgh Press, 1962), 17–18.

118 *New York Times,* April 23, 1874.

119 *New York Times,* May 18, 1887.

120–21 Jacob Riis, *How the Other Half Lives* (1890; repr., New York: Bedford/St. Martin's, 1996), 167.

122 Jacob Riis, "Playgrounds for City Schools," *Century Illustrated Monthly Magazine* 48 (1894): 663.

124–25 Rochester anti-smoke law quoted in *The City of Rochester v. Macauley-Fien Milling Company,* 199 N.Y. 207; 92 N.E. 641; 1910 N.Y. (Lexis 1231).

127 *Brooklyn Eagle,* June 23, 1877.

128 Tree Planting Association discussed in Charles R. Lamb to Mrs. Russell Sage, June 17, 1908, RSF, 10.1, box 85, folder 823, Rockefeller Family Archives, Rockefeller Archives Center, Sleepy Hollow, N.Y. (hereafter RAC).

128 George Waring quoted in Martin V. Melosi, *Garbage in the Cities: Refuse, Reform, and the Environment* (Pittsburgh: University of Pittsburgh Press, 2005), 49.

129 Richard Gilder quoted in *New York Times,* July 7, 1896.

132 For the cholera cure claim, see *New York Times,* July 23, 1876.

133 On Ozone Park, see *New York Times,* July 30, 1882, October 3, 1886.

133 Forest Hills Gardens advertisement quoted in Susan L. Klaus, *A Modern Arcadia: Frederick Law Olmsted Jr. and the Plan for Forest Hills Gardens* (Amherst: University of Massachusetts Press, 2002), 3.

135 Walter Hines Page quoted in Mark Goldman, *High Hopes: The Rise and Decline of Buffalo, New York* (Albany: State University of New York Press, 1983), 7.

Chapter 5

142 On tenements, see Theodore Roosevelt, *An Autobiography* (New York: Macmillan, 1913), 219.

142 On the country and raising children, see Roosevelt, *Autobiography,* 365.

142–43 On being governor, see Roosevelt, *Autobiography,* 313.

143 For Roosevelt's annual message, see *Autobiography,* 338.

143 On Sagamore Hill, see Roosevelt, *Autobiography,* 355.

143 John Burroughs, *Camping and Tramping with Roosevelt* (Boston: Houghton Mifflin, 1906), 79–80.

144 On serving the commonwealth, see Theodore Roosevelt, "Special Message from the President of the United States," in Henry Gannett, ed., *Report of the National Conservation Commission,* vol. 1 (Washington, D.C.: U.S. Government Printing Office, 1909), 3.

145 Park survey quoted in New York State Association, *The State Park Plan for New York...* ([New York?], 1924), 19.

146 Frederick Franklin Moon and Harold Cahill Belyea, "Forestry for the Private Owner," *Bulletin No. 13 of the New York State College of Forestry at Syracuse University* 20 (July 1920): 3.

147–48 Goodsell and Dunning quoted in Karl Jacoby, *Crimes against Nature: Squatters, Poachers, Thieves, and the Hidden History of American Conservation* (Berkeley: University of California Press, 2001), 64.

148 Campaign against Vermin described in *Annual Report of the Conservation Commission, 1918* (Albany: J. B. Lyon Company, Printers, 1919), 51.

148 *Annual Report of the Conservation Commission, 1921* (Albany: J. B. Lyon Company, Printers, 1922), 65.

150 On certifying oysters, see *Second Annual Report of the Conservation Commission* (Albany: J. B. Lyon Company, Printers, 1913), 38.

152 Harry R. Melone, *Souvenir of the Finger Lakes Region* (Auburn: Cayuga County News Co., 1921), 30.

152 For the map, see the cover of Cherry Valley Turnpike Association, *The Cherry Valley Turnpike* (Waterville, N.Y.: 1929).

153 New York State Association, *State Park Plan for New York*, 6.

154 Bob Marshall quoted in Phil Brown, ed., *Bob Marshall in the Adirondacks: Writings of a Pioneering Peak-Bagger, Pond-Hopper and Wilderness Preservationist* (Saranac Lake: Lost Pond Press, 2006), 134.

155 Association for the Protection of the Adirondacks, *Roads in the Forest Preserve* (New York: APA, 1933), 5.

155 Al Smith quoted in *New York Times*, March 19, 1928.

158 Roosevelt to William Overfield, December 2, 1923, in Edgar B. Nixon, *Franklin D. Roosevelt and Conservation, 1911–1945*, vol. 1 (Hyde Park, N.Y.: National Archives and Records Service, Franklin D. Roosevelt Library, 1957), 51.

158–59 Speech by Roosevelt before the Berkshire Bankers' Association, Lenox, Mass., June 20, 1921, in Nixon, *Franklin D. Roosevelt and Conservation, 1911–1945*, 1:47.

160 Franklin D. Roosevelt, "Address at State College of Agriculture, Cornell University (Excerpts), Ithaca, N.Y., February 14, 1930," in *The Public Papers and Addresses of Franklin D. Roosevelt*, vol. 1 (New York: Random House, 1938), 143.

160 On the scientific allocation of school facilities, see Franklin D. Roosevelt, "The Annual Message to the Legislature (Excerpts), January 6, 1932," in *Public Papers and Addresses*, 1:119.

160 For the Roosevelt quotation on acreage, see *New York Times*, January 22, 1931.

160 On the distribution of population, see Franklin D. Roosevelt, "The Annual Message to the Legislature (Excerpts), January 6, 1932," in *Public Papers and Addresses*, 1:116.

162 For Roosevelt on abandoned lands, see *New York Times*, April 2, 1931.

162–63 On conservation policy, see Franklin D. Roosevelt, "Radio Address Urging Voters to Support the Reforestation Amendment to the Constitution, October 26, 1931," in *Public Papers and Addresses*, 1:530.

164   Civilian Conservation Corps, *Two Years of Emergency Conservation Work (Civilian Conservation Corps), April 5, 1933–March 31, 1935* (Washington, 1935), 1.

Chapter 6

173   Thomas Dewey quoted in *New York Times,* July 12, 1946.

174   "Remarks by Dr. Evarts B. Greene at Hudson River Valley Conference," June 1946, RG 2, Cultural Interests, box 62, folder 621, Rockefeller Family Archives, RAC.

175   HRCS mission statement in William H. Osborn, "Hudson River Conservation Society, Inc.," May 1961, RG 2, Cultural Interests, box 62, folder 623, Rockefeller Family Archives, RAC.

176   E. B. White in *New Yorker,* May 16, 1959, 180.

176   Ada Louise Huxtable in *New York Times,* December 29, 1969.

181   Real estate advertisement in *New York Times,* August 31, 1954.

181   Editorial, *New York Times,* January 17, 1947.

182   Tom Huddleston in *New York Times,* November 25, 1951.

182   E. B. White, *Writings from the New Yorker, 1927–1976,* ed. Rebecca M. Dale (New York: HarperCollins, 1990), 204.

182   Irate housewife, letter to the editor, *New York Times,* August 13, 1949.

183   Elizabeth Robinson quoted in *New York Times,* May 20, 1951.

183   "The Next Breath You Take" (New York: Committee for Smoke Control, 1951), unpaginated pamphlet.

184   Editorial, *New York Times,* November 24, 1953.

184   Florence Loozis, letter to the editor, *New York Times,* March 22, 1958.

184   Worried mother, letter to the editor, *New York Times,* March 28, 1959.

187–88   Carl Carmer testimony in *Hearing before the Federal Power Commission in the Matter of Consolidated Edison, Washington, D.C., Project no. 2338, May 5, 7, 8, 12, 1964* (Washington, D.C., 1964), 990–93.

188   *Scenic Hudson v. Federal Power Commission and Consolidated Edison,* United States Court of Appeals, 2d Circuit, 354 F.2d 608; 1965 U.S. App. (Lexis 3514).

189   FPC examiner quoted in *New York Times,* August 7, 1968.

191   *Murphy v. Benson,* United States District Court, 164 F. Supp. 120; 1958 U.S. Dist. (Lexis 3790).

192   William O. Douglas dissent in *Murphy et al. v. Butler,* 362 U.S. 929; 80 S. Ct. 750; 4 L. Ed. 2d 747; 1960 U.S. (Lexis 1435).

192–93   *Yannacone v. Dennison,* Supreme Court of New York, Special Term, Suffolk County, 55 Misc. 2d 468; 285 N.Y.S. 2d 476; 1967 N.Y. Misc. (Lexis 1039).

194   Remarks by Governor Nelson Rockefeller at Ceremonies Held at Jones Beach State Park, Commemorating the Thirty-fifth Anniversary of the State Parks System, August 20, 1959, RG 15 Nelson A. Rockefeller (hereafter NAR), Gubernatorial Series 17.2, box 25, folder 141, Rockefeller Family Archives, RAC.

196 Joint Legislative Committee on Natural Resources, "Wilderness in the Forest Preserve" (1961), RG 2, Cultural Interests, box 80, folder 749, Rockefeller Family Archives, RAC.

197 Robert Moses, "The Philosophy of the New York State Park System," National Conference of State Parks, Bear Mountain, N.Y., October 7, 1947, RG 2, Cultural Interests, box 79, folder 746, Rockefeller Family Archives, RAC.

197 Robert Moses to Gerald P. Hull, July 28, 1961, RG 2, Cultural Interests, box 80, folder 749, Rockefeller Family Archives, RAC.

199 Robert Moses, "New York City Traffic Relief," RG 4L, NAR, box 185, folder 1859, Rockefeller Family Archives, RAC.

200 Jane Jacobs, *The Death and Life of Great American Cities* (New York: Vintage Books, 1961), 6–7.

202 Paul Goldberger in *New York Times*, July 2, 1976.

202–3 Jacobs, *Death and Life of Great American Cities*, 187.

204 John Lindsay quoted in *New York Times*, April 23, 1970.

Chapter 7

205 Quotations about Brownsville in *New York Times*, June 21 and May 6, 1971.

207 John V. Lindsay, *The City* (New York: Signet, 1970), 59–60.

209 "Rats cause riots" chant reported in *New York Times*, August 8, 1967.

213 Michael H. Brown, *Laying Waste: The Poisoning of America by Toxic Chemicals* (New York: Pantheon Books, 1980), 29.

215 Love Canal mother quoted in Martha R. Fowlkes and Patricia Y. Miller, *Love Canal: The Social Construction of Disaster* (Washington, D.C.: Federal Emergency Management Agency, 1982), 95.

219 Williamsburg high school student quoted in *New York Times*, November 16, 1998.

221 Anne LaBastille, "Report on Acid Precipitation," in House of Representatives Subcommittee on Oversight and Investigations, *Acid Rain*, 96th Cong., 2nd sess., 1980, serial no. 96–150 (Washington, D.C., 1980), 784.

222 Acid rain advertisement, *New York Times*, May 20, 1999.

224 Bill McKibben, *The End of Nature* (New York: Random House, 1989), 45.

225 Betty Smith, *A Tree Grows in Brooklyn* (New York: Harper & Brothers, 1943), 3.

226 Charles O'Neill quoted in *New York Times*, October 12, 1998.

Epilogue

238–39 Robert Boyle, *The Hudson River: A Natural and Unnatural History* (1969; repr., New York: W. W. Norton & Company, 1979), 17.

239 Bill McKibben, "Full Circle: An Adirondack Canoe Route Traces the Return of the Wild," *Nature Conservancy Magazine* (Summer 2006): 36–40.

Bibliographical Essay

The historical literature on New York State is vast, but relatively few works examine environmental history, and much of the environmental history of the state focuses on one region: the Adirondacks. I have relied largely on secondary works in writing this book; but given the paucity of books on the state's environmental history, this bibliographical essay includes a wide range of historical works, many of which are in no way environmental histories. This essay is not intended to provide anything approaching a complete description of New York State historiography but instead describes the materials I found most useful in writing this book.

This essay mostly links resources with the topics covered in individual chapters, but some resources deserve mention upfront because they provided guidance across many chapters. For example, researching the history of New York is made considerably easier by the electronic availability of ProQuest's historical *New York Times* (1851–2005), which I used more than any other single source. I also made frequent use of reference works, including *The Encyclopedia of New York City*, edited by Kenneth Jackson (New Haven: Yale University Press, 1995); and *The Encyclopedia of New York State*, edited by Peter Eisenstadt (Syracuse: Syracuse University Press, 2005). For wonderful visual resources, I used the collection of photographs made available on the Web through the New York State Archives Digital Collections, http://iarchives.nysed.gov/PubImageWeb/listCollections.jsp?id=6128.

Many histories of particular locations in New York describe aspects of environmental history, some of them covering long periods of time. Among the best of these is Michael Kudish, *The Catskill Forest: A History* (Fleischmanns: Purple Mountain Press, 2000), which is remarkably detailed. For a broader perspective on that region, see Alf Evers, *The Catskills: From Wilderness to Woodstock* (Woodstock: Overlook Press, 1982); and my own *Making Mountains: New York City and the Catskills* (Seattle: University of Washington Press, 2007). Norman J. Van Valkenburgh and Christopher Olney have created a wonderful work on the Catskills that focuses on the state's role in forest preservation; see *The Catskill Park: Inside the Blue Line, The Forest Preserve and Mountain Communities of America's First Wilderness* (Hensonville: Black Dome Press, 2004). Tim Duerden's *History of Delaware County, New York: A Catskill Land and Its People, 1797–2007* (Fleischmanns: Purple Mountain Press, 2007) is an excellent local history with considerable attention to environmental issues.

Of the many books on the Adirondacks, I found Philip Terrie's two works of most use; see *Forever Wild: A Cultural History of Wilderness in the Adirondacks* (Syracuse: Syracuse University Press, 1994), and *Contested Terrain: A New History of Nature and People in the Adirondacks* (Syracuse: Syracuse University Press, 1997). Students of the Adirondacks should also seek out the works of Barbara McMartin, who has published many books on the region, most of which are guidebooks with ample history; see particularly *The Great Forest of the Adirondacks* (Utica: North Country Books, 1994).

New York's other great landscape—the Hudson River Valley—has also attracted considerable attention. Robert Boyle's *Hudson River: A Natural and Unnatural History* (1969; reprint, New York: W. W. Norton & Company, 1979) is among my favorite books on any topic. It is beautifully written, richly detailed, and an early example of environmental history, a field that did not yet exist when Boyle began his project. Among the many other works on the Hudson, those helpful to me were Frances F. Dunwell, *The Hudson River Highlands* (New York: Columbia University Press, 1991); Carl Carmer, *The Hudson* (New York: Farrar & Rinehart, 1939), part of the Rivers of America Series; and Tom Lewis's more recent and very readable book *The Hudson: A History* (New Haven: Yale University Press, 2005).

I referred frequently to Edwin G. Burrows and Mike Wallace, *Gotham: A History of New York City to 1898* (New York: Oxford University Press, 1999), which contains a wealth of information on the founding and growth of the city.

Other helpful books on New York City include Matthew Gandy, *Concrete and Clay: Reworking Nature in New York City* (Cambridge: MIT Press, 2002); Max Page, *The Creative Destruction of Manhattan, 1900–1940* (Chicago: University of Chicago Press, 1999); and David M. Scobey, *Empire City: The Making and Meaning of the New York City Landscape* (Philadelphia: Temple University Press, 2002). On New York City's suburban development, see the classic work by Kenneth Jackson, *Crabgrass Frontier: The Suburbanization of the United States* (New York: Oxford University Press, 1985); and on the city's long relationship with oysters (and the region's waters that produced them), see Mark Kurlansky, *The Big Oyster: History on the Half Shell* (New York: Ballantine Books, 2006).

Several other works on particular regions provide at least some discussion of environmental history across a long chronology. See Ann Botshon, *Saving Sterling Forest: The Epic Struggle to Preserve New York's Highlands* (Albany: State University of New York Press, 2007); Robert O. Binnewies, *Palisades: 100,000 Acres in 100 Years* (New York: Fordham University Press, 2001); and Tom Andersen, *This Fine Piece of Water: An Environmental History of Long Island Sound* (New Haven: Yale University Press, 2002), which I used primarily as a bibliographical aid.

In addition to these monographs, primary sources that offer insight into the state's environmental history abound. Many of these have been published by the state of New York, including the state's own census, conducted periodically throughout the nineteenth century and into the early twentieth century. These records contain valuable information regarding industry, agricultural production, and land use, among other things. I made use of the state censuses of 1845, 1855, 1865, 1875, and 1925. See the New York State Fish Commission Annual Reports from the late 1800s, and the State Forest Commission Annual Reports, which began in 1885. In 1895, with a change in bureaucracy, the reports began to appear from the New York State Fisheries, Game and Forest Commission, and then as the *Annual Report of the Conservation Commission* through the early twentieth century. Since 1970 the Department of Environmental Conservation has published *The Conservationist*, filled with interesting stories concerning numerous types of environmental issues. In addition to these bureaucratic sources, see the many publications from the New York State College of Forestry at Syracuse University, including its helpful *Bulletin*. Those interested in agriculture might browse the Cornell University Agricultural Experiment Station *Bulletin* and study the agricultural census data available at www.agcensus.usda.gov.

1. This Comes of Settling a Country: European Colonization and the Market's Arrival

For colonial environmental history, see William Cronon, *Changes in the Land: Indians, Colonists, and the Ecology of New England* (New York: Hill & Wang, 1983); Alfred W. Crosby, *The Columbian Exchange: Biological and Cultural Consequences of 1492* (Westport, Conn.: Greenwood Press, 1972); and Crosby, *Ecological Imperialism: The Biological Expansion of Europe, 900–1900* (New York: Cambridge University Press, 1986). For a good general history, see Michael Kammen, *Colonial New York: A History* (New York: Charles Scribner's Sons, 1975). The classic account of the Anti-Rent Wars is Henry Christman, *Tin Horns and Calico: A Decisive Episode in the Emergence of Democracy* (New York: Henry Holt and Company, 1945). Readers may find of interest Oliver A. Rink's *Holland on the Hudson: An Economic and Social History of Dutch New York* (Ithaca: Cornell University Press, 1986), though I made little use of it. See also Sara S. Gronim, *Everyday Nature: Knowledge of the Natural World in Colonial New York* (New Brunswick: Rutgers University Press, 2007). I also used the reprint of Robert Juet, *Juet's Journal: The Voyage of the Half Moon from 4 April to 7 November 1609* (Newark: New Jersey Historical Society, 1959); and Daniel Denton, *A Brief Description of New York: Formerly Called New Netherlands* (London, 1670). Both of these are available on the Web.

Native Americans

I found several very useful works on Native Americans in New York State, including Matthew Dennis, *Cultivating a Landscape of Peace: Iroquois-European Encounters in Seventeenth-Century America* (Ithaca: Cornell University Press, 1993); and John A. Strong, *The Montaukett Indians of Eastern Long Island* (Syracuse: Syracuse University Press, 2001). William Engelbrecht, *Iroquoia: The Development of a Native World* (Syracuse: Syracuse University Press, 2003), provides useful archeological evidence of prehistoric Iroquois. John A. Strong, *The Algonquian Peoples of Long Island from Earliest Times to 1700* (Interlaken: Empire State Books, 1997), offers a wealth of information. Although I didn't make use of it, readers may also find Donna Merwick, *The Shame and the Sorrow: Dutch-Amerindian Encounters in New Netherlands* (Philadelphia: University of Pennsylvania Press, 2006), of interest, along with Evan T. Pritchard's nonacademic *Native New Yorkers: The Legacy of the Algonquin People of New York* (San Francisco: Council Oak Books, 2002).

I referred to several valuable articles on Native Americans in the state, including Dean R. Snow and Kim M. Lanphear, "European Contact and Indian Depopulation in the Northeast: The Timing of the First Epidemics," *Ethnohistory* 35 (Winter 1988): 15–33; and William Engelbrecht, "Factors Maintaining Low Population Density among the Prehistoric New York Iroquois," *American Antiquity* 52 (1987): 13–27. I also consulted several essays in *American Indian Environments: Ecological Issues in Native American History*, edited by Christopher Vecsey and Robert W. Venables (Syracuse: Syracuse University Press, 1980). In addition, I used one contemporary piece, translated and published much later: *A Brief and True Narrative of the Hostile Conduct of the Barbarous Natives Toward the Dutch Nation*, trans. E. B. O'Callaghan (Albany: J. Munsell, 1863). The fur trade has garnered a great deal of attention from historians. Thomas Elliot Norton's study *The Fur Trade in Colonial New York, 1686–1776* (Madison: University of Wisconsin Press, 1974), is the most complete on that topic, but it says little about the environment. Interested readers might also seek out Calvin Martin's *Keepers of the Game: Indian-Animal Relationships and the Fur Trade* (Berkeley: University of California Press, 1978).

Settlement and Deforestation

By far the most important work on colonial and early national New York's environmental history is Alan Taylor, *William Cooper's Town: Power and Persuasion on the Frontier of the Early American Republic* (New York: Vintage Books, 1995), which richly details the relationship between William Cooper, his son James Fenimore Cooper, and the town they helped create, in fact and fiction. James Fenimore Cooper's novels are very instructive; see in particular *The Pioneers* (1823) and *The Last of the Mohicans* (1826), both of which have been repeatedly reprinted. I also made considerable use of Alan Taylor, "'Wasty Ways': Stories of American Settlement," *Environmental History* (July 1998): 291–310.

Readers interested in forest history should begin with Michael Williams, *Americans and Their Forests: A Historical Geography* (New York: Cambridge University Press, 1989), which is a wonderfully detailed work. On New York specifically, see William F. Fox, *A History of the Lumber Industry in the State of New York* (Washington, D.C.: Government Printing Office, 1902); and Leslie C. Wood, *Rafting on the Delaware River* (Livingston Manor: Livingston Manor Times, 1934). On the tanning industry, see Lucius F. Ellsworth, "Craft to National Industry in the Nineteenth Century: A Case Study of the Transformation of the New York Tanning Industry" (Ph.D. diss., University of Delaware, 1971);

Barbara McMartin, *Hides, Hemlocks, and Adirondack History: How the Tanning Industry Influenced the Region's Growth* (Utica: North Country Books, 1992); Patricia E. Millen, *Bare Trees: Zadock Pratt, Master Tanner, and The Story of What Happened to the Catskill Mountain Forests* (Hensonville: Black Dome Press, 1995); and the autobiography of one the state's great tanners, *Memoirs of Col. William Edwards* (printed 1847), available on the Web.

Readers will learn much from Thomas E. Burke Jr.'s very detailed and useful *Mohawk Frontier: The Dutch Community of Schenectady, New York, 1661–1710* (Ithaca: Cornell University Press, 1991). I also learned a great deal about western New York from Charles E. Brooks, *Frontier Settlement and Market Revolution: The Holland Land Purchase* (Ithaca: Cornell University Press, 1996). Interested readers should also seek out Brooks's informative article "Overrun with Bushes: Frontier Land Development and the Forest History of the Holland Purchase, 1800–1850," *Forest and Conservation History* 39 (January 1995): 17–26. I consulted but found less useful for understanding environmental changes William Wyckoff, *The Developer's Frontier: The Making of the Western New York Landscape* (New Haven: Yale University Press, 1988); and Paul Demund Evans, *The Holland Land Company* (Buffalo: Buffalo Historical Society, 1924). For contemporary nonfiction settlement accounts, see Jeptha R. Simms, *Trappers of New York* (Albany: J. Munsell, 1850), which includes biographies of two Adirondack hunters, and William Reed, *Life on the Border, Sixty Years Ago* (Fall River, Mass.: Robert Adams, 1882), which concerns the North Country.

Colonial and Early National Cities

I know of no strictly environmental history of colonial New York cities, but several books give a good understanding of the environmental consequences of urban development. Among the best are Gerard Koeppel, *Water for Gotham: A History* (Princeton: Princeton University Press, 2000); Stuart M. Blumin's classic work on Kingston, *The Urban Threshold: Growth and Change in a Nineteenth-Century American Community* (Chicago: University of Chicago Press, 1976); and Jill Lepore's engaging and insightful *New York Burning: Liberty, Slavery, and Conspiracy in Eighteenth-Century Manhattan* (New York: Alfred A. Knopf, 2005). Interested readers should also seek out Diane Shaw, *City Building on the Eastern Frontier: Sorting the New Nineteenth-Century City* (Baltimore: Johns Hopkins University Press, 2004). The most complete book on early New York City is *Gotham,* by Burrows and Wallace, mentioned earlier.

The American Revolution

Those interested in the role of geography in the Revolutionary War should consult Gerald C. Stowe and Jac Weller, "Revolutionary West Point: 'The Key to the Continent,'" *Military Affairs* 19 (Summer 1955): 81–98; and Lincoln Diamant, *Chaining the Hudson: The Fight for the River in the American Revolution* (New York: Carol Publishing Group, 1989).

2. This Wilderness Becomes a Fertile Plain: Engineering the Empire State

Many firsthand accounts give excellent descriptions of New York's environment in the early 1800s. Some of the most helpful were gathered together by Roger Haydon and published as *Upstate Travels: British Views of Nineteenth-Century New York* (Syracuse: Syracuse University Press, 1982). Curious readers should also seek out John Fowler, *Journal of a Tour in the State of New York in the Year 1830; with Remarks on Agriculture in those parts most Eligible for Settlers* (London: Whittaker, Treacher, and Arnot, 1831); and Basil Hall, *Travels in North America in the Years 1827 and 1828,* vol. 1 (Philadelphia: Carey, Lea & Carey, 1829). I also read Anne McVickar Grant, *Memoirs of an American Lady: With Sketches of Manners and Scenes in America as They Existed Previous to the Revolution* (New York: D. and G. Bruce, 1809); and I made use of Alexis de Tocqueville, *Journey to America* (London: Faber and Faber, 1959), which includes his notebooks from his travels in the early 1830s.

The Erie Canal

Not surprisingly, the literature on the Erie Canal is extensive. Carol Sheriff, *The Artificial River: The Erie Canal and the Paradox of Progress, 1817–1862* (New York: Hill and Wang, 1996), pays the most attention to the environmental consequences of the canal. Ronald E. Shaw's *Erie Water West: A History of the Erie Canal, 1792–1854* (Lexington: University of Kentucky Press, 1966) provides all the detail one could want, while Peter L. Bernstein's *Wedding of the Waters: The Erie Canal and the Making of a Great Nation* (New York: W. W. Norton, 2005) is easier to read but less informative. See also Gerard Koeppel's *Bond of Union: Building the Erie Canal and the American Empire* (New York: Da Capo Press, 2009), which covers the planning and construction of the canal in great detail. Two other books on New York canals were helpful to me: Michele A. McFee, *Limestone Locks and Overgrowth: The Rise and Descent of the Chenango Canal* (Fleischmanns: Purple Mountain Press, 1993); and Dorothy Hurlbut Sanderson, *The Delaware & Hudson Canalway: Carrying Coals to Rondout* (Ellenville: Rondout Valley Publishing Company, 1965). For a contemporary source concerning deforestation, engineering, and water flow, see New York State Survey Board of Commissioners, *Report of the New York State Survey for the Year 1883* (Albany: Van Benthuysen Printing House, 1884).

Urban Growth

On mid-nineteenth-century urban development, see Paul E. Johnson, *A Shopkeeper's Millennium: Society and Revivals in Rochester, New York, 1815–1837* (New York: Hill and Wang, 1978); Mary P. Ryan, *Cradle of the Middle Class: The Family in Oneida County, New York, 1790–1865* (New York: Cambridge University Press, 1981); and Mark Goldman, *High Hopes: The Rise and Decline of Buffalo, New York* (Albany: State University of New York Press, 1983). Unfortunately, none of these fine books says much about the urban environment. Charles Rosenberg's classic *The Cholera Years: The United States in 1832, 1849, and 1866* (Chicago: University of Chicago Press, 1962) provides wonderful descriptions of the changing landscape and disease environment of Manhattan. Although it is a narrow work, Joanne Abel Goldman's *Building New York's Sewers: Developing Mechanisms of Urban Management* (West Lafayette: Purdue University Press, 1997) is thorough and useful.

Agriculture

I used several primary sources concerning nineteenth-century agriculture, some of which would be useful to interested readers. Many of Andrew Jackson Downing's contributions to *The Horticulturalist* were collected in *Rural Essays* (New York: Leavitt & Allen, 1856), edited by George William Curtis and published shortly after Downing's untimely death. Because they were part of my grandfather's library, I also made use of two county histories: L. M. Hammond, *History of Madison County: State of New York* (Syracuse: Truair, Smith & Co., Book and Job Printers, 1872); and John E. Smith, ed., *Our County and Its People: A Descriptive and Biographical Record of Madison County, New York* (Boston: Boston History Company, Publishers, 1899). These types of histories were common in the nineteenth century, and they tend to offer wonderfully rich detail concerning agricultural practices and urban growth.

There are several important secondary works on agriculture, including Ulysses Prentiss Hendrick, *A History of Agriculture in the State of New York*

(Albany: J. B. Lyon Company, 1933), which is old but still contains a wealth of useful information. I also consulted Donald H. Parkerson, *The Agricultural Transition in New York State: Markets and Migration in Mid-Nineteenth-Century America* (Ames: Iowa State University Press, 1995); and Neil Adams McNall, *An Agricultural History of the Genesee Valley, 1790–1860* (Philadelphia: University of Pennsylvania Press, 1952). For agriculture just outside New York City, see Marc Linder and Lawrence S. Zacharias, *Of Cabbages and Kings County: Agriculture and the Formation of Modern Brooklyn* (Iowa City: University of Iowa Press, 1999). Interested readers should also seek out Martin Bruegel, "Work, Gender, and Authority on the Farm: The Hudson Valley Countryside, 1790s–1850s," *Agricultural History* 76 (2002): 1–27. Though not strictly about agriculture, Karl Jacoby's *Crimes against Nature: Squatters, Poachers, Thieves, and the Hidden History of American Conservation* (Berkeley: University of California Press, 2001) says a great deal about farming in the Adirondacks.

On the decline of agriculture in the late 1800s, see Paula Baker, *The Moral Frameworks of Public Life: Gender, Politics, and the State in Rural New York, 1870–1930* (New York: Oxford University Press, 1991). On the development of the Grange, see Thomas Summerhill, *Harvest of Dissent: Agrarianism in Nineteenth-Century New York* (Urbana: University of Illinois Press, 2005). I was deeply influenced in my thinking by Hal S. Barron, *Mixed Harvest: The Second Great Transformation of the Rural North, 1870–1930* (Chapel Hill: University of North Carolina Press, 1997). I also made use of John Burroughs's many works. On the topic of agriculture, his autobiography *My Boyhood* (New York: Doubleday, Page & Company, 1924) is the most helpful. See also the fine biography of Burroughs by Edward J. Renehan Jr., *John Burroughs: An American Naturalist* (Hensonville: Black Dome Press, 1998).

3. We Are Still in Eden: Romanticism, Tourism, and the Power of Culture

Of the many works on romanticism, I have been particularly influenced by Marjorie Hope Nicolson's classic *Mountain Gloom and Mountain Glory: The Development of the Aesthetics of the Infinite* (Ithaca: Cornell University Press, 1959).

Those interested in literary romanticism in New York might begin with another classic: James T. Callow, *Kindred Spirits: Knickerbocker Writers and*

American Artists, 1807–1855 (Chapel Hill: University of North Carolina Press, 1967).

Hudson River School

I find Barbara Novak's *Nature and Culture: American Landscape and Painting, 1825–1875* (New York: Oxford University Press, 1980) the most instructive work on nineteenth-century American art. Interested readers should also seek out Angela Miller, *Landscape Representation and American Cultural Politics, 1825–1875* (Ithaca: Cornell University Press, 1993). Dozens of works on the paintings themselves exist, including Kenneth Myers, *The Catskills: Painters, Writers, and Tourists in the Mountains, 1820–1895* (Hanover, N.H.: University Press of New England, 1987); and a beautiful exhibition catalog titled *American Paradise: The World of the Hudson River School* (New York: Metropolitan Museum of Art, 1987). Many biographies of individual artists are extremely useful, including Louis L. Noble, *The Life and Works of Thomas Cole, N.A.* (New York: Sheldon & Company, 1860); Franklin Kelly, *Frederic Edwin Church and the National Landscape* (Washington, D.C.: Smithsonian Institution Press, 1988); and Ila Weiss, *Poetic Landscape: The Art and Experience of Sanford R. Gifford* (Newark: University of Delaware Press, 1987).

Central Park, Frederick Law Olmsted, and Calvert Vaux

The study of Central Park should begin with Roy Rosenzweig and Elizabeth Blackmar, *The Park and the People: A History of Central Park* (Ithaca: Cornell University Press, 1992). Those interested in the broader career of Frederick Law Olmsted should seek out a collection of his work gathered and edited by his son Frederick Law Olmsted Jr., *Forty Years of Landscape Architecture: Central Park* (Cambridge; MIT Press, 1973). See also the fine biography by Witold Rybczynski, *A Clearing in the Distance: Frederick Law Olmsted and America in the Nineteenth Century* (New York: Scribner, 1999). For an analysis of Olmsted's influence on urban America, see Charles E. Beveridge and Paul Rocheleau, *Frederick Law Olmsted: Designing the American Landscape* (New York: Rizzoli International Publications, 1995); and Francis R. Kowsky, *The Best Planned City: The Olmsted Legacy in Buffalo* (Buffalo: Buffalo State College Foundation, 1991). Kowsky has also produced a valuable biography of Vaux: *Country, Park, and City: The Architecture and Life of Calvert Vaux* (New York: Oxford University Press, 2003).

Tourism

Myriad primary sources reveal the importance of the Hudson Valley and New York's springs to the early tourist industry. See in particular Theodore Dwight, *The Northern Traveller: Containing the Routes to Niagara, Quebec, and the Springs, with Descriptions of the Principal Scenes, and Useful Hints to Strangers* (New York: Wilder & Campbell, 1825); G. M. Davison, *The Fashionable Tour: An Excursion to the Springs, Niagara, Quebec, and Boston* (Saratoga: G. M. Davidson, 1825); and Horatio Gates Spafford, *A Pocket Guide for the Tourist and Traveller Along the Line of the Canals and the Interior Commerce of the State of New-York* (Troy: William S. Parker, 1825). I also made use of Solomon Southwick, *Views of Ithaca and its Environs: By an Impartial Observer* (Ithaca: D. D. & A. Spencer, 1835); John Disturnell, *The Travellers' Guide Through the State of New-York, Canada, &c.: Embracing a General Description of the city of New-York, the Hudson River Guide and the fashionable tour to the springs and Niagara Falls, with Steam-Boat, Rail-Road, and Stage Routes* (New-York: J. Disturnell, 1836); Bayard Taylor, *At Home and Abroad* (New York: G. P. Putnam, 1860); *Alexandria Bay and the Thousand Islands: A Summer Resort for Pleasure Seekers* (Watertown: Ingalls, Brockway and Skinner, Printers, 1873); and *Earth's Grandest River, the St. Lawrence, and the Thousand Islands, An Unrivaled Summer Resort* (Watertown: H. H. Coates, 1897). On the condition of Niagara Falls in the late 1800s, see James T. Gardner, *Report of New York State Survey on the Preservation of the Scenery of Niagara Falls* (Albany: Charles Van Benthuysen & Sons, 1880).

On the Adirondacks, the classic tourist guides include Joel T. Headley, *The Adirondack; or, Life in the Woods* (New York: Baker and Scribner, 1853); William H. H. Murray, *Adventures in the Wilderness, or, Camp-Life in the Adirondacks* (Boston: Fields, Osgood & Co., 1869); and Seneca Ray Stoddard, *The Adirondacks: Illustrated* (Albany: Weed, Parsons & Co., Printers, 1874). Interested readers might also seek out Arthur H. Masten, *The Story of Adirondac* (1923; reprinted, Syracuse: Adirondack Museum/Syracuse University Press, 1968); and William James Stillman, *The Autobiography of a Journalist*, vol. 1 (Boston: Houghton Mifflin and Company, 1901). I also consulted Ralph Waldo Emerson, *Collected Poems and Translations* (New York: Library of America, 1994).

The genre of tourist literature continued to flourish in the early twentieth century. See as examples two works by T. Morris Longstreth: *The Adirondacks* (New York: Century Company, 1917), and *The Catskills* (New York: Century Company, 1918), both of which are easily found.

New York's tourist industry has received significant scholarly attention in recent decades. See in particular Jon Sterngass, *First Resorts: Pursuing Pleasure at Saratoga Springs, Newport, and Coney Island* (Baltimore: Johns Hopkins University Press, 2001); and Thomas Chambers, *Drinking the Waters: Creating an American Leisure Class at Nineteenth-Century Mineral Springs* (Washington, D.C.: Smithsonian Institution Press, 2002), which offers a wonderful history of the young Saratoga. See also Theodore Corbett, *The Making of American Resorts: Saratoga Springs, Ballston Spa, Lake George* (New Brunswick: Rutgers University Press, 2001); Richard H. Gassan, *The Birth of American Tourism: New York, the Hudson Valley, and American Culture, 1790–1830* (Amherst: University of Massachusetts Press, 2008); and the reprinted classic by Roland Van Zandt, *The Catskill Mountain House: America's Grandest Hotel* (Hensonville: Black Dome Press, 1991). On the continued development of New York's tourism, consult John F. Sears, *Sacred Places: American Tourist Attractions in the Nineteenth Century* (New York: Oxford University Press, 1989), a seminal work in tourism history. On Niagara Falls, see Elizabeth McKinsey, *Niagara Falls: Icon of the American Sublime* (New York: Cambridge University Press, 1985). I also enjoyed reading Pierre Berton's *Niagara: A History of the Falls* (New York: Penguin, 1992).

I hope readers will find my book *Making Mountains: New York City and the Catskills* (Seattle: University of Washington Press, 2007) useful in understanding how tourism connected the city to rural New York, leading to changes in both places.

4. Tainted and Unwholesome Atmospheres: Urban Environments, Government, and Reform

To understand the environmental consequences of urbanization and industrialization, readers should consult classic texts including John Duffy, *A History of Public Health in New York City, 1866–1966* (New York: Russell Sage Foundation, 1974); Roy Lubove, *The Progressives and the Slums: Tenement House Reform in New York City, 1890–1917* (Pittsburgh: University of Pittsburgh Press, 1962); Christine Stansell, *City of Women: Sex and Class in New York, 1789–1860* (Urbana: University of Illinois Press, 1982); and Paul Boyer, *Urban Masses and Moral Order in America, 1820–1920* (Cambridge: Harvard University Press, 1992), which isn't focused on New York but makes use of considerable evidence from the nation's largest city. Three more recent works describe well many of the environmental changes afoot in industrializing New

York. See Daniel Eli Burnstein, *Next to Godliness: Confronting Dirt and Despair in Progressive Era New York City* (Urbana: University of Illinois Press, 2006); Clay McShane and Joel A. Tarr, *The Horse in the City* (Baltimore: Johns Hopkins University Press, 2007); and Robert M. Fogelson, *Downtown: Its Rise and Fall, 1880–1950* (New Haven: Yale University Press, 2001). Although it doesn't concern New York exclusively, Martin V. Melosi's *Garbage in the Cities: Refuse, Reform, and the Environment* (Pittsburgh: University of Pittsburgh Press, 2005) includes national context and the Waring story in detail. See also Melosi's monumental work *The Sanitary City: Urban Infrastructure in America from Colonial Times to the Present* (Baltimore: Johns Hopkins University Press, 2000). For a fascinating study of upstate cities and the environmental and social impact of railroads, see David O. Stowell, *Streets, Railroads, and the Great Strike of 1877* (Chicago: University of Chicago Press, 1999).

On New York City's slums, readers should begin with Jacob A. Riis, *How the Other Half Lives: Studies Among the Tenements of New York* (New York: Charles Scribner's Sons, 1890), which has been reprinted many times and is available on the Web; and John H. Griscom, *The Sanitary Condition of the Laboring Population of New York* (New York: Harper & Brothers, 1845), which is also available via Google Books. Very interested readers should consult Robert W. DeForest and Lawrence Veiller, eds., *The Tenement House Problem: Including the Report of the New York State Tenement House Commission of 1900* (New York: Macmillan, 1903). For a readable secondary source on nineteenth-century slums, see Tyler Anbinder, *Five Points: The 19th-Century New York City Neighborhood That Invented Tap Dance, Stole Elections, and Became the World's Most Notorious Slum* (New York: Free Press, 2001).

Air and Water Pollution

In describing the coal smoke problem, I relied on some documents I collected while writing *Smokestacks and Progressives: Environmentalism, Engineers, and Air Quality in America, 1881–1951* (Baltimore: Johns Hopkins University Press, 1999). Two of the most useful sources for this work were the Engineers' Society of Western New York, "Abatement of the Smoke Nuisance," *Journal of the Association of Engineering Societies* 30 (January 1903): 41–45; and the Syracuse Chamber of Commerce, "Report upon Smoke Abatement" (Syracuse, 1907), which can be found at the New York Public Library.

On water pollution, see Andrew Hurley, "Creating Ecological Wastelands: Oil Pollution in New York City, 1870–1900," *Journal of Urban History* 20

(May 1994): 340–64. On conditions in nineteenth-century Buffalo, see M. Stephen Pendleton, "A Pipe Dream Comes True: Buffalo's Decision to Make Water a Public Good," *Middle States Geographer* 32 (1999): 48–60; and John V. Cotter and Larry L. Patrick, "Disease and Ethnicity in an Urban Environment," *Annals of the Association of American Geographers* 71 (March 1981): 40–49.

Utopianism and Urban Reform

On the special role of Niagara Falls in inspiring utopian visions, start with a fine secondary source on the topic: Patrick McGreevy, "Imagining the Future at Niagara Falls," *Annals of the Association of American Geographers* 77, no. 1 (1987): 48–62. Interested readers should also seek out King C. Gillette, *The Human Drift* (Boston: New Era Publishing Company, 1894). On urban reform generally in the Progressive Era, see Jon A. Peterson, "The City Beautiful Movement: Forgotten Origins and Lost Meanings," *Journal of Urban History* 2 (August 1976): 415–34; and Raphael Fischler, "The Metropolitan Dimension of Early Zoning: Revisiting the 1916 New York City Ordinance," *Journal of the American Planning Association* 64 (1998): 170–88. Susan L. Klaus, *A Modern Arcadia: Frederick Law Olmsted Jr. and the Plan for Forest Hills Gardens* (Amherst: University of Massachusetts Press, 2002), nicely places Forest Hills Gardens in the context of Progressive Era reform.

On urban infrastructure, see Keith D. Revell, *Building Gotham: Civic Culture and Public Policy in New York City, 1898–1938* (Baltimore: Johns Hopkins University Press, 2003); and Clifton Hood, *Seven Hundred and Twenty-two Miles: The Building of the Subways and How They Transformed New York* (Baltimore: Johns Hopkins University Press, 1995). Those interested in learning more about electrification should begin with David E. Nye, *Electrifying America: Social Meanings of a New Technology* (Cambridge: MIT Press, 1990).

5. A Sound Conservation Program: Theodore Roosevelt, Franklin Roosevelt, and the Power of Individuals

Readers interested in the conservation movement in New York State might start with a fine dissertation by Marvin W. Kranz, completed at Syracuse University in 1961, "Pioneering in Conservation: A History of the Conservation Movement in New York State, 1865–1903"; it is difficult to acquire, but it is full of wonderful detail, especially concerning fish and game regulation as well as forestry and the politics surrounding the creation and management of the

Adirondack Forest Preserve and Park. On conservation generally, see Samuel Hays's seminal *Conservation and the Gospel of Efficiency: The Progressive Conservation Movement, 1890–1920* (Cambridge: Harvard University Press, 1959), even though it says distressingly little about conservation in the East, let alone New York State.

See also David Lowenthal's fine biography *George Perkins Marsh: Prophet of Conservation* (Seattle: University of Washington Press, 2000). Marsh's classic *Man and Nature; or, Physical Geography as Modified by Human Action* (New York: Charles Scribner & Co., 1864) is now available through Google Books. On the oft-overlooked contributions of one of New York's great conservationists, see John C. Devlin and Grace Naismith, *The World of Roger Tory Peterson: An Authorized Biography* (New York: Times Books, 1977).

Theodore Roosevelt

Many fine books can introduce readers to Theodore Roosevelt, but I would start with Roosevelt's own words: *An Autobiography* (New York: Macmillan, 1913). For a more complete portrait, see Edmund Morris, *Theodore Rex* (New York: Random House, 2001). On Roosevelt and the environment in particular, see Douglas Brinkley's massive and thorough account *The Wilderness Warrior: Theodore Roosevelt and the Crusade for America* (New York: Harper, 2009). See also Paul Russell Cutright, *Theodore Roosevelt: The Making of a Conservationist* (Urbana: University of Illinois Press, 1985). John Burroughs's descriptions of Roosevelt, found in *Camping and Tramping with Roosevelt* (Boston: Houghton, Mifflin & Co, 1907), are also rich and instructive.

Franklin Delano Roosevelt

Those interested in learning more about Franklin Roosevelt and the environment should begin with *Franklin D. Roosevelt and Conservation, 1911–1945*, 2 vols. (Hyde Park: National Archives and Records Service, Franklin D. Roosevelt Library, 1957), a collection of Roosevelt's writings and speeches, gathered and edited by Edgar B. Nixon. Very interested readers can also find valuable primary documents in *The Public Papers and Addresses of Franklin D. Roosevelt*, 2 vols. (New York: Random House, 1938), although those most related to the environment are largely contained in Nixon's collection. As for secondary sources, see the collection of fine essays edited by Henry L. Henderson and David B. Woolner, *FDR and the Environment* (New York: Palgrave, 2005); and A. L. Riesch Owen, *Conservation under FDR* (New York: Praeger, 1983). I also made use of

Bernard Bellush, *Franklin D. Roosevelt as Governor of New York* (New York: Columbia University Press, 1955).

The New Deal

On the Civilian Conservation Corps, see *Two Years of Emergency Conservation Work (Civilian Conservation Corps), April 5, 1933–March 31, 1935* (Washington, D.C.: Government Printing Office, 1935).

The Center for Research Libraries has also made available CCC newspapers, which are excellent primary sources on camp life and conservation activities. I read a two-year run of *The Goodnow Breeze* (1936–1938), the newspaper of Company 1297, Camp S-129, in Newcomb, but dozens of titles from dozens of New York camps can be ordered through the Center for Research Libraries. For an excellent discussion of the CCC, see Neil Maher, *Nature's New Deal: The Conservation Corps and the Roots of the American Environmental Movement* (New York: Oxford University Press, 2008). For the national context, see also Sarah T. Phillips, *This Land, This Nation: Conservation, Rural America, and the New Deal* (New York: Cambridge University Press, 2007). On the CCC in New York specifically, see Diane Galusha, *Another Day, Another Dollar: The Civilian Conservation Corps in the Catskills* (Hensonville: Black Dome Press, 2008).

State Parks and Parkways

To study the special role of Robert Moses in shaping New York's parks, building its parkways, and shaping metropolitan New York more generally, see Robert Caro's seminal biography *The Power Broker: Robert Moses and the Fall of New York* (New York: Vintage Books, 1975). For a critique of Caro's portrait, see Hilary Ballon and Kenneth T. Jackson, eds., *Robert Moses and the Modern City: The Transformation of New York* (New York: W. W. Norton & Company, 2007). On planning in New York generally, see David A. Johnson, *Planning the Great Metropolis: The 1929 Regional Plan of New York and Its Environs* (London: Chapman & Hall, 1996); and on building the park system, see New York State Association, *The State Park Plan for New York*... (New York[?], 1924).

Automobiles and Tourism

For a sense of the automobile's role in changing tourism and the tourist landscape, see the many publications meant to attract tourists around the state, including Harry R. Melone, *Souvenir of the Finger Lakes Region* (Auburn: Cayuga County News Co., 1921); and Cherry Valley Turnpike Association, *The Cherry Valley Turnpike* (Waterville, 1929). William Copeman Kitchin's *Wonderland of the East* (Boston: Page Company, 1920) is a fascinating firsthand account of auto touring in the Catskills and central New York. On the automobile and tourism generally, consult Marguerite S. Shaffer, *See America First: Tourism and National Identity, 1880–1940* (Washington, D.C.: Smithsonian Institution Press, 2001). On automobiles in the Adirondacks, see Association for the Protection of the Adirondacks, *Roads in the Forest Preserve* (New York: APA, 1933).

6. Tracing Man's Progress in Making the Planet Uninhabitable: Environmental Interest Groups and Postwar Threats

On New York City's deepening urban crisis, see John V. Lindsay, *The City* (New York: W. W. Norton & Company, 1969); and Vincent J. Cannato's massive biography *The Ungovernable City: John Lindsay and His Struggle to Save New York* (New York: Basic Books, 2001). On the development of the crisis generally, see John A. Jakle and Keith A. Sculle, *Lots of Parking: Land Use in a Car Culture* (Charlottesville: University of Virginia Press, 2004); and Jon C. Teaford, *The Rough Road to Renaissance: Urban Revitalization in America, 1940–1985* (Baltimore: Johns Hopkins University Press, 1990). On New York City in particular, see Wendell Pritchett, *Brownsville, Brooklyn: Blacks, Jews, and the Changing Face of the Ghetto* (Chicago: University of Chicago Press, 2002). On postwar urban planning, begin with Jane Jacobs' classic *The Death and Life of Great American Cities* (New York: Vintage Books, 1961); and Oscar Newman, *Defensible Space: Crime Prevention through Urban Design* (New York: Macmillan, 1972).

Postwar Air Pollution and Lead Poisoning

On air pollution, see Scott Hamilton Dewey, *Don't Breathe the Air: Air Pollution and U.S. Environmental Politics, 1945–1970* (College Station: Texas A&M University Press, 2000); and David Stradling, *Smokestacks and Progressives: Environmentalism, Engineers, and Air Quality in America, 1881–1951* (Baltimore: Johns Hopkins University Press, 1999). On the lead poisoning crisis in New York City, see Jack Newfield, "Lead Poisoning: Silent Epidemic in the Slums," *Village Voice*, September 18, 1969, 3, 39–40. On lead poisoning more generally, see Christian Warren, *Brush with Death: A Social History of Lead Poisoning* (Baltimore: Johns Hopkins University Press, 2000); and Gerald Markowitz and David Rosner, *Deceit and Denial: The Deadly Politics of Industrial Pollution* (Berkeley: University of California Press, 2002).

Storm King

The Storm King story is best told by Allan R. Talbot in *Power along the Hudson: The Storm King Case and the Birth of Environmentalism* (New York: Dutton, 1972), and is more completely told in Robert Douglas Lifset, "Storm King Mountain and the Emergence of Modern American Environmentalism" (Ph.D. diss., Columbia University, 2005). Very interested readers should consult the court cases themselves, especially *Scenic Hudson Preservation Conference, et al. v. Federal Power Commission*, 1965 U.S. App. (Lexis 3514). On issues related to the Hudson River more broadly, see John Cronin and Robert F. Kennedy Jr., *The Riverkeepers: Two Activists Fight to Reclaim Our Environment as a Basic Human Right* (New York: Scribner, 1997).

Wilderness Preservation and the Adirondacks

Environmental historians have paid a great deal of attention to wilderness issues, although most of the literature concerns the American West. See, for example, Mark Harvey, *Wilderness Forever: Howard Zahniser and the Path to the Wilderness Act* (Seattle: University of Washington Press, 2005). Several important books do address the wilderness movement in the East and in New York in particular, especially through the biography of Robert Marshall. See Paul Sutter, *Driven Wild: How the Fight against Automobiles Launched the Modern Wilderness Movement* (Seattle: University of Washington Press, 2002); and Marshall's own writings, collected and edited by Phil Brown: *Bob Marshall in the Adirondacks: Writings of a Pioneering Peak-Bagger, Pond-Hopper, and Wilderness Preservationist* (Saranac Lake: Lost Pond Press, 2006). Other important New York figures in the wilderness movement have also left us important writings. See *Where Wilderness Preservation Began: Adirondack Writings of Howard Zahniser*, edited by Ed Zahniser (Utica: North Country Books, 1992); and Paul Schaefer, *Defending the Wilderness: The Adirondack Writings of Paul Schaefer* (Syracuse: Syracuse University Press, 1989).

DDT and Other Threats

Those interested in the story of DDT should begin with Thomas R. Dunlap, *DDT: Scientists, Citizens, and Public Policy* (Princeton: Princeton University Press, 1981).

Some primary sources are also of use. Begin with the seminal work of Rachel Carson, *Silent Spring*, first published by Houghton Mifflin in 1962 and reissued many times since. See also Albert C. Worrell, "Pests, Pesticides and People,"

American Forests 66 (July 1960): 39–81. Very interested readers might find the relevant court decisions, beginning with *Robert Cushman Murphy et al. v. Benson, etc., et al.,* 164 F. Supp. 120; 1958 U.S. Dist. (Lexis 3790); and *Murphy et al. v. Butler,* 362 U.S. 929; 80 S. Ct. 750; 4 L. Ed. 2d 747; 1960 U.S. (Lexis 1435).

On the debates surrounding nuclear power, see Dorothy Nelkin, *Nuclear Power and Its Critics: The Cayuga Lake Controversy* (Ithaca: Cornell University Press, 1971).

On roads reshaping New York's economy, see Michael R. Fein, *Paving the Way: New York Road Building and the American State, 1880–1956* (Lawrence: University Press of Kansas, 2008).

7. We Live in This Filth: The Urban Crisis, Environmental Justice, and Threats from Beyond

For recent environmental coverage, see the Department of Environmental Conservation website, http://www.dec.ny.gov/. See also *Final Report of the New York State Invasive Species Task Force* (2005), available at http://nyis.info/PolicyArena/PDFs/NYS_ISTF_Rep.pdf. On the consequences of sprawl, see A. C. Spectorsky's early work *The Exurbanites* (New York: J. B. Lippincott Company, 1955); and the more recent and cutting work of James Howard Kunstler, *The Geography of Nowhere: The Rise and Decline of America's Man-Made Landscape* (New York: Simon & Schuster, 1993). Readers interested in environmental justice might begin with Robert Gottlieb's seminal *Forcing the Spring: The Transformation of the American Environmental Movement* (Washington, D.C.: Island Press, 1993). Julie Sze's more recent *Noxious New York: The Racial Politics of Urban Health and Environmental Justice* (Cambridge: MIT Press, 2007) is also of interest.

Love Canal

The most helpful books on the Love Canal story come from two people who lived through it: Michael H. Brown, *Laying Waste: The Poisoning of America by Toxic Chemicals* (New York: Pantheon Books, 1980); and Lois Marie Gibbs, *Love Canal: My Story* (New York: Grove Press, 1982). Also of special value is the lengthy summary of the case in *United States of America, The State of New York v. Hooker Chemicals and Plastics Corporation,* 850 F. Supp. 993; 1994 U.S. Dist. (Lexis 3237). For a readable summary of the longer story, see Richard Newman, "From Love's Canal to Love Canal: Reckoning with the Environmental

Legacy of an Industrial Dream," in *Beyond the Ruins: The Meanings of Deindustrialization,* edited by Jefferson Cowie and Joseph Heathcott (Ithaca: Cornell University Press, 2003). On the connection between Love Canal and Superfund, see Travis Wagner, "Hazardous Waste: Evolution of a National Environmental Problem," *Journal of Policy History* 16 (2004): 306–31. On postwar dumping near Niagara Falls, see Andrew Jenks, "Model City USA: The Environmental Cost of Victory in World War II and the Cold War," *Environmental History* 12 (July 2007): 552–77.

Acid Rain

I first read about acid rain in college, when I was assigned Robert H. Boyle and R. Alexander Boyle, *Acid Rain* (New York: Nick Lyons Books, 1983), which I think is still a fine introduction to the topic. Jerry Jenkins, Karen Roy, Charles Driscoll, and Christopher Buerkett, *Acid Rain in the Adirondacks: An Environmental History* (Ithaca: Cornell University Press, 2007), offers a more complete and up-to-date explanation of the ecology related to acid rain. On the legal side, I made use of Bernard C. Melewski, "Acid Rain and the Adirondacks: A Legislative History," *Albany Law Review* 66 (2002): 171–205. Very interested readers might use House and Senate publications, which include rich testimony and data entered into the record at various hearings. See in particular *Acid Rain,* Hearings before the House of Representatives Subcommittee on Oversight and Investigations of the Committee on Interstate and Foreign Commerce, 96th Cong., 2nd sess., February 26, 27, 1980; and *Acid Rain,* Hearing before the Senate Committee on Environment and Public Works, 97th Cong., 1st sess., October 29, 1981. For a wonderful rumination on the many consequences of acid rain and global warming, see Bill McKibben, *The End of Nature* (New York: Random House, 1989).

Epilogue

The epilogue is based mostly on my recent travels in the state, but I also consulted the writings of Bill McKibben for the passage on the Adirondacks; see "Full Circle: An Adirondack Canoe Route Traces the Return of the Wild," *Nature Conservancy Magazine* (Summer 2006): 36–40; and *Wandering Home: A Long Walk across America's Most Hopeful Landscape: Vermont's Champlain Valley and New York's Adirondacks* (New York: Crown Journeys, 2005). I also consulted a recent Sierra Club publication, "Imagine: The Great Oswegatchie Canoe Wilderness" (n.d.).

Index